Routledge Revivals

The Enigma of the Fourth Gospel

First Published in 1938, *The Enigma of the Fourth Gospel* by Robert Eisler presents a comprehensive overview of the Fourth gospel, its author, and its writer. In forty-one chapters, it discusses themes like an insoluble enigma; the preface to the Christian reader; the longer Anti-Marcionite preface to the Fourth Gospel; the Greek and the Latin texts of the Anti-Marcionite prologue to Luke; the two traditions about the evangelist John; John killed by King Herod in Jewish tradition; the two tombs of St. John in Ephesus; the confusion of the two Johns; who wrote the Gospel dictated by John; the date of the Fourth Gospel and of the first Epistle of John; traces of Marcionism in the Gospel of John; John the evangelist and the Fourth evangelist identified. This is a must read for scholars and researchers of Christian religion.

The Enigma of the Fourth Gospel
Its Author and Its Writer

Robert Eisler

First published in 1938
by Methuen & Co, Ltd.

This edition first published in 2024 by Routledge
4 Park Square, Milton Park, Abingdon, Oxon, OX14 4RN

and by Routledge
605 Third Avenue, New York, NY 10017

Routledge is an imprint of the Taylor & Francis Group, an informa business

© Robert Eisler, 1938

All rights reserved. No part of this book may be reprinted or reproduced or utilised in any form or by any electronic, mechanical, or other means, now known or hereafter invented, including photocopying and recording, or in any information storage or retrieval system, without permission in writing from the publishers.

Publisher's Note
The publisher has gone to great lengths to ensure the quality of this reprint but points out that some imperfections in the original copies may be apparent.

Disclaimer
The publisher has made every effort to trace copyright holders and welcomes correspondence from those they have been unable to contact.

A Library of Congress record exists under LCCN:

ISBN: 978-1-032-79421-1 (hbk)
ISBN: 978-1-003-49187-3 (ebk)
ISBN: 978-1-032-79423-5 (pbk)

Book DOI 10.4324/9781003491873

C. Gutbier pinx. Sculps. Friedr. Müller

CARL GOTTLIEB BRETSCHNEIDER, D.D.
1776–1848
'*Quo autem locorum et a quonam Christianorum evangelium quartum scriptum fuerit, it expedire nemo facile poterit.*'
Probabilia de Evangelii et Epistolarum Joannis Apostoli Indole et Origine, Lipsiae, MDCCCXX (p. 223)

PLATE I

THE ENIGMA OF THE FOURTH GOSPEL

ITS AUTHOR AND ITS WRITER

BY

ROBERT EISLER, Ph.D.

WITH SIXTEEN PLATES
AND FIVE TEXT ILLUSTRATIONS

METHUEN & CO. LTD. LONDON
36 Essex Street, Strand, W.C.2

First published in 1938

PRINTED IN GREAT BRITAIN

GRATEFULLY DEDICATED

TO THE SACRED MEMORY OF

THOSE WHO BLAZED THE TRAIL

LEADING THE SEEKER THROUGH
A JUNGLE OF
ERROR, CONFUSION AND CONCEALMENT
ON HIS LONG QUEST
OF
THE LIGHT THAT SHINETH
IN THE DARKNESS

★

PREFACE

UNWITTINGLY AND UNWILLINGLY the author seems to have complied with Horace's counsel of perfection: '. . . siquid . . . scripseris . . . nonum . . . prematur in annum, membranis intus positis . . .'

Not until he sat down to write this preface did he realize that he had had the original draft of this little volume on his desk for a full nine years—ever since he received on an auspicious day in 1928 Dom de Bruyne's essay on his startling new discovery. He has been altering and increasing it by following up every side-issue of the problem, answering in advance all possible objections to this new solution of the age-old Johannine problem, analysing every source in the most minute detail, until the manuscript had grown to such a bulk, containing so much Greek text and so many footnotes, that no publisher would so much as look at it.

During all these long years he had been lecturing on the subject in many places, among others before such an august assembly as the French Académie des Inscriptions et Belles Lettres, in Paris (1930) and discussing his views with the foremost living scholars. The lecture before the Academy had, as usual, been fully and intelligently reported by the five leading daily papers of Paris. But there was no sign forthcoming that the public was at all interested in a question so little connected with the daily bread by which men tried to live in these anxious years of depression following upon the world-crisis of 1929. The author was perfectly resigned and, indeed, almost content to go on increasing and improving his manuscript and seeing now and then the text of some of his lectures on the subject printed in a periodical, such as the *Revue de Philologie,* which published in 1930 his Academy paper about the anti-Marcionite prologue to John discovered by Dom de Bruyne.

The situation was suddenly changed as if by magic, as soon as one such lecture—delivered on the 2nd of February, 1936, in London, before the Society for Promoting the Study of Religions—had been reported in a long and able article by *The Times*. On the two following days this paper—the only daily in the world which can afford to print Greek quotations without adding a translation and to devote the better part of one of its giant columns to a problem of New Testament scholarship, to the reading of a new papyrus, or of an inscription on a potsherd found in Palestine—was swamped with Letters to the Editor. Two of them, emanating from distinguished Oxford scholars, were printed, as well as the author's reply, the discussion being closed by an admirable editorial article on the leader-page. The author who had been imprudent enough not only to sign his name, but to give his London address, received postbags full of letters with every mail for days on end. Better still, the distinguished publishers of his book, *The Messiah Jesus and John the Baptist*, became interested.

So the author had to sit down again and to make a serious effort to present the result of so many years of grind in such a shape as might be likely to reach the great English-speaking public, which still seems to be passionately interested in such problems.

How difficult a task it was to write a book which is—he hopes—easy to read and to present an entirely new, in many respects revolutionary, in many respects ultra-conservative thesis, without spreading all the learned material which has gone into the making of the new synthesis in long footnotes at the bottom of his pages, and to condense such an amount of new data between the covers of a handy little volume, need not be told here.

Having tried to reduce the number of notes and appendices to a size that would not frighten away the general reader, and would still satisfy the specialist, the author has finally found that it is impossible to serve two masters, and that it is better to omit the learned notes altogether. Books are written, after all, to be read.

It is, of course, a great convenience for those who want to

criticize and to use them as a basis of their own ulterior research-work, to be presented separately with the bricks and stones that have gone into the construction of the building, and even with the clay and the straw out of which the bricks have been made. But the general reader, who wants to perambulate in a leisurely manner, without stumbling over the tools and materials left lying on the floors, through room after room of the new castle in the air that Jack built—on solid ground or on quicksand, as the case may be—cannot be expected to pay for a convenience to others, which is to him nothing but a very great nuisance. Elaborate notes supporting every word in the text of this little book are in the hands of the publishers, ready to go to press at any moment. If those readers who want them will write to Messrs. Methuen, their orders will be filled in a short time at the lowest possible price, multigraphed if the demand should be limited to a small number of copies, printed uniform with the present volume and at the same price, if enough readers should desire to possess the whole available evidence, completely analysed in every detail.

An elaborate monograph on Fortunatian's translation of the anti-Marcionite prologues to the Gospels, on Marcion's 'Pro-evangel', on his *Summa* or 'Book of the Prefixed Addresses' of the Pauline Epistles is equally offered for subscription.

A monograph on the Evangelists' portraits in our manuscripts illustrating the various extant Gospel-prefaces is ready for publication in book form. The reproductions on our Pls. IX–XIII are a few specimens showing the important contribution which pictorial evidence is able to make to the problem in question.

The analysis of the two main sources of the Fourth Gospel which the author proposes to publish in the following volumes: *The Book of Lazarus* and *The Gospel of the Paraclete* is meanwhile available in the German text of the author's lectures on the subject delivered in August 1935 in Ascona, printed in the *Eranos-Jahrbuch* for 1935, published by the *Rheinverlag* in Zürich in 1936, pp. 323–511.

Due acknowledgement to those who have preceded the author along the path to what he believes to be the final solution of the Johannine problem is made in the explanatory lines added to the portraits on Pls. I, II, VI, XVII–XXI. One of the scholars represented, Adolph von Harnack, spoke—in a letter to Holl (1902)—of the near future 'when Mr. Holl and Mr. Harnack will be no more than convenient abbreviations of a book-title'. Under this sun, where the battle is not to the strong neither yet bread to the wise, nor yet riches to men of understanding, where the memory of the dead is soon forgotten, neither have they any more a reward, the time comes all too soon when nothing is left of a scholar's life-work—even if he has been a martyr of his quest for the Truth—but a footnote, at best a footnote trailed along from book to book.

The almost unbelievable difficulties which had to be overcome in order to conjure from their quite recent graves some of the εἴδωλα of the author's few spiritual ancestors, so as to assemble them all for this shadows' symposium of the quick and the dead, Catholic and Protestant, orthodox and heretic, and to celebrate together the belated unveiling of a memorial statue to the long-forgotten real author of the Fourth Gospel; last, not least, the absolute failure to discover anywhere a portrait of the Rev. Edward Evanson (d. 1805) who ought to have presided at our banquet—are in themselves a sufficient justification of this desperate effort to rescue their memories from oblivion, even if it be only for the short span of time which books and libraries may reasonably be expected to last in a civilization subsisting on sufferance under perpetual menace.

The author's best thanks are due to His Eminence the Cardinal-Prefect of the Vatican Library for the photographs reproduced on Pls. III, IV, V to the Rev. Father Dom Ph. Schmitz, Librarian of Maredsous Abbey, for the photograph reproduced on Pl. II, to the Director of the John Rylands Library for the block printed on Pl. XVI, to Professor Wilhelm Neuss of Bonn University for the photographs reproduced on Pl. VII, to Dr. Christian Delff of Husum for that reproduced on Pl. VI, to Professors Dr. Rudolf Egger, Dr. Joseph Keil, and Camillo Praschniker of Vienna University for the blocks of Pl. VIII and the two plans on pages 120 and facing 122, to Professor Joseph Keil of Vienna and Professor Georgios A. Sotēriou of Athens for the photograph on Pl. X, to the R. Rev.

Canon Van den Gheyn of St. Bavo in Ghent for the reproduction on Pl. XII, to the Librarian of the Pierpont Morgan Library for the photograph reproduced on Pl. XIII, to the directors of the Leningrad Public Library and the State Archives in Moscow for the photographs reproduced on Pls. XIV and XV, to Frau von Zahn-Harnack for the portrait of her great father (Pl. XVII), to M. Félix Sartiaux for the portrait of the Abbé Turmel (Pl. XVIII), to Dr. A. Pupato-Rahn of Zürich for the portrait of his late father-in-law Dr. Kreyenbühl (Pl. XIX), to Misses Ramsey and Muspratt, photographers, in Cambridge and Messrs. Heffer for the portrait of Dr. Swete. To Dom Germain Morin for his expert opinion on the date of the pseudepigraphic *'tractatus Hilarii episcopi'* published by Cardinal Mai (ch. XII), and for his spontaneous, invaluable communication identifying the punctuator and emendator of Fortunatian's prefaces as the 6th-century presbyter Patricius of Ravenna (ch. XXXVI). To his old friend and fellow-student Professor David Ernest Oppenheim of Vienna and to Dr. Heinz Etthofen of Berlin for their unfailing help in verifying quotations and the like without which this book could not have been completed in this mountain hermitage far away from public libraries. To my kind host and friend, the Rev. W. A. Wordsworth, the worthy scion of the family which gave the world both the immortal poet and the learned editor of the Vulgate New Testament, and to Mr. Royle Shore, the erudite connoisseur of ecclesiastical law and music, for reading the typescript of this book, and offering many a helpful suggestion for improving a foreigner's English style. To the Rev. L. B. Cholmondeley of Adlestrop Rectory, Moreton in Marsh, Gloucester, and to Mr. F. T. A. Ashton-Gwatkin, Head of the Economic Section of H.M.'s Foreign Office, for supplying me with a copy of the most important article 'Who was the Loved Disciple?' in *The Spectator* of August 7, 1926, quoted in ch. XL, which would have escaped the author's notice as it has been overlooked by all previous commentators of the Fourth Gospel, had it not been mentioned incidentally by Mr. Ashton-Gwatkin in *The Times* obituary of the Rev. William Kaye Fleming (November 19th, 1937) and discussed by Mr. Cholmondeley in a letter to the editor of that paper on the 25th of the same month, when the proofs of this book had already been divided up into pages. It grieves me to think that a scholar of such rare qualities as the author of *Mysticism in Christianity* (1913) should have had to die in order to obtain a belated recognition of his most important contribution to the solution of the Johannine problem, and that the purely accidental delays which have held up the publication of this book for more than half a year should have deprived my only English predecessor in what I believe to be the correct interpretation of Jo. xxi. 24 and Jo. xi. 3 of the satisfaction of seeing his thesis vindicated by an accumulation of new and, in my opinion, decisive evidence.

I have to thank the Ven. Archdeacon C. E. Lambert, of St. James's in Piccadilly, for a copy of W. K. Fleming's earlier article, 'The Authorship of the Fourth Gospel,' in *The Guardian*, of December 19th, 1906, p. 2118.

Last, not least, I owe a debt of gratitude to my dear wife, who patiently and cheerfully typed—in addition to all her other exhausting work—about five times the number of pages which finally reached the printer's press.

ROBERT EISLER

UNTERACH AM ATTERSEE

St. James's and St. John's Day, the 28th of December, 1937

CONTENTS

		PAGE
Preface	. . . .	vii
I.	An Insoluble Enigma?	1
II.	The 'Preface to the Christian Reader' and the Ancient Bio-Bibliographical Librarian's Notes	4
III.	The Earliest Gospel Prefaces and Summaries discovered by Dom de Bruyne . . .	6
IV.	Breves Fortunatiani	8
V.	Fortunatian's Sources.	11
VI.	The Longer Anti-Marcionite Preface to the Fourth Gospel	13
VII.	The Greek and the Latin Texts of the Anti-Marcionite Prologue to Luke . . .	22
VIII.	Heretic and Catholic Second-Century Testimonies concerning John of Ephesus . .	25
IX.	The Leucian 'Acts of John' on the Beloved Disciple of Jesus	29
X.	Bishop Polycrates of Ephesus on the Ephesian John	36
XI.	'John of the High-priestly Kin' in Acts iv. 6, and in Flavius Josephus' 'Jewish War' .	39
XII.	Pseudo-Hilarius Africanus on St. John—The Boy in Jesus' Arms (Matt. xviii. 2; Mark ix. 36)	46
XIII.	The Two Traditions about the Evangelist John	55

		PAGE
XIV.	THE MARTYRDOM OF THE TWO SONS OF ZEBEDEE IN THE EARLIEST MARTYROLOGIES AND LECTIONARIES	59
XV.	LITERARY TESTIMONIES FOR THE MARTYRDOM OF THE ZEBEDAID JOHN	64
XVI.	JOHN KILLED BY KING HEROD IN JEWISH TRADITION	69
XVII.	THE ORIGINAL TEXT OF ACTS XII. 2	73
XVIII.	THE MEETING OF PAUL AND JOHN THE 'PILLAR' IN GALATIANS AND IN THE ACTS .	78
XIX.	THE TRUE TEXT OF GAL. II. 9, AND THE ALLEGED CONFUSION OF THE TWO JAMESES BY IRENAEUS	81
XX.	THE CHRONOLOGY OF GALATIANS AND THE TRUE DATE OF THE CRUCIFIXION	84
XXI.	THE MARTYRDOM OF THE TWO WITNESSES IN REV. XI. 3–11	86
XXII.	REV. I. 9, REFERRING TO THE ZEBEDAID JOHN DEPORTED UNDER THE EMPEROR CLAUDIUS .	90
XXIII.	THE WORLD-WIDE CONGRATULATIONS IN REV. XI. 10 AND THE HISTORIC DATE OF THE ZEBEDAIDS' EXECUTION	95
XXIV.	THE SOURCE OF REV. XI. 13, THE DATE OF THE ORACLE REV. X. 1–XI. 2, AND THE ORIGINAL MEANING OF THE TWO MURDERED WITNESSES	99
XXV.	THE 'APOCALYPSE OF JOHN'—A PSEUDEPIGRAPHIC WRITING BY THE GNOSTIC CERINTHUS . .	103
XXVI.	THE 144,000 'VIRGINS' IN REV. XIV. 4 AND THE 'VIRGIN' JOHN OF THE 'LEUCIAN' ACTS . .	110
XXVII.	ST. JOHN GOING TO SLEEP IN HIS TOMB .	116
XXVIII.	ST. JOHN'S GRAVE AND THE DUST RISING OUT OF IT —ARCHAEOLOGICAL EVIDENCE FOR A MIRACLE LEGEND	120
XXIX.	THE TWO TOMBS OF ST. JOHN IN EPHESUS .	125

CONTENTS

		PAGE
XXX.	The Confusion of the Two Johns	128
XXXI.	The Identification of John the Son of Zebedee with John Mark and with John the Evangelist in Pseudo-Hippolytus	136
XXXII.	Papias on the Apocalypse of John and the Fourth Gospel	138
XXXIII.	The Quotation from Papias in Fortunatian's Preface to the Gospel of John	145
XXXIV.	Papias 'the Beloved Disciple of John'	147
XXXV.	Who wrote the Gospel dictated by John?	149
XXXVI.	The Punctuator and Emendator of Fortunatian's Prologue—the Presbyter Patricius of Ravenna, instructed by Bishop Ecclesius	157
XXXVII.	The Restored Witness of Papias and the Internal Evidence of the Fourth Gospel	161
XXXVIII.	The Date of the Fourth Gospel and of the First Epistle of John	165
XXXIX.	Traces of Marcionism in the Gospel of John	178
XL.	The Gospel 'published during the Lifetime of John', and the Author's Super- and Subscription	187
XLI.	St. John witnessing the Testimony of the Beloved Disciple	193
XLII.	John the Evangelist—an Eyewitness of the Arrest of Jesus. 'The High-Priests' Present at the Crucifixion	196
XLIII.	The Fourth Evangelist identified	204
	Index	214

ILLUSTRATIONS

PLATE
I   DR. C. G. BRETSCHNEIDER (1776–1848) . . *Frontispiece*
General-Superintendent of the Lutheran Church in Gotha.
The first theologian to question the traditional attribution of the Fourth Gospel to John the son of Zebedee on the very grounds which have been discussed ever since his time (1820), but forced to recant his heresy.
                                                                   FACING PAGE

II   DOM DONATIEN DE BRUYNE (1871–1935) . . . 6
By courtesy of Maison Thill, Brussels.
who discovered the African summaries and the anti-Marcionite origin of the earliest extant prologues to the Gospels of Luke and John.
    Dom de Bruyne was born in Neuf-Eglise October 7th, 1871, ordained in Bruges (1895), Professor of Sacred Scripture at the Grand Séminaire of Bruges (1901), entered Maredsous Abbey in 1905, Member of the Papal Commission for the new edition of the Vulgate version since 1907, died in Bruges August 5, 1935.

III   CODEX VATIC. REG. LAT. 14 SAEC. IX FOL. 144 . . *page* 15
The shorter version of the anti-Marcionite prologue to John (Fortunatian's Preface).

IV & V   CODEX VAT. LAT. 6083 SAEC. XI FOL. 90 R° AND V°
                                                  Between 16 *and* 21
The Monarchianist preface to John, followed by the longer version of the anti-Marcionite prologue to John and the European summary to it.

VI   DR. H. K. HUGO DELFF OF HUSUM (1840–1898) . . 38
Kindly lent by Dr. Christian Delff, Husum.
Dr. Delff was the first scholar who saw that the Evangelist John must have been a former high-priest of Jerusalem, the John of Acts iv. 6.
    He was born on August 11, 1840, in Husum, studied Protestant theology and philosophy in Tübingen (1857) and Munich (1858), Ph.D. of Tübingen (1862), *Privatdozent* of Kiel University (1864), quarrelled with the Protestant faculty, retired to Husum where he lived until November 6, 1898, when he was tragically burnt to death, having fallen asleep over his work and overturned the scholar's midnight oil lamp.
    Converted to Roman Catholicism in 1866. Published a considerable number of philosophic books. In 1889 he wrote and issued in Leipzig (W. Friedrich) his *Geschichte des Rabbi Jesu von Nazareth*, a Life of Jesus based in the main on the Fourth Gospel which he considered as the authentic memoirs of a personal disciple and friend of Jesus, who must have been (pp. 67 ff.) one of the high-priests of Jerusalem. This thesis was further developed in a monograph *Das vierte Evangelium, ein authentischer Bericht über Jesus von Nazareth, wiederhergestellt, übersetzt und erklärt*, Husum 1890, pp. 1 ff. In a supplement *Neue Beiträge zur Kritik u. Erklärung des vierten Evangeliums*, Husum, 1890, he collected a still valuable series of rabbinic parallels to the Gospel of John, intended to prove that the author must have been a learned Jew and cannot have been an illiterate Galilean fisherman.

PLATE		FACING PAGE
VII	BEHEADING OF THE TWO SONS OF ZEBEDEE BY KING HEROD AGRIPPA I	88

By courtesy of Prof. Wilhelm Neuss, of the University, Bonn a. Rh.
Illustration to Rev. xi. 3–7: the 'two witnesses' killed by 'the Beast' ascending from the bottomless abyss, and their corpses lying on the ground. Miniatures from two MSS. of the Commentary to Revelation by Beatus of Liébana.
(a) Cod. Paris. Bibl. Nat. Lat. 8878 (span.s.XI), fol. 155, derived from a North African pre-Hieronymian illustrated MS. of Revelation.
(b) Cod. Berol. (State Library), Theol. lat. fol. 561 saec. XII fol. 67 v° (a palimpsest written in Italy, on parchment formerly covered with Langobardic script).

PLAN OF THE PRE-CONSTANTINIAN, PROBABLY LATE SECOND OR EARLY THIRD CENTURY MEMORIAL CHAPEL (*cella memoriae*) OF JOHN THE EVANGELIST IN THE CENTRE OF THE LATER CONSTANTINIAN AND JUSTINIANIAN BASILICA . . . . *page* 120

By courtesy of Profs. Rudolf Egger and Josef Keil.
Jahreshefte d. österr. archaeologischen Instituts., vol. XXV, Beiblatt cols. 21/22, fig. 10.

VIII THE RUINS OF THE EPHESIAN BASILICA OF ST. JOHN THE DIVINE, BUILT OVER THE TOMB OF THE FOURTH EVANGELIST, EXCAVATED BY THE AUSTRIAN ARCHAEOLOGICAL EXPEDITION IN 1927 120

By courtesy of Profs. Rudolf Egger and Josef Keil.
Ibid., vol. XXV, Beiblatt cols. 5/6 fig. 1.

IX PLAN OF THE CROSS-SHAPED GROUP OF CATACOMBS FOUND UNDER THE ALTAR OF THE BASILICA OF ST. JOHN THE DIVINE IN EPHESUS 122

Jahreshefte d. österr. archaeologischen Instituts, vol. XXIV, Beiblatt cols. 65/66, fig. 36.

X ROCK-TOMB WORSHIPPED BY THE FORMER GREEK POPULATION OF EPHESUS AS THE GRAVE OF ST. JOHN . . 126

Photograph by Kyrios Lampakis in the collection of the National Museum of Athens.
By courtesy of Profs. Keil and Sotēriou.

The general situation of this tomb, which is very likely to be the original resting-place of John the Evangelist, is easy to identify on Baedeker's map of Ephesus, where the stadium is marked No. 5.

On Benndorf's map of Ephesus reproduced as fig. 2 to Bürchner's article *Ephesos* in Pauly-Wissowa's *Realencyclopaedie*, vol. V, between cols. 2780 and 2781, the reader will find the lettering GR (meaning 'grave') immediately on the east of the stadium. About one millimetre due south of the letter G, on the first isohypsic line along the slope of the hill is the exact place of this rock-tomb.

The tomb is cut into the steep slope of the Panajirdagh hill on the east of the stadium. The present photograph was taken by Kyr. Lampakis and reproduced in his book Οἱ ἑπτὰ ἀστέρες τῆς Ἀποκαλύψεως. It is now deposited in the photographic archives of the National Museum in Athens (ἀρ. 5982). My attention was called to it by Prof. Josef Keil, of Vienna University, who was good enough to obtain the loan of it from Prof. Sotèriou.

ILLUSTRATIONS

PLATE		FACING PAGE

To both gentlemen the author is most obliged for their courtesy. If funds were available, Prof. Keil would like to excavate the surroundings of the tomb in order to ascertain whether any traces of early Christian worship subsist beneath the surface of the little mound before the entrance.

XI JOHN THE EVANGELIST DICTATING TO MARCION . . 154

"who brought scriptures to him from the Pontic brethren." Ivory book-cover of an evangel of St. John in the treasury of Halberstadt (about A.D. 1000) made in Cologne. Said to have been added by the treasurer Albert of Langenburg to an evangeliary presented by Charlemagne's son Louis I to Bishop Haymo of Halberstadt in A.D. 840 (Hermes, *Der Dom zu Halberstadt*, 1896, pp. 132, 136; Molinier, *Les Ivoires*, p. 171; Beissel, *Gesch. d. Evangelienbücher*, p. 307; Ad. Goldschmidt, *Elfenbeinskulpturen aus der Zeit der sächs. u. karolingischen Kaiser*, Berlin, vol. II, pl. XIV, fig. 44; ibid., fig. 45, a companion ivory book-cover by the same sculptor for the Gospel of St. Mark, now in the provincial museum of Münster i.W.). Dated by Prof. Goldschmidt about A.D. 1000, and tentatively attributed to a workshop of Liège. The present writer would think it more than a century earlier. Comparison of the composition —especially the cloud supporting the Evangelist's symbol, the crouching attitude of the figures, the frame mounted with gems —with the miniature representing the Four Evangelists in the Carolingian evangeliary given by Louis I and his wife Judith to St. Medard of Soissons in 827 (Die Trierer Ada Hs., Leipzig, 1889, t. VI, pl. 23) shows the kind of miniatures which the Halberstadt Gospel must have contained, and which have influenced the sculpture of this ivory.

XII MARCION, 'WHO BROUGHT SCRIPTURES FROM THE PONTIC BRETHREN TO THE EVANGELIST JOHN' . . 156

Miniature from the 10th-century evangeliary of St. Libuinus in the treasury of the Cathedral of St. Bavo, Ghent, Flanders.

By courtesy of the Right Rev. Canon Van den Gheyn, Ghent.

Canon Van den Gheyn, *Inventaire archéologique de Gand*, MSS., Ghent 25/1, 1915, fiches 561–563; Kervyn de Volkersbeke, *Eglises de Gand*, I pp. 171 f.; Wilhelm Koehler, *Belgische Kunstdenkmäler*, hg. v. Paul Clemens, vol. I, 1923, pp. 11 ff. St. Livinus is not the Irish 7th-century saint of this name, but the hero of an 11th-century legend composed by the monks of the Abbey of St. Bavo. Canon Van den Gheyn (19.6.'36) thinks that the Livinus honoured in Ghent is no other but the monk Libuinus of Deventer in Holland, not a martyr, but an ecclesiastic who died a natural death in the 8th century. According to Dom de Bruyne's opinion the MS. may be old enough to have been the property, if not the product, of Libuinus of Deventer.

XIII MARCION REPROVED AND DISMISSED BY JOHN THE EVANGELIST 158

Miniature from a 10th-century evangeliary of Keiroussis on the Pontic coast of Asia Minor. MS. 748, Pierpont Morgan Library, New York.

By courtesy of the Librarian, Miss Belle da Costa Greene.

Previously published, but not explained, by Dr. Josepha Weitzmann-Fiedler, *Goldschmidt-Festschrift*, 1935, pl. XI, fig. 8; cp. p. 32.

xx THE ENIGMA OF THE FOURTH GOSPEL

PLATE FACING PAGE
XIV JOHN THE EVANGELIST DICTATING HIS GOSPEL FROM HIS AUTOGRAPH ON A PAPYRUS SCROLL TO HIS SCRIBE WHO 'COPIED IT' (*descripsit*) INTO A CODEX 160
Miniature of the 11th-century Codex Coislin CXLVI olim CCXIII, formerly in the Royal Library in Paris. Codex Nr. CI of Muralt's catalogue of the Imperial Library of Petersburg, now Leningrad Public Library.
By courtesy of the Librarian.

The secretary is explained by the accompanying inscription as 'Prochoros'. But the composition does not correspond at all to the Prochoros legend, which describes St. John dictating the Gospel, while standing erect on the top of a mountain on the island of Patmos—as he may, indeed, be seen on our Pl. XV. In this illustration the Evangelist and his scribe are seated on the *solarium* of a house, protected against the sun by a *velum* supported on two columns. See Strack-Billerbeck, *Das Evangelium erklärt nach Talm., Midr.* etc., Munich, 1924, p. 594a on the *solarium* used as a study by scholars.

The secretary is represented as extremely young, the Evangelist as very old, in order to minimize the chronological difficulties facing the reader of the anti-Marcionite prologue, whether it is punctuated so as to suggest that the secretary is Papias or whether it is read as saying that Marcion took John's dictation. On the contrary, there is no reason why Prochoros, one of the deacons selected, Acts v. 6, among 'men of honest report, full of . . . wisdom' and clearly distinguished from the 'young men' (οἱ νεώτεροι) of the primitive community, should have been imagined as a very young boy when he set out—twelve years later!—with St. John the son of Zebedee on his missionary wanderings.

The Evangelist is represented as holding in his hands an autograph draft from which he dictates to the secretary. This reduces the latter's function to that of a scribe copying (*descripsit*!) the evangelist's χειρόγραφον—a papyrus scroll—into a parchment codex. This tends to exalt the value of the Ephesian relic (see pp. 163, 168) and to minimize the consequences of the unfortunate collaboration of the (future) heretic Marcion, represented as having been at that time a mere schoolboy—albeit an unreliable and mischievous disciple.

XV JOHN THE EVANGELIST STANDING ON THE KATAPAUSIS MOUNTAIN ON THE ISLAND OF PATMOS AND DICTATING HIS FOURTH GOSPEL TO HIS DISCIPLE, THE DEACON PROCHOROS 162
By courtesy of the Librarian of Moscow Public Library.
Illustration to Ps.-Prochoros 'Acts of John.' Cod. Mosq. 41 (42 of Matthej's catalogue).

From the end of the 11th century onwards this composition is frequently found as frontispiece miniature to the Fourth Gospel. See the list given by Dr. Josepha Weitzmann-Fiedler in the *Adolph Goldschmidt-Festschrift*, 1935, p. 30, note 3, and the reproductions in Prof. A. M. Friend, jun.'s essay on the Evangelists' Portraits, *Art Studies*, 1927, pls. XVIII and XX; Gerstinger, *Griech.* Buchmalerei, pls. XX and XXII; Baumstark, *Monatsschr. f. Kunstwiss.*, vol. VIII, 1915, pl. XXX.

XVI THE JOHN RYLANDS LIBRARY PAPYRUS FRAGMENT OF THE FOURTH GOSPEL, ROUGHLY CONTEMPORARY WITH THE FIRST EDITION OF THE GOSPEL 168
By courtesy of the Librarian, Dr. Henry Guppy.

The papyrus was acquired, together with other fragments in Egypt by the late Prof. Bernard P. Grenfell, in 1920. To Mr. C. H.

ILLUSTRATIONS

PLATE — FACING PAGE

Roberts, Fellow of St. John's College, Oxford, belongs the credit of having identified the text of the fragment, which is the earliest known MS. of any part of the New Testament, and the earliest witness to the existence of the Gospel according to St. John. According to the editor's judgment, supported by Sir Frederic Kenyon, D. W. Schubart, and Dr. H. I. Bell, the papyrus was written in the first half of the 2nd century. It is thus about contemporary with Papias and Marcion. It contains chapter xviii, vv. 31-33 *(recto)* and vv. 37-38 *(verso)*: Pilate hailing Jesus as the king of the Jews, and Jesus admitting 'I am a king' . . . a passage which is, beyond doubt, derived from the Lazarus source (below, p. 202 ff.), the testimony of the eyewitness.

XVII ADOLPH VON HARNACK (1851–1929) 178

Reproduced by courtesy of his daughter and biographer, Frau Agnes von Zahn-Harnack, and of her publisher, Hans Bott Verlag, Berlin.

The first to attribute the Fourth Gospel to Papias' 'Elder John,' the author of the great standard work on Marcion; the first to perceive the Marcionite elements and affinities in the Fourth Gospel and the first to recognize the paramount importance of Dom de Bruyne's discovery of the anti-Marcionite origin of our earliest Gospel prologues. Adolph Harnack was born on the 7th of May, 1851, in Dorpat, educated in Dorpat and Erlangen, studied in Leipzig (1872 ff.), Doctor of Divinity Leipzig (1873), *Privatdozent* Leipzig (1874), professor in Giessen (1879-1886), in Marburg (1886), finally in Berlin (1888). In his *Dogmengeschichte* (1885) and in his *Chronologie der altchristlichen Literatur*, vol. I (1897), Harnack adopted and developed the thesis—first proposed by the French theologian Michel Nicolas, *Etudes critiques sur la Bible*, 1864—that the Fourth Evangelist must be the man whom Papias calls the Elder John. Although he wrote that the evangel might be described as 'the Gospel of John the Elder according to John the Apostle', even this conciliatory formula aroused a storm of protest in German orthodox circles. The ecclesiastical authorities entered a protest against his appointment as professor of theology in Berlin. The conflict developed into a full-blown political thunderstorm (W. Wendland, *Die Berufung Ad. Harnack's nach Berlin, Jahrb. f. Brandenburg. Kirchengesch.*, vol. XXIX, 1934); 1890 Member of the Prussian Academy of Sciences; 1905 Director-General of the Royal Library, Berlin. Seventy years old, he finished his masterpiece—the monograph on Marcion—for the first draft of which he had got the gold medal of the theological faculty of Dorpat as a student of nineteen years! In 1928 he presented Dom de Bruyne's discovery of the anti-Marcionite origin of our earliest Gospel-prefaces to the Academy, immediately recognizing—alone among the theologians of all nations—the epoch-making importance of the learned Benedictine's great find. Died on the 10th of June 1929 in Heidelberg.

XVIII THE ABBÉ JOSEPH TURMEL OF RENNES 182

Reproduced by courtesy of Turmel's biographer (Joseph Turmel, prêtre, historien, Paris, 1930), M. Félix Sartiaux, and of his publishers, Editions Rieder, Paris.

Born 1859, tried—in 1925—to show, independently from Harnack and without knowing the anti-Marcionite prologue to the Evangel of John, that the Fourth Gospel is a Marcionite book revised by a Catholic. Turmel was the second son of seven children of an unskilled labourer who could not write and of a dearly beloved mother who could not even read. Taught Latin by the parish priest from 1870 onwards, while he had to cut,

PLATE		FACING PAGE
	bundle, and hawk about sticks of firewood for a living. At thirteen, during his prayers, he had a vision of Jesus Christ, looking silently and steadily at the adoring child. Entered in 1876 the great clerical seminary of Rennes, 1880 the Catholic theological faculty of Angers, ordained in 1882. Professor at the Rennes Seminary from 1882–1892. Denounced by one of his pupils to his superiors, deposed in 1892, he obtained the humble post of an almoner of the congregation Petites Soeurs des Pauvres of Rennes, 1893; published a long series of extremely learned and competent books and essays on the history of dogma under his own name and fourteen different pseudonyms. They were condemned by the Index Congregation in 1908. In 1930 the author himself was excommunicated *latae sententiae* and declared *haereticus vitandus*. In 1925 he published under the pseudonym Henri Delafosse his translation and commentary of the Fourth Gospel. Many of his observations hold good even now that the alleged 'editor' of a Marcionite gospel of John has been recognized as the author responsible for the evangel.	
XIX	THE LATE DR. JOHANNES KREYENBÜHL OF LUZERN AND ZURICH (1846–1929)	190
	Reproduced by courtesy of his son-in-law, Dr. Med. A. Pupato-Rahn of Zürich.	
	The first to see that the 'Beloved Disciple' was Lazarus (John xi. 3, 5: 'Lord, behold, he whom thou lovest'). Dr. Kreyenbühl was born in 1846 in Luzern, as the scion of an old family of Pfaffnau, Canton Luzern; Professor of Philosophy at the Lyceum of Luzern, lost his post because he preferred the philosophy of Plato to the speculations of the Church-fathers, had to live for years as an elementary schoolmaster in Zurzach. Obtained the degree of Ph.D. from the University of Bâle for a monograph on Plato's *Theaitetos*, became *Privatdozent* at Zürich University, earning a living as a free-lance writer, dramatic, literary, and art critic. In 1896 he published a book, *Freies Christentum und ethische Kultur*; in 1897 a two-volume book, *Das Evangelium der Wahrheit*, on the Fourth Gospel, which he tried to identify with the 'Gospel of Truth' of the Gnostic Valentinus. A number of his essays appeared in the *Zeitschrift für neutestamentliche Wissenschaft*. Occupied until the end of his life with the preparation of an (unpublished) Life of Jesus. Died in Zürich in October 1929.	
XX	THE LATE DR. H. B. SWETE OF CAMBRIDGE (1835–1917)	208
	Photograph by Ramsey and Muspratt, Cambridge.	
	who first identified the 'Beloved Disciple' and the 'rich young man, whom Jesus loved, when he saw him' of Mark x. 21.	
	Professor H. B. Swete was born on the 14th of March, 1835, educated at King's College, London, and at Caius College, Cambridge; Dean, Tutor and Theological Lecturer of Caius College, 1869–1877, Fellow of the British Academy, 1902; Editor of Theodore of Mopsuhestia's Commentary on the Epistles of St. Paul (1880–2), of the Septuagint Version of the Old Testament (1887–94); of the Akhmim Fragment of the Gospel of Peter; wrote on the *History of the Doctrine of the Holy Spirit*, on the *Gospel of Mark*, on the *Apocalypse of John*, etc. The first to identify (1916) the Beloved Disciple with the Rich Young Man, whom Jesus loved at the first glance, in Mark x. 21.	

THE ENIGMA OF
THE FOURTH GOSPEL

I

AN INSOLUBLE ENIGMA?

Quis, quid, ubi, cur, quomodo, quando?

THE MOST ELEMENTARY and inescapable duty of the historian facing any source-document whatsoever is, admittedly, to ascertain its author, date, place of origin, meaning, tendency and *raison d'être*.

The authors of the best text-book on historical method, from which every French student is taught the rules of the game, MM. Ch.-V. Langlois and Ch. Seignobos, have laid down the law in one terse and impressive sentence:

'A document whose author, date and provenance cannot be determined, is just good for nothing.'

In view of this universally recognized canon of sound historical research, it is extremely disconcerting to find that the Rev. Dr. Carl Gottlieb Bretschneider, the first German theologian to question the traditional belief in the authorship of John the son of Zebedee, says (1820) in so many words:

'Where on earth, and by which of the Christians of old, the Fourth Gospel was written—nobody is ever likely to find out!'

Probably nobody would mind what this very learned and perspicacious scholar said, more than a century ago, were it not that his words have been echoed until this day by a long series of the most qualified experts, obviously independent of each other and of old Carolus Theophilus Bretschneider (Pl. I).

Among German critics, we find the late Professor Julius Grill, of Tübingen (1902), telling us that the author of the Fourth Gospel

'wanted to be anonymous and will, therefore, remain unknown for ever'.

THE ENIGMA OF THE FOURTH GOSPEL

The late world-famous Adolf von Harnack (1909) speaks of the Johannine problem as:

'the greatest enigma in the entire field of Christian history'.

'It is a riddle', says Professor Rudolf Bultmann, of Marburg (1923), 'which has, unto this day, not yet been solved.'

Finally, the great Albert Schweitzer (1930) delivers the following hopeless verdict:

'The Hellenistic doctrine of salvation through the communion with Christ is presented in wonderful perfection in the Gospel of John. But the literary problem of this book remains an insoluble enigma. Never shall we know who was its author, nor how it occurred to him to present John, the disciple of the Lord, as the witness for the truth of his story.'

An equal resignation has been manifested by French scholars. In 1867 Ernest Renan, in the thirteenth edition of his *Life of Jesus*, said and repeated the statement in all the following editions: The Fourth Gospel cannot have been written by John the son of Zebedee. It must have been an esoteric book containing the mystic doctrines of a particular, otherwise unknown Christian community in Asia Minor, where it was used for a long time before it was offered to the Church at large:

'to pierce the mystery of this school or to know how the document in question issued from it, is impossible'.

No less finally Jean Réville (1901) despaired of deriving from ecclesiastical tradition any trustworthy information about the author of the enigmatic evangel.

As late as 1928 the French Academician, M. Aimé Puech, said in his voluminous and lucid *Histoire de la Littérature Chrétienne:*

'The Fourth Gospel shows only such affinities to the three Synoptics as are inevitable. Whilst the other three, with certain individual differences, express in the simplest form the common faith of all Christians, the Gospel of John contains a mystic doctrine which goes far beyond it. It spiritualizes the life and teaching of Jesus. The material facts which it mentions are, indeed, not infrequently different from those recorded in the Synoptics, or else otherwise arranged. The difficulties of interpretation, which are sometimes considerable, are increased by the mystery which shrouds the author of the book and the milieu out of which it issued. This mystery has not yet been fathomed, and doubtless never will be.'

As to the Higher Critics in the English-speaking countries—where a 'turbulent priest' of the Church of England, the Rev. Edward Evanson, M.A., of Cambridge, had been the first modern theologian to deny the apostolic origins of the Fourth Gospel in a book '*The Dissonance of the Four Generally received Gospels*' published in 1792 at Ipswich—it will be sufficient to quote the Lamplough professor of New Testament Language and Literature in Birmingham, Dr. W. F. Howard, who wrote only two years ago:

'We shall never know who wrote this Gospel.'

The present writer hopes to show in the following chapters that this apparently insoluble riddle *was* already solved when the last among the above-named eminent judges delivered his verdict of despair—thanks to the momentous discovery (in 1928) of a learned member of the famous Maurine Congregation of Benedictine scholars, the late Dom Donatien de Bruyne (Pl. II). He hopes to prove that the Fourth Gospel, far from being an anonymous or pseudepigraphic book, undatable, unlocalizable and therefore obscure and unprofitable to the critical historian, is, on the contrary, a priceless document, the real author, writer, date, address, tendency and sources of which can be perfectly well determined. However paradoxical this may sound to readers who have been taught to accept the hesitant humming and hawing of an aimless and frequently baseless scepticism as the final verdict of the so-called Higher Critics, he has convinced himself that the evangel of John is actually the work of the man who could truthfully claim, in the dedicatory epistle once prefixed to it, to have heard, seen and touched the incarnate Word of Life, and that it is really derived, in certain essential parts, from the testimony of an eyewitness of the crucifixion of Jesus.

II

THE 'PREFACE TO THE CHRISTIAN READER' AND THE ANCIENT BIO-BIBLIOGRAPHICAL LIBRARIAN'S NOTES

THE PERSISTENT FAILURE to solve what is known as the Johannine problem is entirely due to the fatal neglect of all the information supplied by the Gospel manuscripts themselves.

While the few *obiter dicta* of the earliest Church Fathers on the origins of the Gospels were carefully gathered and all the old bones of contention chewed and gnawed again and again *ad nauseam*, nobody ever thought, throughout the whole 19th century, of analysing carefully the various old prefaces to the Gospels which profess to impart to the reader all the information he needs about the authors of these precious books.

This lack of interest in what has now been proved to be the most valuable source of information is all the more astonishing in view of the fact that the bulk of all the data in ancient and modern histories of Greek and Latin literature can be shown to be, in the last instance, derived from the little bio-bibliographical introductory notices which the librarians of the great Hellenistic libraries, foremost among them that remarkable scholar and poet, Callimachus, the author of the great subject and authors' catalogue of the Royal Library of Alexandria, and his successors, systematically inserted into the standard editions prepared for these central treasure-houses of classical and contemporary thought. Copyists have transcribed, compilers combined them again and again into ever new patterns, and finally lexicographers like Suidas have inserted them into their dictionaries. There we can still find many biographical prefaces to books which have long ago been lost to us through the destruction of the great public and private libraries of the Greek and Roman cities where many of these introductory notes had been first composed. What should we know of Aeschylus, Sophocles and Euripides, what of Thucydides and Herodotus, not to speak of a host of minor authors known to us only through fragmentary quotations, if no subscriptions and superscriptions—cataloguing the names and patronymics of the authors, their nicknames distinguishing them from homonymous colleagues, the dates of their birth, the dialect they used, the main incidents of their career and the catalogue of their 'previous works'—and no summaries or 'tables of contents' had ever been added at the beginning or at the end either of the original editions or of the standard texts subsequently prepared by well-informed learned editors, revisers and librarians?

There is no reason to suppose that the books of early and later Christian authors were originally published and later on copied and distributed, privately or commercially, in a manner different from the methods used for issuing and circulating non-Christian Greek or, for the matter of that, early Latin or any other ancient books published throughout the Hellenized Mediterranean world.

Had this fact and its implications been realized, the systematic collection of the various Greek and Latin prefaces to the single books of the New Testament would not have been left over to the 20th century and a due appreciation of the earliest among these texts would not have been delayed until 1928.

III

THE EARLIEST GOSPEL PREFACES AND SUMMARIES DISCOVERED BY DOM DE BRUYNE

IT WAS in the year 1928 that a learned Benedictine scholar, Dom Donatien de Bruyne, of the Abbey of Maredsous in Belgium, finally succeeded in determining the primitive character and early origin of certain texts which he had identified as 'the most ancient Latin prefaces to the Gospels' and in convincing the greatest authority among his Protestant contemporaries, Adolf von Harnack, of the incomparable importance of this discovery.

In 1910 he had had the great good fortune to discover in a Vatican and in a Munich manuscript a series of hitherto unknown summaries prefixed to a slightly revised form of the pre-Hieronymian Latin New Testament, known as the 'African text' because of its close correspondence with the quotations found in the writings of the martyr Cyprian (*d.* A.D. 258). These obviously African summaries of a post-Cyprianic, but pre-Hieronymian text, attributed by Dom de Bruyne tentatively to the end of the 3rd century A.D., were preceded in both MSS. by three little prefaces to the Gospels of Mark, Luke and John, which had been known and printed long ago, but never properly noticed and understood.

Dom de Bruyne has been able to show to von Harnack's satisfaction that the prologues to Mark and to Luke of this incomplete series have been used as the nucleus for the composition of the so-called Monarchianist prologues to the Second and Third Gospels, which had been known for some time already to have been written by a friend of the heretic Priscillian, the Spanish bishop Instantius, beheaded together with Priscillian in A.D. 385.

He could further prove that all three were translations from Greek originals; that a Greek preface preserved in an

DOM DONATIEN DE BRUYNE, O.S.B.,
OF MAREDSOUS ABBEY
1871–1935

'. . . aucun motif d'ordre apologétique ne doit pas nous empêcher d'admettre. . . .'—*Revue Bénédictine*, 1928, p. 203

PLATE II

Athenian 11th-century MS. of the Acts was the Greek original of this Latin introduction to the Third Gospel; that the prologues to Mark and Luke or (as we must add now) their primary sources had already been known to Irenaeus; finally, that the prologue to Luke showed a definite, implicit, and the preface to John an equally strong, but explicit, bias against Marcion.

Dom de Bruyne and von Harnack have, therefore, called the whole series 'the anti-Marcionite prologues to the Gospels', although, strictly speaking, this epithet does not apply to the original form of the short prefatory notice to Mark.

IV

BREVES FORTUNATIANI

ON THE BASIS of the invaluable spade-work done by Dom de Bruyne, the present writer could gradually advance a number of steps beyond the achievements of his distinguished predecessor.

To begin with, it was found possible to substitute for Dom de Bruyne's tentative guess 'towards the end of the 3rd century' an at once more precise and more plausible date for these African summaries, the three extant prologues prefixed to them and the 'slight' revision of the Cyprianic text to which all this introductory matter had been attached. However 'slight' this revision of the 'African' text used by Cyprian may have been, it stands to reason that we have to look for some definite reason why a new edition of the Gospels should have been prepared and why a summary and bio-bibliographical prefaces should have been added to it.

While no such reason is discoverable anywhere throughout the last years of the 3rd century, the initial years of the 4th century are marked by the fatal persecution *librorum tradendorum*, more exactly Diocletian's edict of the 23rd of February, A.D. 303, ordering the wholesale confiscation and destruction of the sacred books of the Christian Church.

Having been deprived of most of their Bibles, the various dioceses of the Roman Empire, among them the African Church, where the persecution had been particularly severe, must have had to satisfy a great and urgent demand for new books as soon as the Constantinian rescript of Milan (A.D. 313) restored their freedom of worship. Though there would be no time for a thoroughgoing new recension of the text as found in the few surviving manuscripts, the opportunity for a 'slight revision', such as could be achieved without too much delay, in the course of the process of dictating from the best available copies, would certainly not be missed on such an occasion.

At the time when Eusebius of Caesarea and Athanasius of Alexandria were commanded by Constantine—probably at their own suggestion—to prepare for his imperial majesty the standard edition of the Greek Bible, of which our earliest great uncial codices seem to be representative specimens, something analogous has certainly been done about the Latin text of the Western part of the Empire by the bishops of Carthage, probably also of Rome.

The preparation of the new African standard edition and of the summaries and prefaces attached to it was obviously not a job to be left to some obscure clerk or to some unauthorized speculative bookseller.

As we should have expected, we find that their author was perfectly well known to St. Jerome, the final reviser and editor of the Latin Bible. He praises as a real gem, and confesses to have used himself the 'short notes' to the Gospels which 'Fortunatian an African by birth, Bishop of Aquileia under the Emperor Constantius, wrote in rustic language, having arranged their chapter-headings (*tituli*) in due order'.

It is natural that African prologues to the Gospels should be encountered in a number of manuscripts in Spanish, so-called Visigothic Bibles. We learn from Prudentius that the destruction of the Christian books had been duly carried out in Spain too. Knowing the close relation of the Spanish and the African Churches, we should expect that many copies of the newly revised African edition of the Gospels, with Fortunatian's summaries and prefaces, would immediately be exported to Spain.

The fact that we find these prologues in Spanish manuscripts interpolated with large extracts from St. Jerome's short history of Christian literature '*De viris inlustribus*' is equally easy to understand for those who remember that this book was dedicated by the author in A.D. 392 to the *praefectus praetorio*, Numerianus Dexter (the son of Bishop Pacianus of Barcelona), a gentleman to whom the municipality of Barcelona has erected a monument, and that a Spanish admirer of St. Jerome, the rich and generous Lucinius of Baetica, sent no less than six accomplished scribes from Spain to Palestine where Latin copyists were scarce, in order to copy whatever the Church

Father had written until then (A.D. 391), especially Jerome's revised text of the Latin Gospels.

No doubt, Lucinius put the archetypes obtained from St. Jerome at great cost through his six scribes to good use in his native country, circulating copies of them wholesale throughout the six episcopates of Christian Baetica, and probably also throughout the communities of the five other provinces of Spain.

V

FORTUNATIAN'S SOURCES

AS DOM DE BRUYNE has seen, all the three African prologues show manifest signs of being translated from the Greek. So they cannot have been composed by Fortunatian.

The present writer has shown, moreover, that he did not even himself translate the short introductory notice to Mark, ending with the phrase '*descripsit hoc in partibus Italiae evangelium*', but copied it, without the slightest compunction, from the Latin version of Marcion's 'proevangel' in the Bible of the Marcionites, just as he or another editor of the Latin collection of the Pauline Epistles lifted the Marcionite preface to the *Apostolos* unchanged out of Marcion's Bible into his copy of the Catholic canonical New Testament.

Yet this pompous redundancy '*in partibus* . . .', which seems to have been an idiom or rather a peculiar mannerism of the Latin translator of the Marcionite Bible, must have pleased Fortunatian. For he imitated it in what appears to be his own translation of a Greek preface to the Acts, prefixed to his own 'slightly revised' Latin text of the Gospel of Luke, where he says that the Apostle wrote his evangel '*in partibus Achaiae*'.

If Fortunatian derived his little preface to Mark from the Marcionite 'proevangel', he certainly borrowed the two prefaces to Luke and John from an anti-Marcionite, more probably from two different anti-Marcionite controversialists. Two sources rather than one are suggested by a somewhat striking discrepancy between what we read in the prologue to Luke and what we are told in the preface to John about the origins of the Fourth Gospel; the one authority saying that the Apostle *wrote* first the Apocalypse, and then the Evangel, while the second one does not breathe a word about 'Revelation', but stresses the fact that the Gospel was *dictated*—

correctly dictated indeed—by the author to a scribe, which is not at all the same thing as writing it *manu propria*.

Accepting a suggestion of von Harnack, the present writer would be inclined to suppose that the Greek preface to 'Acts', translated and used as a preface to the Third Gospel by Fortunatian, is derived in part—that is to say as far as it is directed against various tenets of the Marcionite Church—from a letter of Bishop Dionysius of Corinth 'to the Nicomedians in which he combated the heresy of Marcion and compared it with the true Canon', i.e. with the four canonical Gospels as opposed to Marcion's single allegedly 'true evangel'.

The preface to the Fourth Gospel is equally obviously translated from a Greek original. A characteristic phrase of it '*adhuc in corpore constitutus*' has been matched by Lightfoot with a *verbatim* parallel in the old Latin translation of Origen's Commentary to Matthew.

In another line of it, a characteristic alternative translation '*scripta vel epistulas*' is offered for the Greek word γράμματα, which can mean both, just as the earliest German translations of the Bible frequently offer two different German versions side by side for one difficult Latin word.

Accepting the views of Dom de Bruyne and von Harnack, the present writer is convinced that the Greek original of this preface too is extremely old, in other words, that it belongs to the later half of the 2nd century, when the controversy between Catholics and Marcionites had reached the height of bitterness.

VI

THE LONGER ANTI-MARCIONITE PREFACE TO THE FOURTH GOSPEL

THE THREE PREFACES to Mark, Luke and John, dealt with in the preceding chapter, exist in two forms:

(*a*) The shorter one, connected with the African summaries, which the present writer attributes to Fortunatian the African (*c*. A.D. 313) and proposes to quote henceforward under this name (Pl. III).

(*b*) The longer one, found in a group of Spanish MSS. (Pl. IV), the so-called Visigothic Bibles, expanded by interpolations taken from St. Jerome's *De viris inlustribus*. Were it not for the striking difference between St. Jerome and this expanded form of Fortunatian's prefaces, which we shall have to explain below, the latter might reasonably be attributed to St. Jerome himself, who admits having used Fortunatian's introductory notes and summaries, who has, demonstrably, had personal discussions with Marcionite heretics and was certainly more concerned about the Marcionite heresy than one would expect of a late 4th-century author. Because of the said important divergence and because of the multiple corruption disfiguring the title of Papias' *Exegetica* (below ch. XXXIII) —which St. Jerome has known from Eusebius and correctly translated in his *De viris inlustribus*, ch. 18, as '*Explanatio sermonum Domini*'—it seems more plausible to attribute their composition to some local clerk employed by Lucinius of Baetica and to quote them, for the sake of convenience, henceforth as the 'Lucinian prologues'.

In this longer form all three prefaces are editorially linked together, so as to form a reasonably coherent prologue dealing with all the Gospels. The preface to Mark—originally borrowed from Marcion's 'Pro-evangel' and therefore free from any anti-Marcionite tendency—is now expanded into an apology for the second evangel against all possible attacks by a Marcionite critic.

Since the existence of these two different versions has been rather obscured by Dom de Bruyne's and Harnack's attempt to construct a single text out of both and to relegate the variants into the *apparatus criticus*, they are here printed side by side on the folder inserted between pp. 16 and 17.

The third column shows St. Jerome's text, the footnotes its dependence on Eusebius and on the chapter (LI) of Epiphanius' *Panarion* directed against those who reject the Fourth Gospel. Epiphanius' arguments are known to be derived from the book of Hippolytus of Rome (A.D. 203) against Gaius of Rome, the principal critic of the Fourth Gospel. Epiphanius was in personal contact with St. Jerome in Palestine. Eusebius is used throughout the whole of St. Jerome's rather hurriedly written booklet, and indeed is its recognized principal source.

On the reverse of the said folder the reader will find four columns of text, demonstrating *ad oculos* how the original text of the preface to John has been modified so as to harmonize its beginning with the end of the prologue to Luke and to join the two together.

The assertion of the longer preface that the Fourth Gospel was written by its author in order to refute certain heretics is an old story without any foundation in the contents of the Gospel or in the Epistles of John, the first one of which had been said by Tertullian to have been directed against '*precoces et abortivi Marcionitae*', as we should say, 'against Marcionites before Marcion'. According to Irenaeus, John wrote in order to contradict or to forestall the errors of Cerinthus, of the enigmatic Nicolaitans, mentioned in the Apocalypse, of Marcion and the Valentinians, altogether quite a large order. Because the 'Ebionites'—the 'Poor' or proletarian Jewish-Christians of the primitive type—claimed to have a book of the Apostle John, rejected as apocryphal by the orthodox Church, Epiphanius—or perhaps his source, Hippolytus of Rome—chose to assert that the canonical Gospel of John was intended by its author as a refutation of the 'Ebionite' heresy.

To reproduce all or some of these entirely baseless imaginations of the later heresy-hunters is, however, quite in the style of the Greek bio-bibliographical notes to the editions of famous orators. It is customary to indicate in these '*hypotheses*' who was

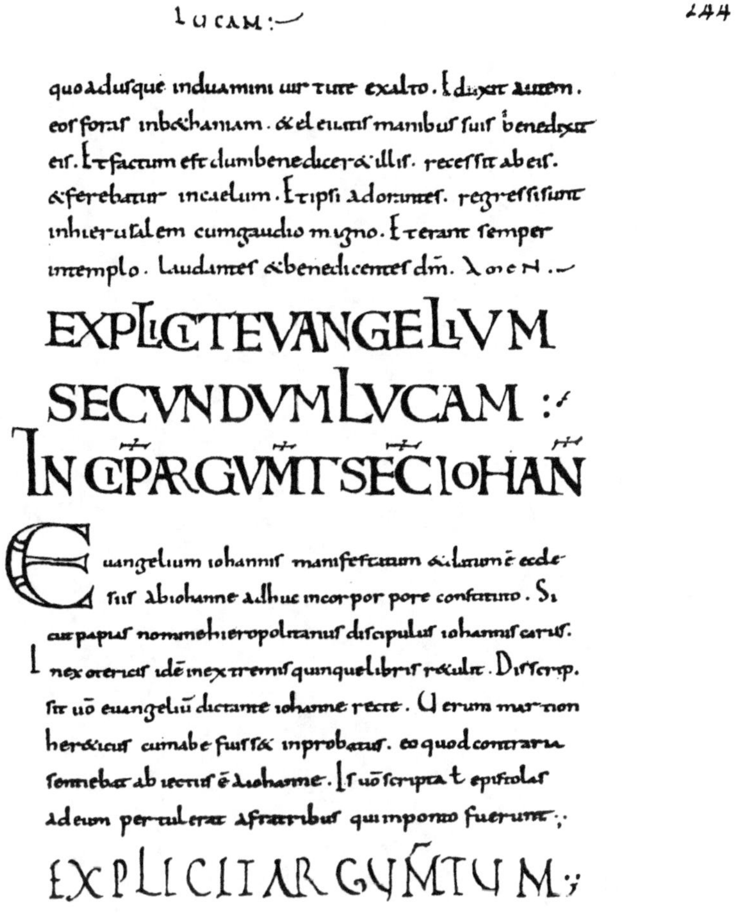

LUCAM

quoadusque induamini uirtute exalto. Eduxit autem
eos foras inbethaniam. & eleuatis manibus suis benedixit
eis. Et factum est dum benediceret illis. recessit ab eis.
& ferebatur incaelum. Et ipsi adorantes. regressi sunt
inhierusalem cumgaudio magno. Et erant semper
intemplo. Laudantes & benedicentes dm. AMEN.

EXPLICIT EVANGELIVM
SECVNDVM LVCAM:
INCP ARGVMT SEC IOHAN

Euangelium iohannis manifestatum &datum est ecclesiis ab iohanne adhuc incorpore constituto. Sicut papias nomine hieropolitanus discipulus iohannis carus. in exotericis ide inextremis quinque libris retulit. Discripsit uo euangelium dictante iohanne recte. Uerum mar-non hereticus cumab eo fuisset improbatus. eo quod contraria sentiebat ab iectus é aiohanne. Suo scripta t epistolas adeum pertulerat a fratribus qui ponto fuerunt.

EXPLICIT ARGVMTVM;

CODEX. VAT, REG. LAT. 14, SAEC. IX, FOL. 144

The shorter version of the anti-Marcionite Prologue to John
(Fortunatian's Preface)

PLATE III

c

INCIPIT PREFAT
euglii scdm iohm

HIC EST IOHS EVANGLISTA

unus ex discipulis
xpi. qui uirgo elect'
est ado. que denupqis
uolentem nubere uocauit dr̄. cui
uirginitas inhoc duplex testimonium ineug'lo datur. qd̄ & pre
ceteris dilectus adeo dicitur. &
huic matrē suam iēsus adcrucem
commendabit dr̄. ut uirginem
uirgo seruaret. Deniqi manifestans
ineug'lo quod erat ipse incorruptibilis uerbio post inchoans
solus uerbū caro factum ee nec
lumen atenebris cōprehensum
fuisse testatur. Primum signū
ponens quod innupnis fecit ōs
& ostendens quod erat ipse legentibs demonstrans. Q d̄ ubi dn̄s
inuitatus deficere nuptiarum
uinum uidebat &cueterib; in
mutatis. noua om̄a que axpo
ministruuntur apparent. hoc
autem eugl'm scripsit inasia.
postea qui inpathmos insula
apokalipsin scripserat. ut cui
inprincipio canonis incorrupta
bile principium ingenis & &
incorruptibilis finis puirginem
inapokalipsi redderetur. dicente
xpō egosū A & w. Et hic est ioh's
quiscians supuenisse diem recessus sui conuocatis discipulis in
epheso. promulta signorū experimenta promens xp̄m. descendens
indefossum sepulturę suę loci
Facta oratione. positus est ad
patres suos. tam extraneus adolore mortis quam acorruptione
carnis inuenitur alienus. Tam
post om̄s eugl'm scripsit. & hoc
uirgini debebatur. Quorū tam
uel scripturarū tempore dispositio. ut librorū ordinatio. ideo
persingula anobis non exponit
ut sciendi desiderio collocato. &
querentib; fructus laboris & dō
magisteri doctrina seruetur.
EXPLICIT PREFATIO.

INCIP PROLOGUS SCD'S
OHS APLS QUE DNS
ih̄s amauit plurimum.
Nouissimus omium scripsit
hoc eugl'm. postulantibus
asię episcopis aduersus cerinthum aliosqi hereticos. &
maxime tunc ebionitarum
dogma consurgens. qui asserunt
stultitię suę prauitate. Si ceni
ebionite appellantur. xp̄m ante
quam de maria nasceretur n̄ fuisse. nec natū ante scl̄a. de deo
patre. Unde etiam copulsus est
diuinam eius apatre natuitatē
dicere. Sed & aliam causam conscripta huius euangelii ferunt.

CODEX VAT. LAT. 6083, SAEC. XI, FOL. 90 RECTO

The Monarchianist preface to John, followed by the longer version
of the anti-Marcionite Prologue to the Fourth Gospel.

PLATE IV

quia cū legisset mattha marci & lu-
cę de euglo uolumina; pbauerit
quidem textū historię. & uocū cor-
duxisse firmauerit. Sed unius tan-
tum anni inquo & passus e post
carcerem iohīs historia texuisse.
Pretermisso itaq; anno cuius acta
atnb; exposita fuerant superioris
temporis antequā iohīs claude-
retur incarcere gesta narrauit.
Sicut manifestum ee poterit
his qui quattuor euglioȝ uolumina legerint diligenter. hoc igit
euangłm post apokalipsin scriptum manifestum & datum est
ecclīs ī asīa ioħe ad huc īn corpore constituto. sicut papias nōīe
ieropolitanus eps discipulus ioħr
& carus ī exoterīcis suis id est in
extremis quinq; libris retulit
qui hoc euglm ioħe sibi dictante conscripsit. Uerū marcion
hereticus cum ab eo fuisset repro-
batus eo quod contraria sentire-
pro iectus e a ioħe hic uero scripta ut epīas ad eū pertulerant a
frib; missas qui in ponto erant
fideles. in xpō ihū dño nr̄o
FINIT PROLOGUS.
Incipit elencus eiusdē.
Pharisei leuite interro-
gunt ioħm   I
Ioħs ihm uidens agnū
dei dicit.   II
Et andreas petro dicit. inue-

nimus messiam   II
Ihr iudeam de aqua uinum
facit.
De templo nummularios eicit.
soluite templum hoc dicens.
II Nichodemo loquitur de bapti-
smo & aliis multis.   III
Ihr in iudea baptizat.
I Et ioħs meion quiq; dicit xpm
crescere se aūt minorari IIII
Ihr cum muliere samaritana
loquitur.
I Propham in patria sua sine ho-
nore ee dicit.
II Reguli filiū a morte suscitat.
Apud natatoriam bezeta xxx
octo annoȝ infirmitate homi-
nis sanat.
I A dicit scrutamini scripturas.
II Et si crederetis moysi crederetis
forsitan & mihi.   III
O e quinq; panib; & duob; piscib;
I Et quod eū regem facere uoluer
II Ihr supra mare ambulabat
III Et de manna & pane cęli loqr̄.
IIII A cedentib; ab eo discapulis.
Unū ex duodecim diabolū dicit.
Scenophegia.   VII
I Ihr medio die festo ascendens
in tēplū docet.
II Multas cui de turba credentib;
idem clamat.
III Si quis sitit ueniat & bibat.
IIII Cū ministris & nichodemo princi-
pes contendunt.

CODEX VAT. LAT. 6083, SAEC. XI, FOL. 90 VERSO

End of the longer version of the anti-Marcionite preface to the Fourth Gospel, followed by the 'European' summary to it. The reader will notice that, curiously enough, this summary does not mention the famous logosophic prologue to the evangel.

PLATE V

the adversary against whom the speech in question was delivered and what had been the debated subject. The *'hypothesis'* of Zosimus to Isocrates' *Praise of Helen of Troy* discusses, e.g., the question whether this panegyric was directed against Polycrates of Athens, Anaximenes of Lampsacus or Gorgias, who had all previously, but wrongly or inadequately, praised the fair heroine. Considering the various Gospels as a *kerygma* or rhetoric proclamation of the Glad Tidings by the individual evangelist and as *'aretalogies'* praising the miraculous deeds and reproducing the admirable speeches of Jesus Christ, they would be classified as rhetorical literature, and the writer of a bio-bibliographical preface would consider it his duty to inform the reader 'against whom' they had been directed by their author.

For our particular purpose these expansions of the original preface could be completely disregarded were it not that the comparison of the 'Lucinian' preface with St. Jerome's chapter on John the Evangelist (Folder 1) reveals a most remarkable fact: St. Jerome's text has evidently been copied *verbatim* with certain additions corresponding exactly to Jerome's source Epiphanius. They might have been thought to indicate that the preface was not compiled in Spain, but by St. Jerome himself for the revised Gospel text he sent to Lucinius—were it not for one most significant exception:

The words *'filius Zebedaei et frater Jacobi apostoli, quem Herodes post passionem Domini decollaverat'* used by St. Jerome for the purpose of identifying the fourth evangelist, the favourite disciple of Jesus with 'the son of Zebedee the brother of the Apostle James whom Herod beheaded after the passion of the Lord' are deliberately omitted.

This means that the editor of a Spanish edition of the Vulgate Gospels—anterior to the *De ortu et obitu Patrum*, i.e. to the Bible prefaces attributed to St. Isidore of Sevilla (570–636), whose encyclopedic learning is so fully reflected in these so-called Visigothic Bibles and whose preface to John shows no objection to St. Jerome's identification of John the Evangelist with John the son of Zebedee—flatly refused to accept an equation which could have been supported by St. Jerome with quotations from Epiphanius, Eusebius, Origen and Dionysius of Alexandria (A.D. 262).

VII

THE GREEK AND THE LATIN TEXTS OF THE ANTI-MARCIONITE PROLOGUE TO LUKE

THE REMARKABLE attitude taken by the author of the 'Lucinian' preface is by no means unparalleled. Dom de Bruyne has printed in parallel columns the Greek text of the anti-Marcionite prologue to Luke—copied from a 9th-century autograph of Patriarch Methodius of Constantinople—and the Latin, early 4th-century translation by Fortunatian:

ὕστερον δὲ 'Ιωάννης ὁ ἀπόστολος ἐκ τῶν δώδεκα	Postmodum Iohannes apostolus
ἔγραψεν τὴν 'Αποκάλυψιν ἐν τῇ νήσῳ Πάτμῳ καὶ μετὰ ταῦτα τὸ εὐαγγέλιον	scripsit Apocalypsin in insula Pathmos deinde evangelium in Asia.

If we compare the two texts we find that on the one hand the Greek preface does not say where the Fourth Gospel was written—probably because the original writer of this preface, prior to Irenaeus, who says definitely that the evangel was written in Ephesus, did not know it, or because he thought that both the Gospel and the Apocalypse had been written on the island Patmos. On the other hand, Fortunatian, who remembered his Irenaeus and added '*in Asia*' as a counterpart to the preceding assertions that Matthew had been written '*in Judaea*', Mark '*in Italia*', either deliberately omitted the words 'one from among the Twelve' in his translation or did not read them in the Greek text he was rendering into Latin.

In the latter case it would be necessary to suppose that the words 'one of the Twelve' were interpolated by some Greek copyist, posterior to the translation of Fortunatian (A.D. 313), but prior to the autograph copy of the Greek prologue made by the patriarch Methodius of Constantinople in

THE ANTI-MARCIONITE PROLOGUE TO LUKE

the latter half of the 9th century. The object of this interpolation would have been to make it clear that the Apostle John the Evangelist was—according to this reviser's opinion—'one of the Twelve', and not the other John from among the Seventy-Two, said to have been ordained Bishop of Ephesus by John the son of Zebedee, who is first mentioned in the Apostles' Catalogue of the so-called 'Apostolic Constitutions', written at some time before A.D. 394, probably in Transjordania.

It is this second John, Bishop of Ephesus, who is said by Solomon of Basra to have written the Apocalypse according to 'what he had heard from John the Evangelist'. This story (handed down by a 13th-century compiler of much earlier legends about the Apostles) is an obvious and rather naïve reply to the irrefutable demonstration of Origen's pupil, Dionysius of Alexandria, proving that for reasons of language, style and ideology the author of the Gospel and the Catholic Epistle of John cannot have written the Apocalypse. It seems reasonable to attribute its invention to Dionysius' adversary, Bishop Nepos of Arsinoë, shortly after A.D. 262.

Knowing this story of a second John of Ephesus, the hypothetical interpolator might very well have thought it necessary to emphasize his conviction that both the Apocalypse and the Gospel were written by the first John 'the Apostle, one of the Twelve'.

It is, however, contrary to a recognized canon of sound philological method to assume an interpolation in a text which can perfectly well be understood without resorting to such an expedient.

In our case this is certainly possible. Fortunatian may well have omitted to translate the words 'one of the Twelve', simply because he refused to accept the identification of John the Evangelist with John the son of Zebedee, an 'illiterate and unlearned' Galilean fisherman—just as did the author of the preface to John in the Spanish Bibles when he was transcribing St. Jerome's chapter on the first evangelist.

As to the Greek prologue, the original author of it may very well have insisted so energetically on telling his readers that both the Apocalypse and the Gospel of John were written by 'one of the Twelve' because even in his time—before A.D. 180—the contrary opinion was widely held. As a matter of fact, Adolf von Harnack has clearly seen—and attached great importance to this observation—that the rather clumsy apposition 'one of the Twelve' after the words 'John the Apostle' (᾽Ιωάννης ὁ ἀπόστολος ἐκ τῶν δώδεκα) must have been meant to distinguish this John from a second John, presumably from the much discussed 'Elder John' or 'older John', whom the famous fragment of Papias mentions, together with a certain Aristion, and clearly differentiates from the John whom it groups with his brother James.

Two years after von Harnack had discussed this problem, Dr. Mingana published the following superscription to the Gospel of John discovered in a Peshiṭṭô codex finished on the 23rd of September 1749, but faithfully transcribing with all its most minute details a parent manuscript of about A.D. 750:

> 'The Holy Gospel of our Lord Jesus Christ
> the preaching of John the Younger.'

This remarkable Syrian title line is a perfect counterpart to the 'Lucinian' prefaces in the Spanish Bibles, and to Fortunatian the African's prologue to Luke. It proves that in the east and in the west of the Mediterranean, as well as on its southern coasts, from the 4th to the 8th, and even to the 18th century, unmistakable traces have been left behind in still extant manuscripts of the Gospels by different men who, each one in his time and independently from one another, stubbornly refused to accept the identification of John the Evangelist with John the son of Zebedee.

If the African and the Iberian satisfied their conscience by the purely negative attitude of excluding the contested equation from the prefaces in the editions of the evangel which they had to superintend, the Syrian went one better and dared to distinguish plainly and unequivocally John the Evangelist, as the 'younger John', from the Zebedaid, as the 'older one', just as the Callimachean bio-bibliographic library-tags differentiate an Athenian playwright Euripides the Younger from his 'older' more famous namesake, or an 'Astydamas the Younger' or 'the young one' from an Astydamas 'the Older' or the 'Old one'.

VIII

HERETIC AND CATHOLIC SECOND-CENTURY TESTIMONIES CONCERNING JOHN OF EPHESUS

READERS INTENT upon defending the traditional point of view might refuse to be impressed by the testimonies discussed in the preceding chapter. Fortunately we are in a position to demonstrate by positive, safely dated evidence that in the very second century when the Fourth Gospel was published, a definite diversity of opinion existed about the personality of its ostensible author, John.

It may surprise scholars, no less than laymen, to be told that the identification of John the son of Zebedee with the Ephesian John, supposed to be the beloved disciple of Jesus mentioned in John xxi. 24 as the writer of the Fourth Gospel, is not found —whatever they may have read to the contrary in all the current text-books and commentaries—in any orthodox author of this period, but only and exclusively in the heretical, so-called Leucian 'Acts of John' which are generally attributed to the years round about A.D. 160.

There is not a word of truth in the usual assertion that John the Zebedaid is identified with John the Evangelist by Irenaeus, Theophilus of Antioch, the *Canon Muratori*, or the presbyters of old quoted by Clement of Alexandria.

As to Irenaeus, the late Professor C. F. Burney, of Oxford, had already carefully tabulated all the passages concerning John the Evangelist. There is not a line in Irenaeus that will bear such an interpretation, let alone one that says explicitly anything of the sort. The other quotations are so short and easy of access that the reader can verify for himself without any difficulty the following facts:

In none of the above-quoted passages is John the Evangelist ever identified with John the son of Zebedee. He is identified— quite naturally—on the strength of John xxi. 24 and 20 with 'the beloved disciple of Jesus'. But there is no proof whatsoever for the assumption that the Fourth Gospel itself intends to suggest the identity of the 'beloved disciple of Jesus' with one of the two Zebedaids, who are never mentioned in it but in the Appendix xxi. 2. It means simply running round in a vicious circle of arguments to read into every statement of Irenaeus, Theophilus of Antioch, Clement of Alexandria or the *Muratorianum* concerning John the beloved disciple, the equation—never implicitly or explicitly stated in any of them—of Jesus' favourite with one of Zebedee's twin sons.

It is obvious that those who call the author of the Fourth Gospel 'John the beloved disciple' connect the title of the book 'Evangel according to John' with the statement in John xxi. 24: 'this is the disciple who testifieth of these things and who wrote these things'. But it does not follow at all that even one of them ever thought of equating the writer mentioned in John xxi. 24 with one of the two Zebedaids, incidentally named in xxi. 2, where they are clearly distinguished from the unnamed 'two others of his disciples'. It may very well have been as clear to all our ancient witnesses as it must be to the modern, moderately attentive reader that the unnamed 'two other disciples' of the Appendix xxi. 2 hark back to the equally unnamed 'two of his disciples' in John i. 35, one of whom was Andrew (John i. 40), while the other was currently identified by early commentators even before John Chrysostom (A.D. 347–407), Theodor of Mopsuhestia, and Ishodad with the 'beloved disciple', 'who wrote this' and who is, elsewhere too, mentioned but not named.

Other ancient authors beside the Fourth Evangelist had occasionally introduced an anonymous figure about the identity of whom readers and critics could go on speculating and offering more or less plausible conjectures. We find, e.g., the grammarian Thrasyllus, author of a bibliography of the philosopher Democritus, telling us: 'If the Rivals ($Ἀντερασταί$) be a work of Plato, the unnamed bystander, different from Oenopides and Anaxagoras, who makes his appearance when conversation is going on with Socrates about philosophy and to whom Socrates says that the philosopher is like the all-round athlete, might be Democritus.'

In the same way ancient 2nd-century readers have certainly been speculating from the start about the identity of the anonymous 'beloved disciple' of Jesus. Nothing prevented them—unless they knew some definite fact incompatible with this conjecture—from identifying him with John the son of Zebedee, as Origen, Dionysius of Alexandria, Eusebius, Epiphanius and St. Jerome did in the third and fourth centuries. But nothing either opposed their equating this anonymous figure with one of the unnamed two disciples mentioned alongside with the Zebedaids. The latter identification presupposes simply that among the most intimate circle of primitive disciples of Jesus there were two men, bearing the extremely common Jewish name John—John the son of Zebedee and John the beloved disciple, the alleged writer of the Gospel—just as there were in this small group two men with the equally common name Simon—Simon Peter and Simon the Zealot—and again two men with the very common name Judah—Judas Thomas, in Greek *Didymos*, the 'Twin', and Judas the traitor, called 'The Sicarian' (*Iskariōtēs*). What objection could anyone raise against such a very plausible interpretation of John xxi. 2 on the basis of the equally plausible, analogous interpretation of John i. 35, 40 f.? Was the trustworthiness of the eyewitness who had leaned against the bosom of the Master in any way lessened, if he was identified, not with the one of the passionate and irascible 'Sons of Thunder' who was, according to Acts iv. 13, an 'illiterate and unlearned man' and of whom not a single word is reported throughout Luke's Acts, but with another disciple, presumably better able to write a 'spiritual gospel'? Had not the identification of the evangelist with a John, other than the son of Zebedee, the signal advantage that it did not force the reader to suppose that Jesus had given at the Last Supper the place of preference at His side to one of the ambitious twins whom He had rebuked for their claim to sit on the thrones right and left of the Master's seat in His Kingdom? Is it not a welcome relief not to be compelled any longer to suppose that John the son of Zebedee, the strong and silent 'Pillar' of the Jewish-Christian community of Jerusalem, siding with Peter against Paul in the discussion concerning the admission of the Gentiles to the communion of the believers in Jesus the Christ, had written in his later life an openly anti-Jewish book speaking with the coolest indifference, nay with unmistakable Pauline hostility of the Jewish Law?

Knowing the opinions of Origen, Dionysius of Alexandria, Eusebius, Epiphanius and St. Jerome, nobody will want to deny that it was quite possible for the apostolic and other early Fathers of the Church to identify 'the beloved disciple' with John the son of Zebedee.

But it is absolutely unwarrantable to presuppose that those who say nothing more than that 'John the beloved disciple' or 'John the Apostle' is the author of the Fourth Gospel implied *ipso facto* that he was John the son of Zebedee, when the identification with another John, one of the unnamed disciples or Apostles in John xxi. 2 is at least equally possible, if not vastly preferable.

What we want, therefore, is definite 2nd-century evidence of the equation of the beloved disciple of Jesus with John the son of Zebedee, or with some 'other John', be he 'a younger' ($\nu\epsilon\omega\tau\epsilon\rho\sigma s$) or an 'older' ($\pi\rho\epsilon\sigma\beta\upsilon\tau\epsilon\rho\sigma s$) John. We do find both, but in two original documents only: as a matter of fact, the first one only in the heretical Leucian 'Acts of John', the second in the letter of Polycrates, the orthodox Bishop of Ephesus, to Pope Victor of Rome.

IX

THE LEUCIAN 'ACTS OF JOHN' ON THE BELOVED DISCIPLE OF JESUS

THE SO-CALLED 'Leucian' Acts or 'Wanderings' *qui appellantur Joannis, quos sacrileg⟨us⟩ Leucius ore ⟨eius⟩ conscripsit* are known to have been used as Holy Scripture by the so-called Encratites, the so-called Ebionites, the Montanists, the Manichaeans and the Priscillianists of Spain. According to the late Provost of Eton, Dr. M. R. James, they are 'not later than the middle of the second century'.

All the characteristic views and aims of their author can be derived from the teachings of Marcion, who prohibited marriage and every sort of sexual intercourse and admitted to baptism and communion only bachelors, spinsters, widows and widowers and such married people as would promise to separate and to lead henceforth a life of absolute chastity, who abhorred the eating of meat and the drinking of wine, praised poverty as blessed, and cursed wealth as an obstacle to salvation.

All these features, as well as Marcion's dualism and docetism are prominently displayed in the Leucian 'Acts of John', where the Apostle is represented as preaching against the gathering of earthly treasures, as dissuading the rich from rejoicing in their wealth, commending a married woman for living with her husband in total sexual abstinence, converting even a harlot to perpetual chastity, celebrating the Eucharist with water and bread only and thanking God in his last hour for having preserved him from any contact with women by endowing him with a congenital bodily impotence and for having prevented him from marrying; where the Jews are said to have received their Law from a godless serpent, and Judas the traitor to worship another god than John; where Jesus reveals to John that He has not an ordinary human body, but an immaterial, Protean shape, able to assume the most different aspects and to be felt at one time as intangible as air, at another time as hard as stone, and where, finally, John alone sees that Jesus is not really crucified, while His enemies nail an imaginary phantom-body to the cross.

Conversely, not a trace can be detected in this book of the tenets of any other sect. The beautiful mystic hymn in ch. 95 is one of the songs composed by Arsinous, Valentinus and Miltiades '*qui novum librum psalmorum Marcioni conscripserunt.*

It is in this edifying *vie romancée*, a typical ψευδὴς ἱστορία, which nobody has ever considered for one moment as a document from which any trustworthy information could be derived either about the life and passion of Jesus or about the life and character of the Apostle John, that we meet for the first time the clear and unequivocal identification of the 'beloved disciple' of Jesus with the Galilean fisherman John the son of Zebedee.

The crucial passage—manifestly devoted to the exposition of the author's Docetic creed—begins with the statement of one Drusiana to whom the Lord had appeared 'in the likeness of John'. The audience is 'perplexed' about this report, but John explains to them that similar experiences have been vouchsafed to him. When Jesus

'had chosen Peter and Andrew which were brethren, he cometh unto me and James my brother saying: I have need of you, come unto me. And my brother, hearing that, said: John, what would this child have that is upon the sea-shore and calls us? And I said: What child? And he said to me again: That which beckoneth to us. And I answered: Because of our long watch we have kept at sea, thou seest not aright, my brother James; but seest thou not the man that standeth there comely and fair and of a cheerful countenance? . . .'

'And so when we had brought the ship to land, we saw him also helping along with us to settle the ship: and when we departed from that place, being minded to follow him, again he was seen of me as having (a head) rather bald, but the beard thick and flowing, but of James as a youth whose beard was newly come. . . . And after that, as we followed him, both of us were by little and little (yet more) perplexed as we considered the matter. Yet unto me there then appeared this yet more wonderful thing: for I would try to see him privily, and I never at any time saw his eyes closing (winking), but only open. And oft-times he would appear to me as a small man and uncomely, and then again as one reaching unto heaven. Also there was in him another marvel: when I sat at meat he would take me upon his own breast; and sometimes his breast was felt of me to be smooth and tender, and sometimes hard like unto stones, so that I was perplexed in myself and said: Wherefore is this so unto me? And as I considered this, he . . . etc.

'And at another time he taketh with him me and James and Peter unto the mountain where he was wont to pray, and we saw in him a light such as it is not possible for a man . . . to describe what it was like.'

Clearly in this passage the disciple whom Jesus loved, who leaned against his breast, is unequivocally identified with John the brother of James. Both are the fishermen in the boat on the Galilean Sea whom Jesus called away from their nets. To make the identification doubly certain, the author introduces, in addition, the scene of the Transfiguration on the Mountain, witnessed by Peter, John and James only—a chapter of the most fundamental importance in the Synoptics, since it describes the revelation of Jesus' Messianic glory to his most intimate disciples, which is, however, paradoxically enough, entirely wanting in the evangel supposed to have been written by one of the three!

Yet it would be very rash to say that the author of these pseudepigraphic heretical 'Acts of John' wanted to identify John the son of Zebedee with the Evangelist John. Not only is there no mention whatsoever of the writing of the Gospel by John in these Acts—an omission which has been rectified in the later 'Acts of John' by the Pseudo-Prochoros, and which the reader might feel tempted to explain as possibly due to the fact that large parts of the Leucian 'Acts of John' are lost—but the apostle is made to say clearly:

'I am neither able to declare unto you nor to write the things which I both saw and heard'

thus evidently and flatly contradicting the introductory words of the First Epistle of John (i. 3 f.):

'that which we have seen with our eyes and our hands have handled . . . we declare unto you and these things we write unto you'.

If this means anything, it means that John the son of Zebedee is made to say by the Ps.-Leucius: I am unable to compose a Gospel, let alone to write one, and I have no intention to try it.

As if that were not enough, he is made to give another, more weighty reason for not even trying: Jesus has forbidden it

'for all His magnificent and wonderful deeds ought, for the present, to be concealed in silence, since they are ineffable and cannot, perhaps, altogether be either told or heard'.

Concerning everything that has been revealed to John about the mystic drama of the Passion, Jesus is said to have told His beloved disciple:

'... That suffering which I showed unto thee and the rest in the dance, I will that it be called a mystery. What I am, I alone know' —a remarkable paraphrase of the 'I am who I am' in Exodus!— 'and no man else. Suffer me then to keep what is mine.'

If John is made to say that he will not write a Gospel, that Jesus has forbidden him to divulge the mystery of 'what He is'—i.e. that He and the Father are one—and the secret of his wonderful deeds; if he is made specifically to contradict 1 John i. 3 f., the conclusion is unavoidable that the author of the Leucian 'Acts of John' intended to discredit the canonical Gospel of John as spurious and unduly attributed to the Apostle.

Now this doctrine is precisely the central and essential dogma of the Marcionite Church. According to Adamantius, Marcion taught that the original Apostles 'preached without writing' (ἐκήρυξαν ἀγράφως) and that the names of their ostensible Apostolic authors have been prefixed to them by Judaizing forgers.

It follows that the identification of the anonymous 'beloved disciple of Jesus' mentioned as the writer of the Fourth Gospel in the Appendix John xxi. 24 with John the son of Zebedee, the fisherman stigmatized in the Acts as an 'illiterate and unlearned' man, serves in the one 2nd-century text where we can find it, the purpose of denying that there ever was an Evangelist John. It has been introduced into an in itself spurious and obviously heretical romance merely for the purpose of contradicting the claim of the Fourth Gospel to have been written by the favourite disciple of Jesus.

It is certain that no reader knowing only the Fourth Gospel, in which the individual names of 'those of Zebedee' (xxi. 2) are not so much as mentioned, could ever have hit upon the idea of identifying the beloved disciple with the one of the two brothers who happened to be called with the same frequent name of John, as the author of the book mentioned in its superscription.

Had the author of the Appendix John xxi. intended to throw out a hint as to the identity of the anonymous disciple by mentioning 'the (sons) of Zebedee' in verse 2, he could only have aimed this cryptic allusion at readers who were already fully conversant with the Synoptic Gospels. It would be entirely misleading to say that, whatever they might have read or not read, every member of a Christian community at the beginning of the 2nd century must have known the names of these most intimate disciples of Jesus. Whether or not this is true, it would mean in any case that the Fourth Gospel was destined exclusively for Christian readers, people already converted to belief in Jesus the Christ. Such an assumption is, however, on the face of it absurd, because the Glad Tidings was by definition meant to be brought to those who had not yet heard it. It does not become less nonsensical because it is essentially identical with the theory of those Fathers who assert that the Fourth Gospel was written in order to supplement the three others.

This thesis itself is nothing but the transparent subterfuge of those who try to evade the main problems of scientific exegesis by 'harmonizing' originally independent writings, each of which was meant to be *the* evangel, and each of which has, admittedly, first been used as the one and only Gospel of some particular community.

No Jew or Gentile hearing the Fourth Gospel read or reading it himself in a province of the Church which used this Gospel only, could ever have hit upon the idea that the beloved disciple was one of the Zebedaid brothers. Unless the author of John xxi. 2, 20, 24 wrote exclusively for Christian communities using one of the Synoptic Gospels, intending to supplant this evangel by a better one, he cannot possibly have meant to suggest this identification. Whether any unbiased Christian reader of the Tetraevangel who had no axe to grind would ever have stumbled upon such an entirely unlikely interpretation, if the Marcionite forger had not intentionally misled all those who read his 'Acts of John', cannot be decided experimentally in our days in Christian countries brought up on the uncritical belief in this Marcionite thesis.

That this Marcionite interpretation of John xxi. 2, 20, 24 is a natural and unsophisticated explanation of the text or that it was based on a true tradition, would only be plausible if it could be established that this equation had been simply and straightforwardly stated in some orthodox document before the Marcionite 'Acts of John' were published. But that is exactly what cannot be done. Not only is it impossible to prove that the anti-Marcionite preface to Luke is anterior to the Leucian 'Acts of John'—the reverse being much more likely—but the statement that the Fourth Gospel was written by 'John the Apostle from among the Twelve' is the very contrary of a simple unsophisticated *obiter dictum*. It is not as if the author had said simply: 'And after that John the son of Zebedee wrote the Apocalypse'. . . . The very words 'and after that John, the Apostle from among the Twelve . . .' are evidence of an already existing divergence of opinion on this point, such as would have been immediately caused by the publication of the Pseudo-Leucius between those who accepted and those who rejected the new theory.

There is, moreover, a strong argument against the attribution of the words 'one of the Twelve' after 'John the Apostle' to the original author of the preface to Luke, which could not yet be taken into consideration when we compared the Greek and the Latin text on our p. 22. Dom de Bruyne and Harnack have shown conclusively that Irenaeus knew and utilized the anti-Marcionite preface to Luke: yet as Burney has pointed out with equal certainty, there is not the slightest trace of Irenaeus having anywhere or at any time identified the John, to whom he attributed—as did the preface to Luke—both the Apocalypse and the Fourth Gospel, with the son of Zebedee whom he mentions twice (*adv. haer.* I. 21, 2; and III. 12, 15) without connecting him in any way with either of the two books. On the contrary, there are definite reasons for supposing that Irenaeus wanted to make a difference between the Evangelist

John, the '*disciple* of Jesus' and the Evangelist whom he calls 'the *Apostle* Matthew'.

All this is best explained by the assumption that the crucial words 'one from among the Twelve' were added to the preface of Luke's Gospel after Irenaeus (*c.* A.D. 180), most probably by a scribe of the Alexandrian school who had read the passages attributing all the Johannine writings to the Zebedaid John in the anti-millenniarist pamphlet of Dionysius of Alexandria, (A.D. 262), albeit possibly before Fortunatian (A.D. 313), who may deliberately have rejected them.

As we said before: it is not absolutely certain whether or not the crucial words are an original part of the old pre-Irenaean preface to Luke; but if they are, they are proof of the existence of a controversy on this point, which arose before this preface was written. They cannot therefore be quoted as evidence for the existence of a simple and unanimous tradition handed down by those who had known the John in question.

X

BISHOP POLYCRATES OF EPHESUS ON THE EPHESIAN JOHN

LET US SEE now what, on the other side, the most trustworthy witness among the catholic, orthodox writers of the 2nd century, better qualified than anybody else for knowing all there was to know at the time about the Ephesian John, has to say about the Lord's beloved disciple.

We are fortunate enough to possess in Eusebius' *Ecclesiastical History* (III. 31, 2; V. 24, 7) an official letter which Polycrates, Bishop of Ephesus, then a man of sixty-five years, sent to Pope Victor of Rome in A.D. 196 or 198. The writer was a bishop from a family of bishops, seven of whose kinsmen had been bishops before him, not necessarily in Ephesus, but presumably there and in other Churches of Asia Minor.

In order to exalt the glory of his own Church in the face of Roman claims, the Ephesian bishop says:

'... in Asia, too, great foundation-stones (στοιχεῖα) are laid (to rest) and they will rise on the day of the coming of the Lord when He shall ... raise up all the saints. Such were Philip of the twelve Apostles (τῶν δώδεκα ἀποστόλων), who sleeps in Hierapolis ... and a daughter of his who ... rests at Ephesus. Moreover, there is also John who lay on the Lord's breast, who had been a priest who had worn the golden frontlet (ὃς ἐγενήθη ἱερεὺς τὸ πέταλον πεφορηκὼς) and a martyr and a teacher (διδάσκαλος = *rabbi*). He sleeps at Ephesus. And there is also Polycarp of Smyrna, both bishop and martyr. ...' (Follows a long list of further martyrs.)

Now here is a letter of the greatest solemnity, written by the bishop of the diocese, which was or became very soon the Metropolitan See of Asia, addressed to the Pope of Rome, in which every word may be supposed to have been weighed and pondered upon and chosen with the greatest care: in it Philip is introduced as 'one of the twelve Apostles', but John is not! The reader may say: John is given a higher title: 'he who lay on the Lord's breast'. But the two titles might so easily have been juxtaposed without difficulty by saying, e.g. 'the one from among the Twelve who leaned against the Lord's bosom'! Yet, in an enumeration meant to cumulate all the titles to glory of Asia, this one is omitted. Still, this is admittedly again a purely negative observation.

But there is more to come: the John who sleeps in Ephesus is said to 'have been a priest who had worn the frontlet'. Now at that time the Christian Church had bishops, it had presbyters or 'elders' and it had deacons. But the Church had no hereditary sacerdotal caste serving at the altar, and the word ἱερεύς, in Latin *sacerdos*, was exclusively employed either for pagan idol-priests, or for the hereditary caste of the Jewish priests, the *kohanîm*. It was used specifically of the Jewish high-priest —'Ἀάρων ὁ ἱερεύς—as it is found in the Septuagint version alternatively with ἱερεὺς μέγας and ἀρχιερεύς. The phrase 'who had been' (or 'become') 'a priest who had worn the frontlet' can have only one meaning: a man who had been a ruling Jewish high-priest.

The long discussion in the Epistle to the Hebrews vi. 20–vii. 28 about Jesus in heaven being now the eternal 'high-priest for ever after the order of Melchisedec' proves that the Church was, as we should expect, perfectly familiar with the Jewish priestly law according to which none but the High-Priest, none but a descendant of Aaron, could wear the frontlet. It was equally well known, as Heb. vii. 6, 12, 13 proves, that the priesthood itself was the hereditary privilege of the descendants of Aaron, and that of 'other tribes'—e.g. Judah—'no man gave attendance at the altar'.

Are we then to suppose that a bishop of Ephesus, of a family of bishops, the writer of this letter, and the Pope of Rome, who received it, were so ignorant of the Scriptures as to believe that some of the *kohanîm*, the priestly nobles of Jerusalem, had to earn their living as fishermen in Galilee or that a Galilean reeking of the fish-net could ever have become a High-Priest of the Jews in Jerusalem?

Or have we not rather candidly to admit the unavoidable conclusion—first drawn by the late Dr. Hugo Delff of Husum (Pl. VI)—that Polycrates could no more dream of identifying the Ephesian John, 'who had been a ruling high-priest and a rabbi' (διδάσκαλος), with the 'illiterate and unlearned' fisherman of Galilee, than a modern English writer, speaking of a member of the Royal Family buried in Westminster Abbey, could be imagined to refer with these same words to a former herring-fisher who had plied his trade in Yarmouth?

One would think there should be no doubt about the proper answer to this question. Yet, there seems to be an amazingly obstinate reluctance to face these plain facts.

Having given us two different translations of the crucial words—both equally erroneous—Professor Kirsopp Lake adds a footnote to p. 271 of his edition of Eusebius' *Ecclesiastical History* in the Loeb Classical Library (1926), saying that 'it has never been discovered' what Polycrates' allusion to the high-priest's πέταλον, worn by the Ephesian John, 'means here'.

HEINRICH KARL HUGO DELFF
(c. 1880)

'One of the best-authenticated extra-canonical sayings of Jesus is the commandment γίνεσθε δόκιμοι τραπεζίται, διακρίνειν τὸ νόθον ἀπὸ τοῦ γνησίου: the Lord Himself has ordered us critically to separate forgery from genuine truth.'
—*Das vierte Evangelium*, Husum, 1890, p. v.

PLATE VI

XI

'JOHN OF THE HIGH-PRIESTLY KIN' IN ACTS IV. 6, AND IN FLAVIUS JOSEPHUS' 'JEWISH WAR'

IT IS VERY UNLIKELY that there should be anything to 'discover' in an official letter of a Bishop of Ephesus to a Pope of Rome. The Bishop of Ephesus is not propounding riddles to the Pope of Rome like King Hiram of Tyre to King Solomon of Jerusalem, but basing a claim on a statement of facts which he supposes to be as well known to the Pope as they are to himself. If Polycrates had been referring to any esoteric or local tradition unknown to the addressee, he would have had to say so. He says nothing of the sort, and expects with legitimate confidence the Pope of Rome to be fully informed about the great teachers and martyrs of the Churches of Asia. He was equally entitled to expect the Bishop of the Church of Rome, a large section of which consisted of Jews and proselytes to Judaism converted to the Christian faith, to know that the John in question had actually been one of the Jewish high-priests officiating under the Herodean and Roman rule.

There had not been such an innumerable host of them as to make it difficult to check Polycrates' statement. According to Flavius Josephus (Ant. XX. 10), there were in all twenty-eight, every one of whom is mentioned by name in Josephus, in the school-book of the Christian Josephus of Tiberias, the contemporary of Epiphanius, and in the chronography of Nicephorus of Constantinople. Moreover, Dr. Hugo Delff has seen, nearly fifty years ago, that the man in question is clearly and unmistakably mentioned in Acts iv. 6:

'. . . there assembled the rulers and the senators (or 'Elders', πρεσβύτεροι) and the scribes in Jerusalem and Annas' (=Ḥanan, Ḥananiah) 'the high-priest and Caiaphas and John ('Ιωάννης= Joḥanan) and Alexander and as many as were of the kindred of the high-priest (ἐκ γένους ἀρχιερατικοῦ) in Jerusalem' . . . (to judge Peter).

The famous Codex Bezae in Cambridge and the 'giant-codex' ('Gigas') have 'Jonathan' instead of this 'John' 'of the high-priestly clan', a variant which has sometimes been explained as a learned correction with reference to the six passages in Josephus mentioning this Jonathan, the son of Annas, high-priest of the year 36–37, later on assassinated at the instigation of the Roman governor Felix. Such a correction would be entirely uncalled for, since a John, son of Annas ('Ἀνανίου Ἰωάννης), as well as this Alexander, are equally mentioned in Josephus (B.J. II. §§ 568 and 235).

As to this Alexander, he was the comrade-in-arms of a certain 'Ele'azar, son of Deinaeus, i.e. *ben Daianaiah*, of whom more will be said elsewhere, in an attack of a mixed band of Galileans and Jerusalemite Zealots on the Samaritans who had killed a Galilean at the time of the Roman governor Cumanus. The result of the unhappy affair was that the old high-priest Annas, his son Annas II, Captain (*sagan*) of the temple-police, later on himself an acting high-priest, and the high-priest Jonathan, son of Annas I—the one mentioned with Annas and Caiaphas in the Codex Bezae of Acts iv. 6—were sent in chains to Rome, to be judged by the Emperor. This procedure seems harsh and unjustified in Josephus, but is entirely understandable on the basis of the list of names in Acts iv. 6, which shows this Alexander to have been one 'of the high-priest's kin'. Alexander's comrade 'Ele'azar escaped into the mountains and was not captured until some years later by the Governor Felix.

As to 'Annas' son John' ('Ἀνανίου Ἰωάννης), the chapter in which this name occurs (B.J. II. § 538) purports to give a list of those who were in command of the various districts in Palestine and of the national levies in each, at the moment of the insurrection of A.D. 66. It says: 'Josephus, son of Gorion, and Ananus the high-priest were elected as dictators in the city' . . . 'other generals were selected for Idumaea, namely Jesus [son of Saphia], one of the high-priests, and 'Elea'zar, son of the high-priest ⟨Ana⟩nios, . . . 'Joseph, son of Simon, was sent to take command in Jericho, Menasse to Peraea, John the Essene to the province of Thamna' . . . 'John, son of Ananias, was appointed commander of Gophna and Acrabetta, Josephus, son of Matthias, was given the two Galilees'.

'JOHN OF THE HIGH-PRIESTLY KIN'

Josephus, son of Matthias, claims to be descended from the Hasmonaean high-priest Jonathan. Ananos the high-priest commanding in Jerusalem is the son of old Annas I (also written *Ananos* or *Ananias*), bearing the same name, Ḥanan or Ḥananiah, i.e. Ananos or Annas II, who had been the acting high-priest for three months in A.D. 62.

As to 'Jesus [son of Saphias] one of the high-priests', the bracketed patronymic was not read by the so-called Ambrosiaster—probably a converted Jew named Isaac, latinized as Hilarius or Gaudentius—who translated Josephus's *Jewish War* into Latin (about A.D. 370): '*Idumaeam quoque Jesus unus de sacerdotibus et Eleazarus . . . militiae praepositi tuendam receperunt.*' 'Jesus, son of Saphia,' appears a few pages later (II. § 599) as 'the ruler at that time' (τότε ἄρχων) of Tiberias. The same man cannot have been the chief-magistrate of Tiberias in Galilee, i.e. at the northern end of Palestine, where he was in constant conflict with Josephus, who calls him 'the ringleader of a band of brigands' (III. §§ 450, 452), until he fled to Tarichæ (III. §§ 457, 467), where he was defeated by Titus (III. § 498)—and at the same time have officiated as governor and army commander of Idumaea a hundred miles south of Tiberias. It is therefore obvious that the bracketed patronymic is a reader's gloss and that Josephus meant the high-priest Jesus, mentioned in VI. § 114—again without a father's name—as a refugee from the besieged Jerusalem to the Romans. This Jesus is the high-priest Jesus who succeeded Annas II in A.D. 62 or the next year, and whom Josephus calls in his *Jewish Antiquities* Jesus the son of Daianaios (codd. *Damnaios*).

'Eleʿazar, son of the high-priest Annas II (codd. NEOY for ANANAIOY), is the headstrong young man whose abolition of the imperial sacrifice was the ultimate cause of the war. 'Joseph son of Simon' is obviously Joseph Kami, son of the high-priest Simon, son of Kamithos, of the year 17/18, who had himself been the acting high-priest of the year 61/62.

The whole *ordre de bataille* being such an obvious family affair of acting and former high-priests, with the addition of the superior of the Essene order, and of some local magnates, it would be a very strange coincidence if the commander of the Gophnitis and Acrabatēnē ὁ ᾽Ανανίου ᾽Ιωάννης, i.e. *Joḥanan b.*

Ḥanan or b. Ḥananiah, were not the 'Ἰωάννης . . . ἐκ γένους ἀρχιερατικοῦ, the 'John . . . of the high-priest's kin' named together with Annas (i.e. Ḥanan, Ḥananiah) and with Annas's son-in-law Caiaphas in Acts iv. 6, i.e. another son of old Annas I.

Hypothetically to introduce without any necessity such an otherwise unknown 'Ananias', would mean to sin against a basic principle of historic method. It would, moreover, deprive us of the simplest answer, why the John in question figures as an army-commander on this list. It is natural that a son of old Annas should lead one of the armies, while it would require an explanation if such a post had been given to an otherwise unknown Ḥanania's son. Besides, such an otherwise unknown upstart would not have been introduced as ὁ 'Ανανίου 'Ιωάννης, 'the John of Annas', but as 'Ιωάννης τις υἱὸς 'Ανανίου, 'a certain Joḥanan b. Ḥananiah'.

Since we know from Josephus (Ant. XX. § 198) that all the sons of Annas I had been acting high-priests at one time or another, the plausible assumption that ὁ 'Ανανίου 'Ιωάννης, the army-leader of A.D. 66, 'John son of Ananias' was one of the sons of the high-priest Annas I, identifies him at once with the John, buried in Ephesus, who had worn the high-priest's diadem according to Polycrates of Ephesus. He must have finished his life as an exile in Ephesus, just as the high-priest Jishma'el b. Phiabi died in Cyrene, and as we find—according to a crucial line in the Acts (xix. 14)—in Ephesus the 'sons of a Jewish high-priest Σκευᾶς exorcizing 'in the name of Jesus'. Whether this Jewish high-priest—whose Latin nickname *Scaeva* is but a translation of this Egyptian Jew's epithet $\Phi IABI = p\cdot i\cdot bj$ 'the Left-handed'—was the elder Jishma'el b. Phiabi, high-priest in A.D. 15/16 or his above mentioned younger namesake, and whether this high-priest and father of two (or seven) sons converted to the faith in Jesus came to live himself with them in Ephesus, after the capture of Jerusalem in A.D. 70, we do not know. But the fact that sons of a Jewish high-priest who believed in Jesus had settled or lived temporarily in Ephesus is a sufficient analogy to the high-priest John whom Polycrates mentions as a Christian martyr buried in Ephesus.

It is a pity that Josephus does not say directly what became of this John, son of Ananias, Governor of Gophna and Acrabetta. Just as Josephus' own Galilean army corps, the forces commanded by this John were defeated by the Romans in A.D. 68, Josephus does not fail to mention (B.J. IV. §§ 551 f.) that Vespasian 'moving from Caesarea ascended into the hill-country and subdued the two provinces which take their name from Gophna and Acrabetta'. Gophna was garrisoned by the Romans and Titus rested there for one night on the way to Jerusalem (B.J. V. § 50 f.). The Jewish commander may have been able to arrange a surrender on generous terms and to stay on, since Josephus does not mention any battle and since we find Titus (B.J. VI. § 115) sending to Gophna the high-priests Joseph (Kabi) and Jesus (b. Dajanajah), three sons of the high-priest Jishma'el (b. Phiabi), four of the high-priest Matthias son of Theophilus, and one son of the high-priest Matthias son of Boethos, who had been able to escape from the besieged, mob-ridden city of Jerusalem. Josephus says that 'Caesar received them with all courtesy and recognizing that they would find life distasteful amidst alien customs, dispatched them to Gophna, advising them to remain there for the present and promising to restore every one's property as soon as he had leisure after the war'. This procedure looks very much as if he had sent all these high-priestly, reputedly conservative, and Romanophile magnates to Gophna, because they would be received there by their kinsman, the high-priest John son of Annas, to whom Vespasian may have made a similar promise.

The only objection which could be raised against the identification of Polycrates' former high-priest John with 'Ananias' son John' the army-commander of A.D. 66, the 'John of the high-priests' clan' in Acts iv. 6, is the fact that, again according to Josephus, the high-priest Annas had five sons, all high-priests:

' I. 'Ele'azar, son of Ananos, high-priest.
      No. 12 in the list of the twenty-eight, in the year A.D. 16–17.
II. Jonathan, son of Ananos—the one mentioned in Acts iv. 6 (Cod. D).
      No. 15 of the series, ruling from A.D. 36 to 37.
III. Theophilos, son of Ananos.
      No. 16, successor of Jonathan, ruling from A.D. 37. to 41.

44   THE ENIGMA OF THE FOURTH GOSPEL

 IV. Matthew, son of Ananos.
  No. 18 of the series, ruling about A.D. 42 or 43, anyhow before A.D. 44.
and finally
  V. Ananos, son of Ananos, Captain of the Temple-Guard, High-Priest.
  No. 24, for three months in A.D. 62.

There seems to be no room for a high-priest John, i.e. Joḥanan, son of Ananos or Ananias in this list.

The difficulty is, however, only an apparent one and disappears immediately if the reader will only remember that, at that time, as well as to-day, occidentalized Jews adopting a foreign, be it a Greek or Latin, or in our days a German, French or English name, always need to have, for ritual purposes, a Hebrew name. The Occidental name was and still is either roughly homonymous—*Mnaseas* for *Menashe*, *Jason* for *Jeshu*, like *Maurice* or *Morris* for *Moses*—or roughly synonymous, e.g. *Theodōros, Theodotos, Theodosios, Theudas* for *Jonathan, Nathanael, Nathanjah, Matthanjah, Mathaia,* etc.

If we find as No. 6 of the list in 4 B.C. a Joʻazar, son of Boethos, and as No. 8 an ʼEleʻazar, son of Boethos, it is obvious that those names were chosen in the family because *Boethos* 'Helper' is the Greek equivalent of ʼEleʻazar and of Joʻazar, 'God helps' (the German name *Gotthilf*) and 'Jahve helps'. Considering the clannish character of the whole list—all of the men belonging more or less to a small family-group—it seems probable that No. 5, 'Matthew son of Theophilus' (5–4 B.C.) was a son of No. 1 Ḥanan-el, who was, according to rabbinic tradition, an Egyptian Jew, according to Josephus, from Babylon, therefore obviously a native of the Egyptian Babylon, who may easily have hellenized his name Ḥanan-el = 'God's favour', 'God's grace' or 'God is gracious' to *Theophilus*. If *Theophilus* is the Greek translation for Ḥanan-el or Jo-ḥanan, as *Boethos* stands for ʼEleʻazar and Joʻazar, then Joḥanan, in Greek transcription *Jōannēs*, son of Annas (Ḥanan), commander of the Jewish army-corps in A.D. 66, may very well be the 'Theophilus son of Annas', whom Vitellius made high-priest in A.D. 37, and whom Herod Agrippa I deposed in

A.D. 41, in favour of Simon the son of Boethos. Indeed, Léon Hermann, in a note to Theodore Reinach's French translation of Josephus, proposed to identify this 'Theophilus' with the above-mentioned Jonathan, son of Annas—the one mentioned in Acts iv. 6, according to the Bezan and the Giant Codex—although he had to admit that the Hebrew *Jo-nathan* should be better translated *Theodore* than *Theophilus*! This imaginary difficulty vanishes entirely if this Theophilus is identified, not with Jonathan b. Ḥanan, but with his brother Joḥanan b. Ḥanan, the 'Ἰωάννης of Acts iv. 6, in all the other manuscripts.

There is not the slightest difficulty in supposing that he was called alternatively 'John' or 'Theophilus' in the various sources utilized by Josephus in his *Jewish War*—where Theophilus does not occur—and in his *Jewish Antiquities*—where John son of Ananias is not found—just as the John Mark of the New Testament is mentioned as 'John' only in Acts xiii. 5, 13, but as 'Mark' only in Acts xv. 39 and in various epistles.

XII

PSEUDO-HILARIUS AFRICANUS ON ST. JOHN—THE BOY IN JESUS' ARMS (MATT. XVIII. 2; MARK IX. 36)

IF POLYCRATES' 'John who had been a high-priest, a rabbi and a martyr and who is buried in Ephesus', was the 'John . . . of the high-priests' kin' mentioned in Acts iv. 6, if he was 'John the son of Ananias', the governor of Gophna in A.D. 66 and if he was the high-priest Theophilos (= Joḥanan) of A.D. 37–41, he would have had to be very young at the time of the Crucifixion, in order to be still able to write a gospel in Ephesus under the reign of Trajan (98–117), as Irenaeus reports on the authority of Papias, Polycarp and the Elders who saw and heard John there and then.

Now that is exactly what is implied by a most interesting assertion to be found in a typical 'preface' or 'proevangel' to John, hitherto not recognized as such, which has been used as introduction to an anti-Arian '*Tractatus Sti. Hilarii episcopi*', inserted between various works of St. Augustine in a 9th-century MS., the Codex Vatic. 4222 (fol. 46). The curious document, discovered and published by Cardinal Angelo Mai is—according to the expert opinion of Dom Germain Morin—by the same author as another anonymous treatise on the genealogy of the Christ in Matthew, found in the same manuscript and equally published by Cardinal Mai. Dom Germain Morin has pointed out that the typically Byzantine prodigal use of the epithet *sanctissimus* ('the most holy') attached to all and sundry biblical names, both in the treatise on Matthew and in that on St. John, is not found in Western texts before the 6th or 7th century A.D.

'Both treatises are visibly translations from the Greek, and exhibit a somewhat exotic character, foreign to the Latin West. The nature of the biblical quotations would suggest that they were imported from the East, not later than the 6th century,

JOHN—THE BOY IN JESUS' ARMS

probably by some African, possibly by one of those who were in Constantinople in the company of Grimasius and Junilius about the middle of this century'.

Accepting this verdict of the most competent authority on such questions, we propose to quote this anonymous author, for the sake of convenience, as 'Ps.-Hilarius Africanus'.

He begins his treatise on John with the following words:

'John the most holy evangelist was the youngest among all the apostles, Him the Lord held (in his arms) when the apostles discussed who among them was greatest and when He said: He who is not converted as this boy, will not enter the kingdom of Heaven. It is he who reclined against the Lord's breast. It is he whom Jesus loved more than the others and to whom he gave his mother Mary, and whom he gave as son to Mary.'

Nobody is more likely to have resorted to such an equation than an apologist like Hippolytus, who had to counter—as we can see from Epiphanius—the objections of Gaius, pointing out the alleged 'dissonances' between the Fourth and the three Synoptic Gospels as well as the chronological objections against the attribution of the latest of all the four evangels to a direct disciple of Jesus.

Anyhow, whether it was Hippolytus or somebody else who introduced this argument into the discussion, he must have been interested in the particular kind of synchronism which follows from the identification of the anonymous child with the Evangelist John.

We know that Callimachus and the Alexandrian librarians following his example did not content themselves with building up their chronological authors' list by cataloguing merely whatever they could find about one man coming into contact with another. They had refined their method by noting carefully what could be gathered about the age of the two persons at the time when they met or associated in one way or another. Thus we read, e.g. in Suidas' bibliographical note about Philochoros, 'he lived at the time of Eratosthenes, being in touch ($\dot{\omega}$s $\dot{\epsilon}\pi\iota\beta\alpha\lambda\epsilon\hat{\iota}\nu$) with Eratosthenes as a very old man ($\pi\rho\epsilon\sigma\beta\dot{\upsilon}\tau\eta$) while he himself was young ($\nu\dot{\epsilon}o\nu$ $\ddot{o}\nu\tau\alpha$)'.

There would have been no point in mentioning a synchronism

of this sort, bringing Jesus into touch with John while the latter was still a child, unless the statement itself could be substantiated by reference to an older source. It is most unlikely that an apologist for the Fourth Gospel and for 1 John i. 1, intent upon demonstrating the chronological possibility of an eyewitness of the Passion surviving until the reign of Trajan, should have invented an interpretation of the incident in question which is *prima facie* incompatible with the equation between the beloved disciple and John the son of Zebedee, after this identification had been accepted and repeated by Origen, Dionysius of Alexandria, Eusebius and St. Jerome. If, on the contrary, it was found in an old source, anterior to this confusion, it could easily be quoted and repeated in spite of its incompatibility with the conflicting 'tradition', owing to the incapacity of ancient exegetes to notice even the most manifest contradictions, a weakness resulting from their being trained in harmonizing the most incompatible statements of their various sources of information.

Were it not for this extraordinary readiness to put up with the most glaring discrepancies, we should hardly find St. Jerome, identifying in his *De viris inlustribus* the Evangelist John with Zebedee's son, a Galilean fisherman, but explaining nevertheless in one of his Epistles (cxxvii), that the Beloved Disciple was 'familiar to the high-priest' (John xviii. 15 f.) *propter generis nobilitatem*—'because of the nobility of his family'—by the way, another bit of information, more likely than not derived from Hippolytus' lost apology of the Fourth Gospel, and anyhow wholly incompatible with the belief that John was a poor illiterate fisherman, full of a plebeian climber's ambition.

At the first glance, the curious saying of Jesus quoted in the beginning of the proevangel utilized by 'Pseudo-Hilary' seems to be taken from some gospel-harmony. It is not to be found in John and does not correspond exactly to any one of our synoptic evangels. Matt. xviii. 2 has *parvulus* ('the little one') not *puer* (boy) for Greek παιδίον, it does not state that Jesus 'held' the boy in His arms, but that He placed him (*statuit eum*, ἔστησεν αὐτό) in their midst, and the saying has the plural throughout: '*nisi conversi fueritis* if you are not converted *et efficiamini sicut parvuli* and become like little children you will not enter the

Kingdom of Heaven'. The phrase appears to have been drawn together with the following: *quicumque ergo humiliaverit se sicut parvulus iste*, 'whosoever therefore shall humble himself as this little child, the same is greatest in heaven', and with Mark ix. 36, *accipiens puerum statuit eum in medio eorum, quem cum complexus esset* (cp. x. 16) 'and he took a boy' (the Greek has again παιδίον, not παῖδα) 'and when He had taken him in His arm, He said unto them' (not the word about the necessity of humiliating oneself like this child, but) 'Whosoever shall receive one of such children in my name', etc. In Luke ix. 47 Jesus sets the boy (*puerum*) beside Him (*secus se*, παρ᾽ ἑαυτῷ) without taking him into His arms and again says nothing about the humility of this child. But both in Luke ix. 49 and in Mark ix. 38, not however in Matt. xviii. 21, the words of Jesus are answered by—John: '*respondens autem Johannes dixit // respondit illi Johannes dicens*' ... Without any logical connection with the preceding saying about the child, the disciple says: 'Master we saw one casting out devils in Thy name and he followed us not and we forbade him'. To which Jesus replies, 'Forbid him not'.

It is, of course, possible that Ps.-Hilary's source—Hippolytus or whoever it was—identified the John replying to Jesus with the boy or little child (*puer parvulus*, παιδίον) whom Jesus 'took into His arm' (*complexus est*, ἐναγκαλισάμενος), because the boy had 'leaned against the bosom of the Master'. No other but the 'bosom-friend' (ὁ ἐπιστήθιος μαθητής), the 'beloved disciple' of the Fourth Gospel could have done that! But there may have been more than this at the back of the mind of the unknown writer, harmonizing these parallel passages in the three synoptics: he did not understand Matthew's 'Whosoever shall humble himself as this child' as meaning 'Whosoever shall humble himself to the level of a little child which has blindly to obey all its elders', but he concluded from the saying what, indeed, it seems to mean on the face of it: he inferred that this boy—John— had performed a signal and exemplary act of self-humiliation, which had brought him to Jesus and into the company of the Apostles. If John was the son of Zebedee, *piscator egens, ignarus, indoctus*, 'a miserable, ignorant, and untaught fisherman', as St. Hilary of Poitiers describes him in *De Trinitate* II. 13, and on top of it a very young boy, a mere fisherman's lad, a truant child run away at the bidding of Jesus from his father's boat, how could such a poor little nobody 'humble himself'?

It seems evident that the author of this gospel-harmony—or was it an 'apocryphal' gospel?—did not consider John, the beloved disciple, here too resting against the bosom of his Master, as the son of the fisherman of Galilee, but as the 'John of the high-priest's kin' mentioned in Acts iv. 6, and that John's surprisingly disconnected reply about the 'one who cast out devils in Thy name and followed us not' reminded this interpreter of the Ephesian 'sons of the Jewish high-priest Scaeva' in Acts xix. 14, who 'took upon them to call over them which had evil spirits the name of the Lord Jesus'.

If the boy John, resting his head on Jesus' arm, is 'of the high-priest's kin' and if this John is talking of his kinsmen exorcising demons in the name of Jesus, then, of course, his leaving father and mother and a ruler's home to follow Jesus and the itinerant little group of disciples around him on their wanderings, is a close analogy to the 'spiritual adventure' of Josephus the historian, claiming a Hasmonaean high-priest as his ancestor, who joined in his early youth a baptizing hermit in the desert. In this case it *is* an act of supreme self-abnegation and exemplary self-humiliation, which the Lord may set up as a model to all the other disciples rivalling with each other in an unseemly desire for power to overrule their companions.

It is very remarkable that St. Ambrose of Milan, too, professes to have read in a gospel and in a gospel 'to boot (dictated) by the voice of John himself'—that the Evangelist John was 'a youth' (*adolescens*), and that St. Jerome equally read in certain '*ecclesiasticae historiae*' that the Evangelist John was a mere boy (*puer*), the youngest (*minimus*) of all Apostles. Is St. Ambrose quoting as a 'gospel' the 'Life of John', of which we have only a Syriac translation and in which John refuses to write an evangel lest others, stirred up by the devil, might say 'he is a mere boy'? Or is he quoting Matt. xviii. 2—accepting as true a number of Greek gospel-prefaces asserting that Matthew's Gospel was translated into Greek from the Hebrew original by John—and is he identifying Matthew's παιδίον, the 'child' placed in their midst with St. John? Or is he thinking of the νεανίσκος (*adolescens*) in Matt. xix. 20, whom Jesus loved at first sight (Mark x. 21) and equating this youth with St. John, the beloved disciple, as Dr. Swete (Pl. XX) did in our days?

Is it possible that Ps.-Hilary's source quoted the Gospel of John used, according to Epiphanius, by the Ebionites, or their Aramean Matthew, the so-called 'Gospel of the Hebrews', which St. Jerome translated into Latin and which may very well have said, in the chapter about the Last Supper, that the beloved disciple as 'the youngest of the disciples' had to ask the ceremonial question 'why is this night'—the Passover-night—'different from all other nights . . .'? We do not know. We can only say, so far, that none of the extant canonical or apocryphal gospels says anything about the age of the beloved disciple or, for the matter of that, of the Zebedaid John. On the other hand, it must obviously have seemed desirable to infer from some text or other that the disciple who wrote a gospel in the reign of Trajan was extremely young when Jesus died on the cross under which the evangelist is said to have stood as an eyewitness.

In these circumstances the reader will, of course, object, and we are fully prepared to admit, that the assertions of Ps.-Hilary, St. Ambrose, and St. Jerome cannot be taken as historical evidence at their face value, even if they are all derived from Hippolytus of Rome.

Quite so. But we are not prepared to admit in the least that these assertions are one whit less trustworthy or less credible than the identification of John the Evangelist with the Galilean illiterate fisherman put forward for a transparent polemical and anti-canonical purpose by the Marcionite 'Acts of John', without any other basis than just such an interpretation of one line of a gospel by a number of others (John xxi. 24; 20; 2; xiii. 23). If it is undeniable that the assertions of Ps.-Hilary, St. Ambrose and St. Jerome *may* rest on nothing but on mere *aggadic* combinations of certain gospel texts, the same holds good of the traditional view, supported by St. Jerome, St. Epiphanius, Eusebius and Dionysius of Alexandria and ultimately based on the transparent fraud of a Marcionite ψευδὴς ἱστορία, which has not a leg to stand upon. The alternative identification of John the Evangelist with the exiled Jewish high-priest John—although possibly also based on a mere combination of John xviii. 16 ff. with Acts iv. 6—is at least likely to be derived from an Ephesian local tradition and has, moreover, the advantage of being perfectly compatible, as we shall see later on, with all the other external and internal evidence.

For the moment, we are not concerned with the question whether or not John the Evangelist really was John the son of the high-priest Annas mentioned in Acts iv. 6 and in Josephus' *Jewish War* (II. § 568), but whether it was—as Dr. Howard says—an 'absurdity' (!) for Polycrates of Ephesus to believe and to say that the disciple of Jesus who had reclined against the Master's breast at the Last Supper 'became' ($\dot{\epsilon}\gamma\epsilon\nu\dot{\eta}\theta\eta$) a high-priest, as other sons of Annas I had been high-priests before or after him.

As to the alleged 'absurdity' of Polycrates' assertion, this charge had better be raised against the Marcionite equation between the Galilean fisherman John, the son of Zebedee, with the disciple who was—according to John's Gospel (xviii. 16)— 'known to the high-priest' Annas (John xviii. 13, 24), $\gamma\nu\omega\sigma\tau\grave{o}s$ $\tau\hat{\omega}$ $\dot{a}\rho\chi\iota\epsilon\rho\epsilon\hat{\iota}$, or even 'familiar to him' or 'a kinsman of his' ($\gamma\nu\dot{\omega}\rho\iota\mu\sigma s$) as the Purple Codex of Patmos (*N*) has it, a word which is used in this sense by the Greek translator of the Book of Ruth (iii. 2).

As a matter of fact, nothing could be more amusing and instructive than to read in the poetic paraphrase of the Fourth Gospel by Nonnos of Panopolis in Egypt, a contemporary of St. Jerome, that the fisherman was known to the high-priest as the regular court purveyor—so to say 'by appointment to His Eminence'—of his Friday evening fish; or in a fragment of Ammonius, an Egyptian 6th-century presbyter, that John was known only 'to the girl at the door' (John xviii. 17); or in a Ps.-Hippolytean chronicle that John, having inherited and sold his father's big fish-trawling business in Galilee, had settled in Jerusalem and bought a house owned by the high-priest; and to see finally St. Jerome explain John's 'familiarity' or 'acquaintance' with the high-priest '*propter generis nobilitatem*', as if some member of the priestly nobility of Jerusalem, amply supported by the temple-trade and the temple-banking, could

JOHN—THE BOY IN JESUS' ARMS

have found it profitable to start a wholesale fishing business on the Sea of Galilee!

It is these romantic inventions of the Dionysian poet converted to Christianity, of Ps.-Hippolytus, Ammonius and St. Jerome to which they have been driven by their acceptance of the arbitrary Marcionite equation, and which are still quoted in modern commentaries, that are 'absurd', and not the perfectly straightforward statement of Polycrates of Ephesus.

How difficult it is entirely to overcome the effects of the blind-spot created by an inveterate prejudice in the field of vision, even of an exceptionally learned and perspicacious scholar, may be gathered from the words of the late Dr. H. B. Swete, of Cambridge (Pl. XX), whose momentous discovery concerning the beloved disciple, we shall have to discuss below. He said in an otherwise admirably lucid paper:

'it is scarcely conceivable that a Galilean disciple, drawn from the fishermen of the Northern Lake, could have stood in this relation to the head of the exclusive aristocracy which virtually ruled the Jewish people. This disciple, whoever he was, must have been a person of some wealth and influence, possibly ἐκ γένους ἀρχιερατικοῦ (Acts iv. 6). It was perhaps some confused reminiscence of his early days that gave rise to the tradition that John of Ephesus once served as a Jewish priest.'

How curious that Dr. Swete should not have remembered when he penned these remarkable lines—twenty-seven years after Dr. Hugo Delff, eighteen years after Dr. Fries, of Upsala —that such a John is really mentioned in Acts iv. 6!

What surprises us in the letter of Polycrates is the strange omission in his praise of the Ephesian John of what we should think the chief title to his glory: his authorship of the Fourth Gospel. It is evident that Polycrates knows this evangel since his words ὁ ἐπὶ τὸ στῆθος τοῦ Κυρίου ἀναπεσών are a literal quotation of John xiii. 25 (possibly also of John xxi. 20). But he does not say, however easy and appropriate that would appear to us, that this John wrote a gospel, the 'pneumatic' gospel, superior to all others, or something else of this kind. The only possible explanation of this diplomatic silence is the assumption—anyhow inevitable—that Polycrates was well aware of the controversy about the authorship of this evangel raging in his own province of Asia Minor as well as in Rome, where in these very years the presbyter Gaius stubbornly denied the authorship of John, attributing the alleged pseudepigraphon to the gnostic Cerinthus, while the learned presbyter Hippolytus, the disciple of Irenaeus, was equally obstinately defending its authenticity. Not knowing what opinion Pope Victor was favouring, Polycrates may well have thought it prudent not to express explicitly his opinion on whether or not John wrote the Gospel attributed to him, and to mention nothing but the fact—admitted even by the Marcionite 'Acts of John'—that the Ephesian John had rested his head against the bosom of Jesus.

XIII

THE TWO TRADITIONS ABOUT THE EVANGELIST JOHN

WHETHER OR NOT the explanation we have given of Polycrates' strange silence is the right one, the reader will see now for himself how far from the truth is the usual assertion of a *constans, universalis ac solemnis Ecclesiae traditio iam a saeculo secundo decurrens* concerning the authorship of the Fourth Gospel.

On the one hand, we have the Marcionite 'Acts of John' clearly identifying the beloved disciple with John the son of Zebedee, but rejecting the idea that he wrote a gospel and insisting on his natural death in hoary old age. On the other hand, we have Bishop Polycrates of Ephesus identifying Jesus' favourite and bosom-friend with the 'John of the high-priest's kin' in Acts iv. 6, and thereby implicitly excluding the possibility of his having been a Galilean 'unlearned and illiterate' fisherman, asserting, moreover, that he was a rabbi (διδάσκαλος) and adding to all this the definite statement that he died as a martyr.

Thanks to the hitherto unnoticed survival of the most important fragments of Hippolytus' 'Odes on all the Scriptures' in certain evangeliaries, notably in the Parisian Codex Coislin 195, we can see now that Polycrates' assertion was accepted in Rome and repeated by the most learned presbyter of the empire's metropolitan church; Hippolytus, too, speaks of John as 'a high-priest at Ephesus (ἀρχιερεὺς Ἐφέσιος) and prophet (θεηγόρος)'—a very characteristically Johannine combination, since it is the Fourth Gospel which attributes prophetic character to the utterances of an acting Jewish high-priest (John xi. 51). Not restrained by the considerations which may have weighed on Polycrates' mind, Hippolytus unreservedly praises in a Callimachean distich this 'Ephesian high-priest and prophet'— meaning, of course, the author of the Gospel and the Apocalypse

—as having been the first to say 'In the beginning was the Word . . .'

Hippolytus' witness is all the more important because he was, according to Photius, a disciple of Irenaeus, who must have known not only what writings we still have of the Bishop of Lyons, but the whole of his books of which but fragments survive. All we know of Irenaeus' opinion on the Fourth Gospel and all that Hippolytus knew, he must have considered as entirely compatible with the assertion of Polycrates that the evangelist John was a former Jewish high-priest, resident in Ephesus until the time of Trajan,' whom Polycarp of Smyrna and Papias of Hierapolis had still been able to hear and to see personally.

On the other hand, we have the Montanist Tertullian, writing *On monogamy* (17), about A.D. 220, obviously dependent on the apocryphal Leucian 'Acts of John' used by the Montanists, repeating with obvious relish the mawkish story of John's perpetual virginity and physical impotence, which had been freely invented by the ascetic Marcionite forger of these 'Acts'.

It is hardly necessary to remind the reader that according to Lev. xxi. 21 ff. 'no man that hath a blemish', let alone a congenital *spado* (Tertullian, l.c.), could ever have become a priest, least of all a high-priest. A high-priest could not either be a 'perpetual virgin'. He had to be a married man: 'A maiden of his own people he shall take to wife' (Lev. xxi. 14). To be barren and without issue, he would have counted a misfortune and a curse. Here again there is absolute incompatibility between Tertullian's statement derived from the Marcionite 'Acts of John' and the trustworthy testimony of the Catholic Bishop of Ephesus, Polycrates. While accepting the biographical data about John given in the Marcionite or—as he knew them—in the Montanist 'Acts of John', Tertullian overlooked their significant silence concerning any writings of John and accepted, with the Catholics and the Montanists of his day, the whole *instrumentum Johanneum*—Gospel, Apocalypse, and Epistles of John—as authentic. Like his contemporary, Clement of Alexandria, and later authors such as Eusebius and Epiphanius, he must have followed a 'tradition', i.e. an anti-Marcionite gospel-

THE TWO TRADITIONS ABOUT THE EVANGELIST JOHN 57

preface, stating that John's original unwillingness to write a gospel was finally overcome by the entreaties of his fellow-disciples and by a direct intervention of the Holy Ghost. The latter idea, which occurs in Clement of Alexandria and Epiphanius' chapter li. 'On those who reject the Fourth Gospel'—probably borrowed from Hippolytus' treatise against Gaius—is a typically Montanist doctrine, based on Rev. i. 10 f., 'I, John, was in the Spirit on the day of the Lord, when I heard a voice saying . . . Write!'

Beside Tertullian and roughly contemporary with this African-Latin writer, Clement of Alexandria shows the most definite evidence of more than a bowing acquaintance with the Marcionite 'Acts of John', from which he quotes the Docetic myth about the Lord's intangible body, through which John the beloved disciple could put his hand, as if it were thin air. Whether or not he accepted the identification of John the Evangelist with John the son of Zebedee is not clear from his extant writings.

But the equation is definitely stated by Clement's disciple Origen, the ascetic who inflicted upon himself the bodily defect and the ensuing perpetual virginity which the Leucian 'Acts' had attributed without any historic foundation whatsoever to John the son of Zebedee. The eunuch Origen, 'emasculated for the sake of the Kingdom of Heaven' (Matt. xix. 12), would naturally feel inclined to sympathize with such a survival from the Asiatic religion of the mother-goddess Cybele, her mutilated lover Attis, and her castrate priests.

Origen's disciple, Dionysius of Alexandria, accepted the equation of John the Evangelist with the Zebedaid from his master without any question. It is obvious that he did not know the passage in Polycrates' epistle to the Pope of Rome concerning the Ephesian John, a former Jewish high-priest, nor Papias' lines about an Elder John different from John the brother of James. Both would have been a godsend to him in his search for 'another John' on whom to father the Apocalypse, a work so different in style and thought from the Evangel and the Epistles that he had to attribute it to 'another John', albeit 'a saintly and inspired writer' yet imperfectly conversant with the Greek language. Dionysius is Eusebius' authority, Eusebius is

Epiphanius' and St. Jerome's source for this by now time-honoured and venerable identification invented by the Marcionite author of a *vie romancée* or 'pseudo-history' (ψευδὴς ἱστορία).

The introduction of matter derived from the Marcionite 'Acts of John' into certain Catholic prefaces to the Fourth Gospel—a Greek one based on the commentaries of Theophylactus, definitely identifying John the Evangelist with the illiterate Galilean fisherman, and a Latin preface to John written by the Priscillianist Instantius, which praises the Evangelist's perpetual virginity and describes his peaceful natural death—is an exact parallel to the above-mentioned intrusion of the Marcionite prefaces to the Pauline epistles and of Marcion's criticism of Mark into certain manuscripts of the Vulgate version.

XIV

THE MARTYRDOM OF THE TWO SONS OF ZEBEDEE IN THE EARLIEST MARTYROLOGIES AND LECTIONARIES

WE ARE NOW prepared to understand and to appreciate the attitude of Fortunatian the African, of the Spanish preface-writer of the 'Lucinian' edition, of the Greek and the Syrian scholars, who definitely refused to accept the identification of John the Evangelist with one of the Zebedaid brothers. They were not heretics, dissenting from the opinions of the Catholic Church, but devout Catholics rejecting what they knew to be a Marcionite tendencious invention.

They accepted what the Catholic Bishop Polycrates of Ephesus had implied in a letter to Pope Victor of Rome, of which copies had been sent to all the main churches of the Roman Empire, in the course of the Paschal controversy, and what the learned presbyter Hippolytus of Rome, a disciple of Irenaeus, had approved as true: to wit that the Fourth Gospel had been written by the Ephesian John, who had in his youth been a partaker of the Last Supper, resting his head against the Lord's breast, had 'become a high-priest who had worn the golden frontlet', been a teacher, and died in exile as a martyr and was buried in Ephesus. They also knew a letter of Irenaeus, written to Pope Victor of Rome about the same Paschal controversy and sent to 'many other rulers of churches', in which the Bishop of Lyons says emphatically that the martyr Polycarp (d. A.D. 156) had celebrated Passover after the so-called Quartodeciman reckoning 'in the company of John the disciple of our Lord and the remaining Apostles ($\mu\epsilon\tau\grave{a}$ $\tau\hat{\omega}\nu$ $\lambda o\iota\pi\hat{\omega}\nu$ $\dot{a}\pi o\sigma\tau\acute{o}\lambda\omega\nu$) with whom he had associated'.

They must have known with perfect certainty that the synchronism established by this incidental statement could not possibly apply to the Zebedaid John, for the absolutely cogent reason that the memory of the martyrdom of both the sons of

Zebedee on one and the same day and, therefore, obviously in the same year of the reign of Herod Agrippa I, was celebrated in every church all around the Mediterranean Sea.

The Syrian Martyrology of Edessa (A.D. 411)—based on the pre-Theodosian calendar of the feasts celebrated by the Church of Constantinople and, as far as these last days of December are concerned, derived from a document drawn up in A.D. 341—begins with the protomartyr Stephen's death, 'commemorated according to the Greeks on the 26th of the month *Kanûn*' (i.e. December) and continues immediately: 'on the XXVIIth John and James, the Apostles in Jerusalem' and 'on the XXVIIIth in the same first month *Kanûn* in the city of Rome Paul, the Apostle, and Symeon Kephas, the head of the Apostles of our Lord'.

The Armenian Martyrology has the same martyrs' names, only in the reversed order: 'St. Peter and St. Paul' on December 27th, on the 28th, however,

'James and John, the Sons of Thunder'

the variations being sufficiently important to show that the Armenian calendar is not dependent on the extant text of the Syrian Martyrology, but on some other source.

The Martyrology of Carthage—brought up-to-date until A.D. 505, but certainly much older—has at the end of December, on the 26th: *VII Kal. Jan. sancti Stefani primi martyris*; on the 27th: *VI Kal. Jan. sancti Johannis Baptistae*(!) *et Jacobi Apostoli quem*(!) *Herodes occidit*, although the same Martyrology has the birthday of the Baptist, as usual, on the 24th of June: *VIII Kal. Jul. sancti Johannis Baptistae*, and although the African Church—as all the other Christian churches—celebrated the memory of the Baptist's decapitation on the 29th of August.

The original text of this line was, of course, with the usual abbreviations: *Sanct.(orum) Joannis et Jacobi apostol.(orum) qu.(os) Herodes occidit*.

This is proved by the fragments of the Martyrology of Carmona (about A.D. 480), discovered in 1909 by Don G. Bonsor on an inscribed, coarsely wrought marble column of the *patio de los naranjos* belonging to the church *Sancta Maria*

THE MARTYRDOM OF THE TWO SONS OF ZEBEDEE

la Mayor of Carmona, near Sevilla—that is in the very province of Baetica where the longer anti-Marcionite prefaces seem to have been added to the copies of St. Jerome's revised text of the Gospel distributed by his Iberic patron Lucinius (above, pp. 9 and 13).

The inscription runs:

INCIP	*Incip(it ordo)*
SCRUM	*s(an)c(to)rum (marty-)*
RUMINS	*rum in s(acrata)*
AULACL	*aula cl(ari-)*
TER EXPR	*ter expr(essa. Celebra-)*
TUR	*tur:*
VIII KA	*VIII Ka(lendas Janua-)*
RIAS	*rias (nativi-)*
TAS DNI	*tas D(omini nostri Jesu)*
XRI SECUND	*Chri(sti) secund(um carnem)*
VII K	*VII K(alendas Januarias)*
SCI S . . FANI	*Sancti S(te)fani (martyris)*
VI K . . . ANNIS AP	*VI K(alendas Io)annis ap-*
OSTOLE XII	*ostole XII*
K . . . BRUARIAS	*K(alendas Fe)bruarias*
(etc. etc.)	(etc. etc.)
. . . . . .	. . . . . .
XIII KAL IULIAS	*XIII Kal(endas) Julias*
SCTR GERVASI	*S(an)ct(o)r(um) Gervasi*
ET PROTASI M	*et Protasi M(artyrum)*
VIII KAL IULIAS	*VIII Kal(endas) Julias*
SCI IOANNI B	*S(an)c(ti) Joanni(s) B(aptistae)*

This martyrology of the province Baetica has, exactly as its African counterpart, the Martyrology of Carthage, the Nativity of St. John the Baptist following the day of the martyrs Saints Gervase and Protase, but the day of the Apostle John (the son of Zebedee) on the 27th of December, following St. Stephen's Day and the Nativity of the Christ. No attempt has been made in this case to alter 'John the Apostle' into 'John the Baptist', but the desired effect has been obtained by omitting any mention of the beheading of St. James (see below, p. 63).

The Ethiopic Church commemorates the two brothers together on the 27th, not of December, but of September, obviously through a confusion with the Ephesian St. John's day on the 26th of September (see below, p. 126).

The famous Missal of Bobbio reflecting the pre-Carolingian ritual of the Church of Paris—where Syrians had occupied not only the bishop's seat, but all the most influential ecclesiastical offices under the Merovingian kings—offers, after the mass for Christmas Day (No. 6), as No. 7 the mass for St. Stephen, as No. 8 the mass in memory of the massacre of the Innocent Children, and as No. 9 *Missa Jacobi et Johannis*. The gospel lessons for the day are Matt. xx. 20–23: *accessit mater filiorum Zebedaei* . . . containing Jesus' prophecy of the martyrdom of the two brothers, followed by Acts xii. 1–3: *Misit Herodes rex manus ut affligeret quosdam de ecclesia* . . . the account of how this prophecy was fulfilled in the case of St. James.

The insertion of the epithet 'the Baptist' after 'John' into the original text of the African martyrology might be considered as a mere clerical error for *Evangelistae* or a *bona fide* epexegetical gloss of a scribe, who remembered that according to Acts xii. 3 King Herod (Agrippa I) slew only James, but that John the Baptist was beheaded by a King Herod (Antipas). We find, however, in the so-called *Martyrologium Hieronymianum*—compiled about A.D. 595 in Auxerre—on the 27th of December, i.e. on the old day of the martyrdom of James the son of Zebedee, a wholly invented feast of James the Just

> *Ordinatio episcopatus sancti Jacobi fratris Domini* . . .

substituted for the old commemoration of the decapitated son of Zebedee and joined to the *Assumptio S. Joannis* [*Evangelistae apud Ephesum*]—the last words being a tendentious addition, explained below in chs. XXI, XXVII and XXIX. The same artificial substitution of James the Just for Zebedee's son James can be traced in the Martyrology of Gellone, in a Merovingian martyrology of the abbey Reichenau on Lake Constance, now in Zürich, and in certain Hispanic missals.

The liturgy of Spain is most interesting in this context, because of the reluctance of the Iberic clergy to accept St. Jerome's identification of the Evangelist John with 'the brother of James decapitated by Herod', to which the Lucinian preface

THE MARTYRDOM OF THE TWO SONS OF ZEBEDEE

to the Fourth Gospel in the Spanish so-called Visigothic Bibles testifies. The ritual of the ecclesiastical province of Toledo under St. Ildefonsus (A.D. 657–667) represented by the 11th-century *Liber Comicus* of the Abbey Silos, now in Paris, shows exactly like the martyrology of Carthage on the day after Christmas the office for St. Stephen (with lessons on the miracles of the martyr from St. Augustine's *Civitas Dei*) and, on the day after St. Stephen's, the day of 'the apostle John'. The martyrdom of SS. Peter and Paul, which the Syrian Martyrology places on the 28th of December, is found in the Silos lectionary, just as in the Martyrology of Carthage on the 29th of June, after the nativity of John the Baptist.

As to the prescribed lesson for St. John the Apostle's Day, it is originally Sap. x. 10–14: '*Justum deduxit dominus per vias rectas et ostendit ei regnum Dei . . . et claritatem aeternam,*' which is found in the Ambrosian liturgy with the characteristic title '*In natale unius martyris*'.

This proves that John the son of Zebedee was originally commemorated in Spain and in Africa as a martyr. But the other lesson of the day is John xxi. 21–24: '*vidit Petrus discipulum quem diligebat Jesus,*' which shows that at that time (7th century)—the time when Isidore of Sevilla's preface had been prefixed to the Vulgate Fourth Gospel—the Zebedaid John was already identified with the beloved disciple and with the Fourth Evangelist. Therefore, the commemoration of St. James—later on so famous in Spain as S. Jago de Compostella—has been entirely removed from the lectionary of Silos, which represents the usage of Toledo. Nothing but the harmless Sapiential lesson betrays now to the expert, not however to the ordinary listener in church, that the office once commemorated the joint execution of James and John.

XV

LITERARY TESTIMONIES FOR THE MARTYRDOM OF THE ZEBEDAID JOHN

THE ABOVE-QUOTED ENTRY in the Syrian Martyrology has a parallel in a passage of the Syrian Aphraates '*De persecutione*' (A.D. 343–344), which runs:

'Great and excellent is the martyr Stephen whom the Jews stoned. . . . Simon also and Paul were perfect martyrs. And James and John walked in the footsteps of their master Christ . . . also others of the apostles thereafter in diverse places confessed and proved themselves true martyrs.'

What Aphraates the Syrian knew must have been known to the author of the superscription in Dr. Mingana's Codex 740, who attributed the Fourth Gospel to 'the younger John', knowing that the older John, the brother of James, had suffered martyrdom long before the Fourth Gospel was written.

The Martyrology of Carthage—which must have been known to Fortunatian the African when he translated the prologue to the Fourth Gospel—can be compared with some lines in the epistle '*De rebaptismate*', erroneously attributed to Cyprian and printed among his works, but certainly written by an African contemporary of the martyr about A.D. 250:

'He said to the sons of Zebedee: "Are ye able?" For he knew the men had to be baptized, not only in water, but in their own blood.'

As to the Greek 2nd-century opinion about John's martyrdom, it is well known since de Muralt's edition (1859) of George the Sinner's 'Chronicles' that this Byzantine 9th-century compilation contains the following quotation:

'John the apostle, after he had written his Gospel, suffered martyrdom, for Papias in the second book of the *Logia Kyriaka* says that he was killed by Jews, thus plainly fulfilling along with his brother the prophecy of Christ regarding them and their own consent to it and agreement concerning it.'

The words preceding the quotation and asserting that John was killed 'after he had written his Gospel' are, of course, an expression of George the Sinner's own conviction and have nothing to do with what he quotes from Papias. The latter momentous words are found only in one of the twenty-seven manuscripts of Georgios Hamartolos utilized by de Muralt. In the parent manuscript or manuscripts of all the other twenty-six codices they have been deleted and replaced by the innocuous phrase:

'John the Apostle, after he had written his Gospel, died in peace.'

In 1888, de Boor discovered in a Bodleian manuscript a 7th- or 8th-century epitome, probably of Philippus Sidensis' *Ecclesiastical History* (about A.D. 430), with the following quotation:

'Papias says in his second book that John the Divine (ὁ θεολόγος) and his brother James were slain by Jews.'

Th. Zahn's desperate expedient of presuming that 'Papias was certainly referring here to John the Baptist', because Papias would not have called John 'the Divine' ὁ θεολόγος—an epithet which was not applied to John, again according to Zahn, before the 4th century A.D.—has been repeated quite recently by Dr. W. F. Howard, who says: 'The form of the statement in the Epitomist's alleged quotation from Papias is clearly(!) an anachronism. John was not called "the theologian"(!) as early as Papias—if so, it would imply his authorship of the Gospel.'

The truth is that Hippolytus of Rome (about A.D. 222) called John 'high-priest' and 'Ephesian' θεηγόρος and θεόφωνος or 'divinely inspired prophet'. Now θεηγόρος is absolutely synonymous with θεολόγος and simply preferred to it for the exigencies of the metre of Hippolytus' ode. Like θεηγόρος or θεογλώσσος, 'speaking with the tongue of a god', θεολόγος may mean one who is 'the spokesman of a god'. It is said of diviners and prophets—μάντεις καὶ θεολόγοι, especially of the Delphic oracle-priests and diviners—οἱ τῶν Δελφῶν θεολόγοι. Orpheus, the inspired poet, is called ὁ θεολόγος by the Neo-Platonists. Ὁ θεολόγος, that is 'the θεολόγος', is a Philonian title of Moses, who was not a 'theologian', but ὁ προφήτης,' the prophet' of old, the mouthpiece and speaker of God. Ὁ θεολόγος is no more a Byzantine title of the apostle than ὁ πρόδρομος, 'the forerunner', an epithet bestowed upon John the Baptist in the Greek anti-Marcionite prologue to Luke. It denotes the 'seer', the 'prophet' who saw and wrote down the Revelations in Patmos, a book which Bousset has proved to have been known to Papias and which is entitled Ἀποκάλυψις Ἰωάννου τοῦ θεολόγου in a number of cursives. Since Andrew of Caesarea says in the prologue of his commentary to the Apocalypse (A.D. 515) that Papias, Irenaeus, Methodius and Hippolytus bear witness to τὸ ἀξιόπιστον, 'the trustworthiness' of the Apocalypse, it is probable that Papias knew and mentioned the Apocalypse as a genuine, 'trustworthy' prophecy of its ostensible author and writer John, exiled during a persecution (θλῖψις) to Patmos 'because of the Word of God and the martyrdom (or testimony) for Jesus Christ' (Rev. i. 9). Why on earth should Papias not have called the author of the prophecy of this book ὁ θεολόγος, 'the divine' or 'inspired prophet'?

As to Dr. Howard's argument that 'James the son of Zebedee was not slain "by Jews" but by Herod Agrippa I', the first answer is that neither was Jesus crucified by Jews. Although He was beyond any doubt executed by Pontius Pilate the Roman, *more maiorum*, the Jews are accused in 1 Thess. ii. 15, in Acts iii. 15 and v. 30 of having 'killed' (ἀπεκτείνατε) and crucified Him (κρεμάσαντες ἐπὶ ξύλον). Are we to delete these three verses as spurious from the text of Paul and of Luke because of their intentional historical inexactitude?

Dr. Howard and Archbishop J. H. Bernard have also overlooked that Papias does not blame '*the* Jews' for the death of the brothers. The absence of the definite article is very remarkable and must be conditioned by a particular context. Now Herod Agrippa I, although an Edomite by race, was a Jew, very demonstrative of his Jewish orthodoxy, indeed, and—what is more to the point—one of the Roman governors of Palestine in these years was equally a Jew, Tiberius Alexander, the nephew

THE MARTYRDOM OF THE ZEBEDAID JOHN 67

of Philo of Alexandria. 'Killed by Jews' means 'killed by people who were Jews', words which are probably aimed at Herod Agrippa I and Tiberius Alexander.

The second answer to Dr. Howard is a simple reference to Eusebius' *Ecclesiastical History* III. 5, 2 where this author says: 'Now after the Ascension of our Saviour, in addition to their crime against Him, Jews'—again without the definite article as in the quotation from Papias!—'having contrived numberless plots against His disciples, Stephen was stoned to death by them and next after him James the son of Zebedee and brother of John was beheaded'.

Just as Th. Zahn's hypothesis of Papias meaning not John the Zebedaid, but John the Baptist, is an exact counterpart to the above-mentioned interpolation of the Martyrology of Carthage, Dr. Howard's assumption that 'there has probably been confusion of James the son of Zebedee with James the Lord's brother who was killed by Jews in Jerusalem in A.D. 62' is a parallel to the procedure adopted by the compiler of the Ps.-Hieronymian Martyrology, who replaced the commemoration of James the son of Zebedee by a commemoration of St. James the Just in order to get rid of the inconvenient martyrdom of James' brother John. Both are desperate expedients resorted to in order to safeguard the possibility of the Fourth Gospel having been written by a disciple of Jesus named John, who saw, heard, and touched Him—a possibility which the letter of Polycrates proves to be in no way dependent on the truth of the indefensible Marcionite equation of the beloved disciple with John the son of Zebedee.

Even if there were a legitimate way of discrediting the clear and unequivocal statement of Papias, it would not dispose of the concordant 2nd-century evidence offered by Heracleon (*c.* A.D. 170), an early Valentinian Gnostic and commentator on the Fourth Gospel, preserved by Clement of Alexandria. Heracleon, commenting on the prophecy of Jesus in Luke xii. 11-12, 'when they bring you unto the synagogues and before magistrates and powers' etc., says:

'Matthew, Philip, Thomas, Levi and many others have escaped public martyrdom.'

The omission of the name of John is most significant and cannot, in view of the prominency of the two 'Sons of Thunder', both in the synoptic tradition and in the early martyrologies, be explained away by including him among the unnamed 'many others'.

Finally, Gregory of Nyssa (A.D. 332–400) mentions Peter, James, and John as martyred apostles—dating their passion between the deaths of Stephen and Paul. His testimony is all the more and by no means less valuable because he is puzzled by the calendar of the Church—in his diocese in Asia Minor—attesting the martyrdom of John, and seeks to explain away what so obviously seemed to conflict with the Marcionite legend of John's late and natural death ever since Origen had introduced, into the alleged 'traditions' of the Church, the Marcionite identification of the Evangelist John with the Galilean fisherman John the Zebedaid.

XVI

JOHN KILLED BY KING HEROD IN JEWISH TRADITION

THERE IS independent evidence for the execution of the Zebedaid John by order of King Herod Agrippa I in a Jewish, violently anti-Christian source, the notorious *Toldoth Jeshu*—a crude pamphlet of uncertain age, some versions of which contain elements derived from the Hebrew paraphrase of Flavius Josephus known as the *Josippon*. Its title, meaning 'Generation' or 'Origins of Jesus', proves it to be intended as a Jewish reply to the gospel of Matthew, which begins with the superscription: 'The book of the generation of Jesus . . .' (βίβλος γενέσεως 'Ιησοῦ). It is probably a counterblast to the Hebrew or Aramean version of Matthew used by the so-called Ebionites and translated by St. Jerome into Latin. Its most characteristic features are known already to Tertullian, and there is no sound reason militating against the plausible assumption that the earliest version of this book is not much younger than the Hebrew version of Matthew. Later medieval versions are quoted by Hrabanus Maurus and Agobard of Lyons. Numerous *Toldoth Jeshu* manuscripts are still to be found in various collections and have been analysed in a monograph by Professor Samuel Krauss, of Vienna.

The most interesting of the various recensions was published by Johannes Jacobus Huldricus (Huldreich) in Hebrew and in a Latin translation in Leiden, 1705. It introduces as the chief of the followers of Jesus a certain Joḥanan, who is beheaded by order of King Herod, with the following words (p. 35 f.):

> *Jeshuʻa . . . abiit igitur perfricta fronte impudenter admodum. Legem explicuit non uti ex traditione magistrorum explicari debet.*
> *Wajjithəlaqqəṭū 'ănāshîm rējqîm upōḫăzîm*
> *Wəgham bā'ū 'elājw hap-pārisîm*
> *Shimə'on uMatthāj wə'Elijāqim*

70 THE ENIGMA OF THE FOURTH GOSPEL

uMordəkhai wəThodah
quibus Jeshuʻa nomen immutavit
Simeon—Petrus, Matthiam—Matthai, Eliaqim—Laqum,
Mordəkhai—Marcus, Thodah—Poʻal

'Jesus . . . went away. He taught the Law, not as it should be taught according to the tradition of the teachers, and there assembled (around him) men destitute (or vain) and lightheaded and also there came to him the bandits Sime'on and Matthew and Elijaqim, Mardochaeus and Thodah, whose names Jesus changed, Sime'on into Peter, Matthew to Matthias, *Elijaqim* (= "God will raise up") to *Laqum* (= "Do not arise"!), Mardochaeus to Marc and *Thodah* ("Praise" or "Thanksoffering") to *Poʻal* ("Work").'

> *wəgham bāʼ ʼălējhēm hap-pāriṣ rōʼsh-*
> *barjōnîm Jōhanan wəjasseb shəmo*
> *wajjiqrāʼ Jōhenis ʻal shem han-nissîm*
> *sheʻăśāh Jəshuʻa bəphānājw—ʻălājw shălōm!—*
> *bəshem ham-məphōrāsh.*

'and also there came to them the bandit (*hap-pāriṣ* = ὁ λῃστής) a chief of outlaws (*barjōnîm*) Joḥanan—And he changed his name and called (him) *Jōhenis* (that is *Jahu-, Jō-*, i.e. 'God puts to flight' —*henis, hiphil perf.* of *nws* 'to flee') because of the miracles (*han-nissîm*) which Jesus did in his presence by means of the Secret Name (of God), upon Whom be peace!'

This 'Joḥanan the bandit, the chief of the outlaws'—whom Huldreich confused with John the Baptist, known to the *Josippon* as '*Rabbi Joḥanan ham-maṭbil*', in some manuscripts *Rabban Joḥanan kohen ha-gadol*, 'the high-priest', and never attacked in any version of the *Toldoth Jeshu!*—is said to have been beheaded by order of King Herod:

> *Wajjābhōʼu hărāṣîm wəlōʼ moṣəîm raq Jōhenis*
> *tāphəśu wa-jəbhijʼehu liphənēj*
> *ham-mĕlēkh wa-jəṣaw ham-mĕlēkh lahărōg ʼeth Jōhenis*
> *bassajĭph. wajjahărghu ʼōthō wajitəlū rāʼshaw rōʼśō*
> *nĕghēd shăʻăr Jərūshălājim.*
> *Venientes satellites non invenerunt*
> *(alium) quam Johannem, prehenderunt*

JOHN KILLED BY KING HEROD IN JEWISH TRADITION

*et deduxerunt in praesentiam regis
et dixit rex ut occideretur Johannes
gladio et occiderunt eum et suspenderunt
caput eius ad portam Jerusalem.*

'And there came the (kings) footmen and they found none but John, arrested him and marched him into the king's presence and the king gave the order to kill John with the sword" (= $\mu\alpha\chi\alpha\iota\rho\alpha$, as in Acts xii. 2!), 'And they killed him and hung up his head on the (out)side of a door of Jerusalem.'

That Huldreich should have misinterpreted this story as referring to John the Baptist, beheaded in the fortress Machaerus, whose head was brought on a salver to Salome, is almost unbelievable—but there it is on his p. 41 in so many words!

'Bandit', $\lambda\eta\sigma\tau\acute{\eta}s$, or even chief of outlaws (*barjonîm*), $\mathring{\alpha}\rho\chi\iota\lambda\eta\sigma\tau\acute{\eta}s$, are the well-known opprobrious terms which Flavius Josephus and his Roman sources—accustomed to dub the nationalist insurgents opposing the imperial rule '*latrones*'—habitually apply to the Jewish Messianist revolutionaries and nationalist Zealots. The epithet *barjona*, 'outlaw', 'outcast', is applied by Jesus Himself in the famous saying of Caesarea Philippi to Simon Peter, another of the three Galilean fishermen who constitute, so to say, the innermost circle of the disciples.

The fact that John the son of Zebedee was sentenced by the Roman judge as an insurgent is well known to Christian tradition. The so-called Abdias, a Latin Catholicized version of the Leucian 'Acts of John' says that the Roman proconsul ordered him to be tortured *velut rebellem*. As a matter of fact, the torture confined by Roman republican law to slaves, was applied since the beginning of the rule of the emperors to free men—and women—but only in cases of persons suspected or accused of high treason (*crimen laesae majestatis*).

Characteristically enough, the same manuscript says, further down (p. 59), about the same Joḥanan, i.e. the Zebedaid John, that, while the king wanted to kill him, the disciples of Jesus succeeded in rescuing him. This might be an interpolation added as a concession to the Marcionite legend that John died a natural death at an unusually old age at Ephesus, and it might equally be a reminiscence of John's escape from his exile on the island of Patmos.

But it is more likely to be the Jewish counterblast to the much earlier legend that St. John was executed, but miraculously resuscitated by a descent of the Holy Spirit and ascended into Heaven in the wake of his resuscitated Master, which we shall have to analyse (below, p. 98) in our chapter about Rev. xi. 3–12.

XVII

THE ORIGINAL TEXT OF ACTS XII. 2

IN VIEW of the considerable body of evidence collected in the previous chapters—deeply rooted in the liturgical practice of the Christian Churches all around the Mediterranean and corroborated by an independent Jewish tradition—it would seem paradoxical that the current text of Acts xii. 2 should mention the execution of James the son of Zebedee by order of Herod Agrippa, but not the martyrdom of James's twin-brother John.

As a matter of fact, no less a master of textual criticism than Eduard Schwartz, the latest editor of Eusebius, long ago maintained the thesis—considered as a possibility already by Wellhausen—that the present text of Acts xii. 2 must have been censored at a very early period.

There are several arguments against the integrity of the present text to be added to Eduard Schwartz's general considerations.

First of all, it is quite unusual and irregular that James the son of Zebedee should be introduced, not with his proper name and father's name, but as 'the brother of John', especially if there was no reason for mentioning his brother in this context.

The case is quite different from Mark v. 37 'and he suffered no man to follow him save Peter and James and John the brother of James', where the other brother has been mentioned immediately before; or from John i. 40 ff. '. . . one of the two . . . was Andrew, Simon Peter's brother. He first findeth his own brother Simon . . .', where the name of the father of the two is purposely omitted so as to be revealed by Jesus who 'when He beheld him, said: 'Thou art Simon the son of Jona'; or from the famous passage in Josephus *Antiquities* XX. § 200, introducing James the Just as 'the brother of the afore-mentioned Jesus the so-called Christ', because otherwise his father's name Joseph would have been just as meaningless for the reader as his own, equally frequent name.

This was felt instinctively by Eusebius, who paraphrased Acts xii. 2 in his *Ecclesiastical History* (III. 5, 2) in this way: 'James, who was a son of Zebedee, but a brother of John, was beheaded.' There is indeed no conceivable reason why Luke should have written: ἀνεῖλεν δὲ Ἰάκωβον τὸν ἀδελφὸν Ἰωάννου μαχαίρᾳ instead of ἀνεῖλεν δὲ Ἰάκωβον τὸν υἱὸν Ζεβεδαίου μαχαίρᾳ, 'and he killed James the son of Zebedee with the sword', unless John was somehow mentioned immediately before.

Secondly Origen quotes this line in a still more paradoxical form: 'he killed James of John with the sword'—as if John were James's father and not his brother, and as if James were called 'James the son of John' and not 'James the son of Zebedee'.

The simplest explanation for these otherwise inexplicable irregularities would seem to be that the original ran:

ἐπέβαλεν Ἡρῴδης ὁ βασιλεὺς τὰς χεῖρας κακῶσαί τινας τῆς ἐκκλησίας ἐν τῇ Ἰουδαίᾳ καὶ ἀνεῖλεν ⟨Ἰωάννην καὶ⟩ Ἰάκωβον τὸν ἀδελφὸν Ἰωάννου.

'Herod the king stretched forth his hands to vex certain of the church in Judaea, and he killed ⟨John and⟩ James the brother of John with the sword.'

This seems to have been corrected by expurgating the two words ⟨Ἰωάννην καὶ⟩ 'John and'. Most probably one or more paragraphs have been deleted between Acts xii. 1 and 2, since it is really too grotesque to omit every explanation of Herod Agrippa's action and thus to suggest to the reader that a Roman vassal king could or would just murder anybody *ad lib.* without rhyme or reason.

A careless corrector must have deleted in some copies not only the words 'John and' ⟨Ἰωάννην καὶ⟩, but also τὸν ἀδελφὸν, 'the brother', the apposition to 'James'—a very likely error of a reviser wanting to obliterate the mention of the one brother in this clause and intending, probably, to substitute the correct patronymic 'son of Zebedee' for the deleted words. A mistake of this kind would produce the particularly absurd reading quoted by Origen.

This conjecture would account both for the entirely unusual 'James the brother of John' in Acts xii. 2, and for the still more irregular 'James of John' in Origen's quotation. It would also explain the brevity and lack of all detail in the account of the martyrdom of one of the most prominent members of the original circle of the Twelve Apostles, a feature which has often been observed and contrasted with the long and elaborate report of Stephen's, a mere deacon's passion, and with the amount of space dedicated to the comparatively unimportant story of Peter's arrest and escape during the same persecution.

Now that we have the beautiful Benedictine edition of all the extant 'summaries' of the Latin Bible and are able to compare these short chapter-headings with the text of the Vulgate version, it seems obvious that a short line like

'*Occidit ⟨Herodes Joannem et⟩ Jacobum fratrem Joannis gladio*'

cannot have been the complete account of such a momentous event, but is merely the *titulus* or chapter-heading of it. The chapter itself must have been cut out and replaced by the mere summary of it, minus the mention of John.

To the supposed suppression of the story relating the fate of the Zebedaid John in Acts corresponds logically the omission of Jesus' prophecy foretelling their martyrdom to both the sons of Zebedee in the Gospel of Luke, which has been noticed, but not explained by Eduard Schwartz and by other critics before him.

What seems to have happened is the suppression of the lessons for the office of St. John's and St. James's days—in a community using the two books of Luke only as its lectionary—leaving just the inevitable minimum about the execution of James which was needed in order to bridge the gap and to correspond with the mention of Herod's intention to 'vex some ($\tau\iota\nu\grave{\alpha}\varsigma$) of the Church'—a plural referring originally to ⟨John and⟩ James but now, in the curtailed text, to James and Peter.

Traces of such modifications in the ritual of certain communities are clearly visible in the later Occidental Church. If we compare the above-quoted Missal of Bobbio—representing the Merovingian usage of the Church of Paris—with the 7th-century lectionary of Schlettstadt in Alsatia discovered by

Dom G. Morin, we find that the offices for the martyrs SS. Stephen, John, and James between Christmas and New Year, which are a feature of the Bobbio missal, are missing in the Schlettstadt lectionary.

In the monumental Benedictine edition of all extant Latin summaries to the Old and the New Testaments we can see that there is a whole group of MSS. of the Vulgate in the summaries of which the stoning of St. Stephen and the decapitation of St. James are, most surprisingly, omitted. Since the corresponding chapters in the text are perfectly intact, it is obvious that the parent manuscript of the group was used as a lectionary and that somebody at some time deleted the *tituli* of the lessons for St. Stephen's and St. John's and St. James's days, when these two feasts were discontinued, as they must have been before the Schlettstadt lectionary was written and before St. Gregory the Great composed his Homiliary, which offers no sermons for St. Stephen's, St. James's, and St. John's days after the two homilies for the vigil and the morning of Christmas.

An equally significant case is a missal of the Spanish abbey Silos of the province of Toledo in the British Museum, which has the commemoration of St. James, the brother of John, on the usual day—but the lessons are missing.

This is exactly the state of affairs which might be said to correspond with the present condition of the extant text of Luke: the martyrdom of James is mentioned in Acts, i.e. in Luke's second volume, but the story, how and why he incurred the king's displeasure and how the king managed to get him beheaded—in a country administered under an orderly system of Roman law—is missing, as well as the corresponding 'lesson' in the Gospel—Luke's volume one—commemorating the impressive dialogue between Jesus and the ambitious brothers and the Lord's prophecy of their future baptism in blood.

It is the text of the two books of Luke, curtailed in this particular way and not yet united with the other Synoptic Gospels, which has made it possible for the author of the above-mentioned anti-Marcionite prologue to assert, against the Marcionites and against the *Alogoi*, rejecting the Fourth Gospel as a spurious pseudepigraphon, that it had been written by 'John the Apostle from among the Twelve' after the three other Gospels and after Luke's Acts—a thesis impossible to maintain against the said adversaries as long as they could prove from the Gospel and the Acts of Luke that John had been executed together with James under Herod Agrippa I, i.e. before this king's death in A.D. 44.

Since the statement of the extant anti-Marcionite prologue to Acts about the Fourth Gospel is incompatible with an evangel containing the prophecy of Jesus about the martyrdom of the Zebedaids and with an edition of Acts reporting the inevitable fulfilment of the Lord's forecast, it seems evident that the expurgation of the Lucan parallel to Mark x. 35 ff. and Matt. xx. 20 ff., and of the martyrdom of John in Acts xii must be attributed to the anti-Marcionite and pro-Johannine, in one word, to the Catholic, editor who prefixed the extant anti-Marcionite preface to the two books of Luke.

XVIII

THE MEETING OF PAUL AND JOHN THE 'PILLAR' IN GALATIANS AND IN THE ACTS

EDUARD SCHWARTZ has, of course, been aware from the start of the chronological obstacle which Gal. ii. 9 seems to present to a restoration of the text of Acts xii. 2, harmonizing the account of Luke with the testimony of Papias and the earliest martyrologies about the simultaneous martyrdom of the two sons of Zebedee. If Gal. ii. 9, which mentions John the son of Zebedee as one of the 'pillars' whom Paul met when he came to Jerusalem for the second time, refers to the meeting described in Acts xv. 4–30, it is obvious that the author of Acts cannot have reported the execution of John in xii. 2.

Paul's account in Gal. i. 13–ii. 11 is, however, at variance with the text of Acts, even if Acts xii. 2 is left to stand as we find it in the manuscripts. In a document in which he had every reason to be very accurate, Paul states that up to the date of his meeting Peter, John and James he had been but once before in Jerusalem, for a fortnight only, having met only Peter and 'none of the other Apostles, save James the Lord's brother'. According to Acts, however, the journey to Jerusalem from Antioch (xv. 4 ff.) is preceded not only by the first journey from Damascus to Jerusalem (Acts ix. 26–30 = Gal. i. 18), but by another journey from Antioch to Jerusalem and back again (xi. 27–30; xii. 24 f.). Both accounts cannot be true, and the contradiction between the two has been discussed many times since the Tübingen school of Higher Criticism made it the starting-point for their attack against the trustworthiness of Acts. Since there is no conceivable reason why either Paul or Luke should have purposely distorted the real facts, it is legitimate to suppose that Luke's account has suffered through some accidental confusion. This inevitable conclusion is supported by a very strong argument of historic probability:

Eduard Schwartz has pointed out—and the argument is unanswerable—that the meeting of Paul with the 'pillars' of the Christian community of Jerusalem must have preceded and cannot have followed Herod Agrippa's organized persecution of these very leaders of the Messianist movement which resulted—according to Acts xii. 1–3—in the execution of James, in the arrest of Peter and in this Apostle's flight from his native country.

According to Acts xii. 17, Peter escapes 'to another place' and there is no mention of his having ever returned to Jerusalem, where he is, nevertheless, supposed to have been present at the 'Apostles' council' (Acts xv. 7.)

The meeting between Paul and the 'pillars' may have been —as Eduard Schwartz has very plausibly suggested—the cause of the arrest of both the Zebedaids and of Peter, since we know from Josephus that the Herodian administration had a well-organized system of spying on those 'who came together in the city and in their journeys overland'. Anyhow, it is inconceivable that proceedings such as those described in Acts xv. 7 —Peter addressing an assembly of the Apostles and elders of the Christian community in Jerusalem—should have happened a short time after his arrest and miraculous escape, even if King Herod Agrippa I had died in the meantime.

All these difficulties are by no means insuperable.

Almost a century ago (1838) Fritzsche first identified the journey described in Acts xi. 30 with the occasion to which Paul alludes in Gal. ii. 9. More recently (1896 and 1897) Sir W. M. Ramsay and A. C. MacGiffert have proposed the same solution. So also Spitta (1891)—a conservative theologian otherwise bitterly opposed to Eduard Schwartz's thesis concerning the early death of the Zebedaid John—Wellhausen, and von Soden. This cogent argument forced Schwartz to assume that Acts xi. 27–30; xii. 24 f., and Acts xv. 1–35 are two accounts of one and the same journey 'more accurately described by Acts xv, but chronologically more correctly placed by Acts xi. 27 ff.' (von Soden). For all these reasons Schwartz and, in one way or another, all his above-named predecessors have supposed that the author of Acts has misunderstood what he found in his various hypothetical sources about Paul's second journey to Jerusalem as referring to two different occasions and that he has split into two accounts what he ought to have fused into one story.

But there is a much simpler solution of the problem, which has two great advantages. It is entirely independent of all the various hypotheses about the sources of Acts; and it avoids the necessity of putting the blame for the confusion (in itself undeniable) on an author who shows throughout a considerable skill in presenting a vivid and intelligible picture of a rather complicated series of events.

As the impossible end of the book proves beyond any reasonable doubt, Acts is an uncompleted work, published by some unknown editor—possibly by Theophilus himself, possibly by some clerk whom he employed—after St. Luke's death. The draft was probably written on loose leaves, like the notes of the three Evangelists in the quaint story of the 'Acts of Timothy', which the authors have to submit to John of Ephesus, because they feel unable to join the matter together in the proper order. Or the parts of the scroll, imperfectly glued together, had fallen asunder. Somehow or other, a most ordinary accident happened to the editor of the posthumous publication which the author could not revise any more, an accident which has happened to many a modern typist having to deal with a draft on unnumbered loose pages: certain parts have been inserted into the wrong place.

Once the incompatibility of Gal. i, ii—definitely limiting the number of journeys to Jerusalem to two in fourteen years—with the three ostensible journeys in Acts—ix. 26 (=Gal. i. 18); xi. 30; xii. 25; and xv. 2 ff.—has been observed, the rearrangement of the text in its original logical order is no more difficult than the solving of an ordinary jigsaw puzzle. If the reader will but copy out for himself—by preference in Greek—Acts xi. 25 f; xiii. 1–xv. 2; xi. 27–30; xv. 3–33; xv. 34; xii. 25; xii. 1–24; xv. 35–41, he will see how perfectly the transposed parts dovetail, and how completely the imaginary third journey to Jerusalem before the meeting with the pillars disappears, leaving a perfect concordance between Acts and Galatians and explaining incidentally through the correlation of Acts xii. 17 with Gal. ii. 11 that the 'other place' to which Peter went was Antioch.

XIX

THE TRUE TEXT OF GAL. II. 9 AND THE ALLEGED CONFUSION
OF THE TWO JAMESES BY IRENAEUS

THE SPLITTING of one and the same Pauline journey to Jerusalem into the two apparent journeys Acts xi. 30; xii. 25; and xv. 2–29, through the erroneous editorial transposition of parts of the scroll which had fallen asunder and the consequent shifting of Paul's meeting with the 'pillars' of the Church to a chapter following the execution of the Zebedaid James, is responsible for a fatal corruption of the famous line Gal. ii. 9 concerning the 'pillars' of the Church.

St. Irenaeus has been accused by Archdeacon R. H. Charles of being 'occasionally very inaccurate', having 'confused James the Lord's brother, who in Acts xv. 13 takes part in the Council of Jerusalem, with James the son of Zebedee, who has already been martyred in Acts xii'. As a matter of fact, Irenaeus identifies in the crucial paragraph of his *Elenchus* III. 12, 15, the 'pillar'-Apostles Peter, James and John with the three most intimate disciples of Jesus who are 'throughout found in His immediate neighbourhood', referring, of course, to such passages as Mark v. 37; Luke viii. 51; Mark xiii. 3; Matt. xvii. 1; Mark ix. 2; Luke ix. 28; Mark xiv. 33; Matt. xxvi. 37. It is we who ought to have seen long ago how absurd it is to believe that this 'inner circle' triad in the Synoptic Gospels could possibly be homonymous but not identical with the triad of 'pillars' in Galatians ii. 9! St. Irenaeus read in Gal. ii. 9—as Marcion did before him, and as we still read in the *Codex Bezae*, and the other bilingual MSS. G.E.F., in the *Codex Fuldensis*, in the Gothic Version, in the *Vetus Latina* generally as represented by Origen's translator, Tertullian, Ambrosiaster and St. Jerome: 'Peter and James and John who seemed to be "pillars".' The variant reading 'James and Peter and John', wedging in Peter (or Kephas) between the Zebedaid brothers James and

John and thus suggesting that the James taking precedence before Peter must be James the brother of the Lord, is nothing but a correction, attempting to harmonize Gal. ii. 9 with the text of Acts, absurdly disturbed by a transposition of its columns, according to which the James speaking in Acts xv. 13 must be another than the one beheaded in xii. 2.

Now that the text of Acts is restored to the original order intended by Luke so that xv. 13 precedes xii. 2, it is evident that the Bezan text of Gal. ii. 9—Marcion's and Irenaeus' text and the text of the oldest Latin translator of Paul—is the correct original wording.

The 'pillar'-Apostles are, of course, the same three disciples, Peter and the two sons of Zebedee, who are throughout the Synoptic Gospels the three intimate acolytes of Jesus—as we should have known ever since it had first been noticed that Paul's second journey occurs twice in the extant text of Acts, and that its correct chronological place is before James's execution and Peter's arrest!

Only in Acts xii. 17 and xxi. 18 it is James the Just who must be meant. Paul is taken to see him—just as when he came to see Peter the first time (Gal. i. 19). But now it is not this James who answers Paul, but 'they'—i.e. the assembly of all the elders who have met at James's abode. The James who had been the speaker and laid down in Acts xv. 13 the Noachic law, for the Gentiles to observe, is now no more.

This was perfectly well known to Eusebius where he says: 'There are two Jameses, one James the Just who was thrown down from the pinnacle, the other he who was beheaded.' Paul also mentions the same James the Just when he writes: 'and saw none other of the Apostles, save James the brother of the Lord.' Eusebius does not go on quoting Gal. ii. 9, and telling us that James was one of the 'pillars', because there he read 'Peter and James and John' and did not dream of mistaking one of the pair James and John for James the Lord's brother.

The traditional misinterpretation of Gal. ii. 9 has not only misled Archdeacon Charles into raising the entirely baseless accusation of inaccuracy against St. Irenaeus, but it has also, incidentally, prevented him and other critics from noticing the strong argument which the unjustly incriminated passage offers against the usual assumption that the Bishop of Lyons identified the beloved disciple of Jesus with John the son of Zebedee.

The chapter in question tries to demonstrate that the Apostles most intimately conversant with the teaching of Jesus considered the Old Testament as revealed by the same God as the New Testament and not by another one, as Marcion taught. In order to prove this thesis Irenaeus says:

'Those who allowed the Gentiles, with the Apostle James, liberty of action . . . remained themselves obedient to the old customs, although they professed to believe in the same God, so that Peter too, to avoid scandalizing them . . . separated himself from the Gentiles and did not eat any more with them, when "some came from James". The same was done by Barnabas according to the report of Paul. It follows that, by observing conscientiously the Law, the Apostles whom He had made witnesses of all his deed, and of his entire teaching—for everywhere Peter and *James and John* are found in his immediate presence—testified to the Law having been given by the same God.'

If Irenaeus had considered the John who is mentioned here in connection with his brother James and with Peter to have been John the beloved disciple and Evangelist, he would have been able considerably to strengthen his argument by saying: 'the Apostles whom He had made witnesses of all His deeds and His entire teaching—for everywhere Peter and James and John ‹*the disciple who had rested his head against the Lord's breast*› are found in his immediate presence.' If he says nothing of the sort, it is for two very good reasons: first because it had never occurred to him that anybody could identify James's brother John with the beloved disciple, and secondly because he could not quote the Fourth Evangelist in support of his anti-Marcionite argument, since it is precisely in the Gospel of John that Jesus says to the Jews 'it is written in *your* Law', as if He did not recognize it as the Law given to Him and His disciples by His own God—a fact which we shall endeavour to explain in our chap. XXXIX.

XX

THE CHRONOLOGY OF GALATIANS AND THE TRUE DATE OF THE CRUCIFIXION

IF PAUL'S meeting with the 'pillars' happened, as will be proved below in more detail, towards the end of A.D. 42, i.e. before James was beheaded, Paul's vision of the glorified Jesus in Damascus must have occurred according to the classic method of reckoning, well known to every schoolboy from the *ante Idus, ante Kalendas* calculus of the Romans, but strangely unfamiliar to most Biblical chronologists, either ten or thirteen years before the 'Apostles' Council', according to whether the 'fourteen years' in Gal. ii. 1 are taken as following or as including the 'three years' of Gal. i. 18.

If the second view is taken, that is to say, if we suppose that Paul intentionally said μετὰ τρία ἔτη '*after* three years' in i. 18, but διὰ δεκατεσσάρων ἐτῶν '*in the course* of fourteen years' in ii. 1, meaning that 'in the course' of these fourteen years he had been twice only in Jerusalem, the first time 'three years after his conversion and 'for a fortnight only'—the vision of the glorified Jesus in Damascus would have to be placed in 42 − 10 − 2, i.e. in the end of the year A.D. 30. This date is quite compatible even with the Lucan date for the baptism of Jesus in the fifteenth year of Tiberius (= A.D. 28) and with the resulting date of the Passion at Eastertide, A.D. 29.

Taking the more widely accepted view that the 'fourteen years' must be understood as the interval between Paul's first and his second journey to Jerusalem and not as the space of time between Paul's conversion and his meeting 'the pillars' at the end of the second journey, Eduard Schwartz arrived, by deducting 13 + 2 from 44 at the year A.D. 29 for Paul's conversion, a result which is obviously difficult to combine with the Lucan date of the Passion. He was, however, fully conscious of the fact that the authority of the Lucan date is of the slightest.

He said so quite decidedly, although he confessed not to know how Luke may have hit on this particular date.

Since then the present writer has been able to show that Luke's chronology is simply the result of the search for a year in which the vernal equinox, the 25th of March (VIII° *Kal. Aprilis*) fell on a Friday and therefore without any basis in real tradition.

The whole question is, however, purely academical and otiose, because it is now obvious that the editor of Luke's posthumous Acts was quite hazy about the chronology of Paul's itinerary and of the Apostles' Council in Jerusalem.

As to the true chronology of the events, indelibly engraved upon Paul's own memory, there is in any case—however we choose to interpret the crucial phrase about the 'fourteen years' in Galatians—ample space between the Passion of Jesus and the Apostle's conversion, even if it happened in $42 - 13 - 2 =$ A.D. 27, since the Roman official acts of the lawsuit against Jesus, published from the imperial archives in A.D. 311, date the Passion in the year of the fourth consulate of Tiberius, the seventh year of his reign, which lasted from the 19th of August, 20, to the 19th of August, 21, so that Jesus must have been crucified in the night before Easter, A.D. 21, which fell on a 15th of April. The year, A.D. 26, of Pilate's arrival in Jerusalem in Josephus—which Eusebius quotes, very diffidently indeed, as incompatible with this date—has been proved by the present writer to be a forgery introduced into the manuscripts for the purpose of discrediting the embarrassing official publication of Emperor Maximinus Daia as faked.

XXI

THE MARTYRDOM OF THE TWO WITNESSES IN REV. XI. 3–11

TEN YEARS AGO, the late Professor Benjamin Wisner Bacon of Yale University wrote in his article, 'The Elder John in Jerusalem', commenting on Heitmüller's analysis of the evidence offered by Eduard Schwartz for the martyrdom of both Zebedaids and on its restatement by Archdeacon Charles:

'It does not appear that anyone has yet observed the confirmation offered by Apoc. xi. 8. . . . The implication of the words "their Lord" is unmistakable. . . . The two witnesses of verses 3–8a, who by the description of verses 5 f. are Elijah and Moses *redivivi*, must be understood to represent disciples of Jesus . . . the reader is meant to understand that two Christian martyrs have fullfilled the well-known Jewish expectation that before the great day of judgement Moses (*al.* Enoch) and Elias will be sent from Paradise to preach repentance to the people and that Belial will set the cope-stone on his wickedness by putting the two witnesses to death. Who, then, were these two Christian martyrs? Originally (if we may judge by Mark x. 35 ff.) the two sons of Zebedee.'

This is all wholly admirable, straightforward and unanswerable reasoning. But now we see the author, instead of pursuing his far-reaching discovery to its ultimate consequences, starting off on a tangent and landing in the ditch of utter confusion:

'But since it is certain (!) from Gal. ii. 9, that John did not perish along with his brother James, but at most after a considerable interval, the probable intention of the writer of Apoc. xi. 8 is to indicate that at least the apocalyptic prophecy, if not the Lord's prediction as well, was fulfilled in the martyrdom of James the Lord's brother and John in 62 A.D. For Josephus reports not the death alone of the brother of Jesus called the Christ in Jerusalem at this date, but of this James and some others' (*Antiq.* XX. 9, 1 §200).

Here is another of the various cocksure certainties' which

THE MARTYRDOM OF THE TWO WITNESSES 87

have contributed so much to the obfuscation of the Johannine problem ever since Eusebius wrote that fatal σαφῶς in his notorious discussion of the prologue to the five books of Papias (below, p. 141). In reality, as we have seen before, Gal. ii. 9 does not prove at all, let alone with any amount of 'certainty', that John survived his brother James.

Now that the wholly imaginary obstacle of the erroneous chronology of Paul's meeting with Peter, James, and John in Jerusalem has been definitely removed, it is easy to see that Bacon's original interpretation of Rev. xi. 8 as referring to the two sons of Zebedee is the only possible one, and that the writer of these lines always meant the twin 'Sons of Thunder' and certainly not two men, one of whom died in 44, the other in 62.

Nevertheless, Bacon's first and correct explanation was wholly forgotten, while the ulterior unfortunate perversion of it was repeated by Professor Emmanuel Hirsch of Goettingen, in the most recent analysis of the Johannine problem.

Neither Bacon nor Hirsch has noticed the close correlation of Rev. xi. 5: 'Fire proceedeth out of their mouth and devoureth their enemies' (Jer. v. 14) with the words of the two 'Sons of Thunder' recorded by Luke ix. 54 f.: 'Lord, wilt thou that we command fire to come down from heaven and consume them' —as Elijah did (2 Kings i. 10, 12), although Luke ix. 54 is quoted in the margin of Rev. xi. 5 in Nestlé's Greek New Testament.

Both authors have finally overlooked a significant passage in St. Ambrose of Milan's *Exposition of Luke* and in his *Commentary to Psalm* xlv, where he explains the two witnesses, against whom 'the Beast' will make war, as 'Elijah and Enoch'. In the latter passage a Paris manuscript and an old Paris edition, printed after this or a similar manuscript, have added after the words '*bestia faciet bellum adversus Eliam atque Enoch*', a little awkwardly, but all the more significantly: '*atque Joannem*'. Probably the unknown interpolator of Ambrosius wrote originally, '⟨*Jacobum*⟩ *atque Joannem*', meaning to equate Elijah and Enoch with their Christian reincarnations, the two sons of Zebedee.

This explains at last why we find the 27th of December— the day of 'James and John the martyrs' in the old Syrian

Martyrology (above, p. 60)—called '*Assumptio Joannis*', 'Ascension to Heaven of St. John' in certain German and French medieval documents catalogued in G. Grotefend's invaluable chronological repertories. A commemoration of the *Assumptio Johannis* can only refer to the strange legend in Rev. xi. 11 f. that the two martyrs were miraculously resuscitated and bodily raised up into heaven before the eyes of their enemies.

But the most conclusive proof for the correctness of B. W. Bacon's original explanation of Rev. xi. 3, as well as for the restoration of Acts xii. 2 proposed above (p. 74), are the illustrations to Rev. xi. 3-12, which have been preserved in the manuscripts of the commentary to Revelation compiled by the Asturian abbot Beatus of Liébana (below, p. 90) in A.D. 776. These miniatures (Pl. VII)—one set of which is derived from a North-African illustrated edition of the old Latin, pre-Hieronymian text of Revelation, while another set betrays an Italian ancestry—show regularly the 'two witnesses' beheaded by the sword of a crowned king, explained as the ANTICRISTUS (Pl. VII), although neither the text of the Apocalypse nor the commentary of Beatus says a word about the two witnesses perishing by the sword, simply because this illustration was composed at a time when Acts xii. 2 still ran (above, p. 74): 'Now about that time Herod the king stretched forth his hands to damage certain of the church and he killed ‹*John and*› James the brother of John with the sword' and because at that time '*omnia de apostolis*', 'everything about the two Apostles', notably Rev. xi. 3-12 and Acts xii. 2, were still read on the anniversary of their execution and ascension to heaven, the 28th of December (below, p. 103).

The consequences of a correct understanding of Rev. xi. 5 and 8 are most important and far-reaching.

It is now evident that John the Seer, having to swallow the book and to feel its bitterness, is meant to be understood as one of the Zebedaid twin brothers, receiving the revelation of their own impending martyrdom.

The 'power to shut the heavens that it rain not in the days of their prophecy' is a transparent allusion to the long drought and ensuing famine at the beginning of the reign of the Emperor Claudius. The Messianist Jews and their pagan converts to

BEHEADING OF THE TWO SONS OF ZEBEDEE BY KING HEROD AGRIPPA I
Illustration to Rev. xi. 3–7—'the two witnesses' killed by 'the Beast' 'ascending from the bottomless abyss' and their corpses lying on the ground.
Miniatures from two MSS. of the Commentary to Revelation by Beatus of Liébana.

PLATE VII

the belief that the crucified Jesus was the foretold liberator of Israel and future world-ruler, about to return in glory from heaven, must have attributed this calamity to the prophetic power of the two 'Sons of Thunder', considered as Moses and Elijah *redivivi*, smiting the earth anew with the Egyptian plagues of old and the sore famine of the days of Ahab.

XXII

REV. I. 9 REFERRING TO THE ZEBEDAID JOHN DEPORTED UNDER EMPEROR CLAUDIUS

NOW THAT the chapter on the prophetic activity of 'the two witnesses' in Rev. xi. 3–7 has been understood as a historic reminiscence of the role played by the two sons of Zebedee during the famine of A.D. 41, the conclusion is inevitable that the ancient traditions of the Church explaining Rev. i. 9 as an allusion to John the Zebedaid's deportation to the island of Patmos by order of the emperor Claudius are equally trustworthy.

This is what the earliest Spanish commentators of the Apocalypse, Bishop Apringius of Béja (A.D. 531–548), and the Asturian Abbot Beatus of Liébana (A.D. 776) read in certain *relationes ecclesiasticae*, that is to say in the original preface to Revelation, which has been supplanted in the East by a Ps.-Hippolytean introduction posterior to the writings of the Ps.-Dionysius Areopagita, i.e. to the end of the 5th century, in the West by a repetition of Instantius' Monarchianist prologue to the Fourth Gospel:

'As the traditions of the church have taught (us), at the time of Caesar Claudius when the famine prevailed which was foretold by the prophet Agabus in the Acts, at that time the same Caesar . . . ordained a persecution for the churches. At that time he ordered John the Apostle of our Lord Jesus Christ to be sent into exile. That he has been deported to Patmos the present scripture (Rev. i. 9) also proves.'

This story is now perfectly understandable. If a man either claimed to have the power to 'burn his enemies with fire proceeding out of his mouth' and 'to shut heaven, that it rain not, to turn the waters into blood and to smite the earth with plagues' (Rev. xi. 5 f.), or if he was merely accused of possessing such supernatural faculties, the Roman lawyer would not admire him as a prophet, but prosecute him for *magia* and *maleficium*, for a sacrilegious attempt to 'disturb the forces of nature' (*elementa turbare*) and to 'spirit the harvest away by incantation' (*fruges excantare*). According to Roman Law this is a serious, indeed a capital offence, for which a claim to divine inspiration and a description of visions and auditions experienced by the delinquent would not and could not be accepted as exculpating or even attenuating circumstances.

In normal times an enlightened Roman governor or an educated Hellenized king would not lightly embark on a hunt for alleged witches and wizards. But in times of a world-wide drought and famine—causing that inevitable recrudescence of primitive superstition which is specially mentioned by Livy in his account of the great drought of 325 A.U.C.—the restive and excited Greek population and the simple Italian soldier of the Roman army of occupation would clamour for legal action to be taken against mischievous φθονεροὶ γόητες and *malefici* believed to have destroyed the fertility of the land by spraying it with Stygian water or by criminal invocations of their own vindictive divinity. The least the provincial administration could do in these circumstances was to get the object of public indignation (Rev. xi. 10) out of the way by sending the accused man to Rome, to be judged by the emperor's supreme court of justice. Since Rome itself was seriously affected by the famine, it is difficult to see what else even an emperor priding himself on his humane policy could have done but sentence the Jewish alleged magician to enforced residence on a distant island (*deportatio in insulam*).

As Bousset saw, and as the reference to the famine mentioned in Acts immediately before the story of the martyrdom of James ⟨and his brother John⟩ clearly proves, Apringius is not dependent on the two passages in Epiphanius' book *Against all Heresies*, stating that John wrote his Gospel in his old age after the return from his Patmian exile, this and his death having occurred under the reign of the Emperor Claudius.

In the first place Epiphanius—or rather, the source he uses without quoting his authority—says that John wrote his Gospel 'after his return from Patmos which happened under Claudius Caesar, having lived for a sufficient number of years in Asia' (Minor).

In the second place Epiphanius' source asserts that

'the Holy Ghost foretold prophetically through the mouth of St. John prophesying before his demise in the times of Claudius Caesar and (even) before' (i.e. under Gaius Caligula) . . .

The source upon which Epiphanius drew in his chapter 'On the heresy of those who reject the Gospel of John and his Apocalypse' has been definitely proved to be the treatise *About the Gospel of John and the Apocalypse, chapters against Gaius*, which Hippolytus, the schismatic Bishop of Rome at the time of Pope Callistus, wrote in A.D. 204 as a reply to the *Dialogue against Proclus* published by a presbyter of the Church of Rome under Bishop Zephyrinus (199–217), probably in A.D. 203. Since we know from Dionysius bar Salibi that Irenaeus' disciple Hippolytus believed, as his master had done, in the Apocalypse of John having been written under Domitian, it is certain that it can only have been Hippolytus' adversary Gaius of Rome, who asserted that the Apostle John, the son of Zebedee, returned from Patmos under the Emperor Claudius Caesar, that he died under Claudius, and that his prophetic activity was exerted 'under the reign of Claudius and before'. It must have been Gaius who used this chronological argument as a proof that John could not have written to churches of Asia which did not yet exist at the time of Claudius, etc. To this criticism Hippolytus and Epiphanius replied that it was the Holy Ghost, speaking through John the Prophet, who addressed words of 'warning, praise, and censure to the churches of the future and enabled him to foretell the appearance of the Montanist prophetesses in his words about the Jezebel of Thyatira' (Rev. ii. 20).

In this case, too, the Christian tradition is confirmed by a hitherto overlooked Jewish testimony:

Flavius Josephus says in his *Capture of Jerusalem* preserved in an old Russian version:

'. . . Claudius again sent his officers to those kingdoms, Cuspius Fadus and Tiberius Alexander, both of whom kept the people in peace, by not allowing any departure in anything from the pure laws. But if notwithstanding anyone did deviate from the word of the Law and information was laid before the teachers of the Law, they punished or banished him or sent (him) to Caesar.

And since in his time many helpers of the wonder-worker aforementioned (viz. Jesus) had appeared and spoken to the people of their Master (saying) that he was alive, although he had been dead, and "he will free you from bondage", many of the multitude hearkened to the(ir) preaching and took heed of their directions, for they were of the humble(r sort), some were tailors, others sandal-makers, (or) other artisans.

'But when these noble governors saw the falling away of the people, they determined, together with the scribes, to seize (these helpers) and ruin them, for fear lest "the little might not be little, if it ended in the great".

'And henceforth, for the deeds done by them, they sent them away, some to Caesar, others to Antioch for a trial of the(ir) cause, others to distant lands.'

This story too is quite trustworthy and perfectly correct from the point of view of Roman Law. Because Claudius had given to the proconsular administrator and commander of Syria the supreme jurisdiction over the procurators of the Judaean province, they would naturally send some of the accused to his superior court in Antioch, while others—not only Roman citizens who had the right to appeal to the emperor—would be sent to Rome. Roman Law prescribed for dangerous agitators (*auctores seditionis et tumultus vel concitatores populi*), according to the discretion of the judge and according to the social position of the accused, the penalties of crucifixion, of fighting the wild beasts in the circus, or the milder punishment of *deportatio in insulam*, which was regularly combined with the confiscation of the exile's whole possessions. The latter was, since the reign of Tiberius, applied principally against political offenders for *crimen laesae maiestatis* and *vis publica*.

The provincial administrators were only entitled to propose deportation; the final decision rested with the emperor, who had to determine the place of enforced residence of the condemned offender.

Origen's statement that John was condemned by the Caesar to his exile in Patmos and Hippolytus' rhetorical phrases about

'Babel', i.e. Rome banishing John, are in perfect agreement with the letter of Roman Law.

Reversio illicita from the exile would, of course, render the culprit liable to immediate capital punishment. If we hear that John was condemned by the Emperor Claudius in Rome to banishment on the island of Patmos, that he returned from Patmos under Claudius and was executed with his brother 'in Jerusalem', it seems inevitable to conclude that he was beheaded for having fled from Patmos and returned to Judaea without permission and 'tormented' ($\beta\alpha\sigma\alpha\nu\iota\sigma\alpha\varsigma$) those that dwell in the land (Rev. xi. 10).

The 1,260 days, during which the two witnesses are allowed to prophesy (Rev. xi. 3)—very nearly equal to the 1,290 days in Daniel xii. 11—are evidently meant for the three and a half times, i.e. years ($3 \times 360 = 1080 + 180 = 1260$) of Daniel xii. 7, and for the three years and six months duration of the drought caused by Elijah according to Luke iv. 25 and James v. 17. If the author of Revelation knew that John had been executed shortly before the death of Herod Agrippa I (A.D. 44) and that he had begun to preach the imminence of the Day of Judgement 'under the reign of Claudius and before'—as Epiphanius quotes from Gaius of Rome—and if this 'and before' means 'a little time before' the accession of Claudius in A.D. 41, this span of time would seem near enough to Daniel's 'three times and a half' to strike the apocalyptic imagination of the author of Revelation.

XXIII

THE WORLD-WIDE CONGRATULATIONS IN REV. XI. 10 AND THE HISTORIC DATE OF THE ZEBEDAIDS' EXECUTION

A SURPRISINGLY precise confirmation of Bacon's original and our own interpretation of Rev. xi. 3-13 is offered by the astonishing verse xi. 10 about the world-wide mutual gifts which 'the inhabitants of the earth', men of all languages, races and nations offer to each other after the two witnesses have been dead for three and a half days. Nothing could be plainer than that the 'three and a half days' is the intervening space between the execution of the two Zebedaids on the 28th of December and the Roman New Year (*Kalendae Januariae*), the day on which throughout the Roman Empire public and private banquets were celebrated and mutual congratulatory gifts sent round, in money (*stipes*)—especially old coins—as well as in kind (*strena*).

According to Flavius Josephus, Herod Agrippa died five days after he had celebrated the customary festival in honour of the emperor. Such feasts were celebrated twice every year, on the day of the emperor's accession to the throne (*dies imperii*) and on his birthday (*natalis Caesaris*). Since Claudius was proclaimed as Gaius Caligula's successor on the 24th of January and born on the 1st of August, Herod Agrippa's death must have occurred either on the 28th of January or on the 5th of August. Only the first of the two dates corresponds to Josephus' statement that Agrippa had completed three years of his reign over all Judaea when he arrived in Caesarea, and that he died in the seventh year of his reign, having ruled three years under Caligula over Philip's tetrarchy and obtained the lands of Herod (Antipas) in the fourth year. 'To this he added three years rule over Judaea, Samaria and Caesarea under Claudius, having reigned a total of seven years'. All these indications are only compatible if he lived but a few days of the seventh year of his reign, in other words, if he died in January, A.D. 44.

If the chronology of Acts xii. 3 is correct and if Herod had Peter arrested 'in the days of unleavened bread' after the execution of James, this must have been in A.D. 43, the last Passover week the king lived to see. The execution of the two sons of Zebedee would thus have happened on the 28th of December A.D. 42, and the coincidence that Herod died on a 28th of January could not fail to strike the imagination of those who considered his death a divine punishment for the killing of the 'two witnesses'.

The 'tradition' reported by the anti-Montanist writer Apollonius (c. A.D. 200) and presupposed in the 'Acts of Peter' (ch. v) and equally in the 'Wanderings of John' that the apostles were commanded by Jesus not to depart from Jerusalem for twelve years, would agree perfectly with the date of St. Peter's flight to Antioch in the spring of A.D. 43 on the basis of the usual chronology placing the Passion in A.D. 31 because of the Lucan date A.D. 28 for the baptism of Jesus by John and the mention of three passovers during the ministry of Jesus in the Fourth Gospel.

All this seems to constitute an argument of considerable strength in favour of the historic credibility of the traditional date for the martyrdom of the two Zebedaids in our earliest martyrologies and, *a potiori*, of the tradition itself as we find it in the various hitherto analysed documents.

John's transport to Rome and his exile to Patmos would seem to have happened under the lenient administration of Palestine by Cuspius Fadus and the Romanized Jew Tiberius Alexander in A.D. 41.

Of the same year, A.D. 41, is the letter of the Emperor Claudius to the Jews of Alexandria, which is in the British Museum, and was deciphered by Dr. Idris Bell in 1924 and correctly explained by Franz Cumont and the late Salomon Reinach. They show that it refers to Jewish itinerant or fugitive Messianist agitators coming down by boat from Syria—obviously because of the famine of this year—whom the Egyptian Jews are forbidden 'to invite or to receive, unless they want to incur the emperor's gravest suspicions', as 'propagating a certain world-wide pest'.

THE HISTORIC DATE OF THE ZEBEDAIDS' EXECUTION 97

This 'pest' is not characterized explicitly but is certainly identical with the Naṣōraean 'pest creating sedition among the Jews of the whole world', fomented by 'those who turn the whole world upside down, acting against the decrees of Caesar and saying that there is another king, one Jesus, of whom St. Paul is accused to be the leader in Acts xxiv. 5 and xvii. 6 f.

In the same year, A.D. 41, Herod Agrippa deprived the High-priest John-Theophilos of his office in favour of Simon the Boethusian, possibly because he had excited the king's suspicions by intervening in council, like St. Paul's teacher Gamaliel in Acts v. 34 f., in favour of the Messianist agitators, possibly because he had merely been denounced as a secret sympathiser with the followers of the Galilean Messiah crucified under Pilate.

Considering the inevitable despair of the poorer population in a famine year, one cannot but attribute it to the wise and conciliatory policy of moderation on the part of Tiberius Alexander and Herod Agrippa that no worse punishment than *deportatio in insulam* was meted out to a firebrand like the son of Zebedee who had 'tormented' the country with ceaseless threatening sermons about the immediately impending woes of the Last Days.

That the deported Elijah *redivivus* took the first opportunity to escape from his custodians, probably by a miracle similar to the one which enabled Peter to delude his jailers and to flee to Antioch, and to return to Jerusalem, where he expected the Messiah to arrive at every moment, and that he was recaptured by the king's men and summarily executed together with his brother James, is exactly what we should expect to have happened in due course.

Whatever the reader may think of this chronological reconstruction, Rev. xi. 10 proves at least that at the time when the Apocalypse was written—according to Irenaeus under Domitian, at the latest ever suggested date under Trajan—the Christian Church commemorated the passion of the two sons of Zebedee on the 28th of December and celebrated their resurrection and ascension into Heaven on the 1st of January—when Christians could hardly refrain from taking part in the merriments of the pagan New Year.

H

There is no doubt that Rev. xi. 11 f.:

'And after three days and a half the spirit of life from God entered into them and they stood upon their feet . . . and they heard a great voice from heaven saying unto them "Come up hither". And they ascended into heaven in a cloud and their enemies beheld them.'

is the ultimate source of the later legend about John the son of Zebedee being 'lifted up bodily into Heaven and dwelling there in the flesh like unto and with Elijah and Enoch', as we find it in certain Gospel prefaces and in the collection of short lives of Apostles attributed to Dorotheus of Tyre and Hippolytus of Rome.

XXIV

THE SOURCE OF REV. XI. 13, THE DATE OF THE ORACLE REV. X. 1–XI. 2, AND THE ORIGINAL MEANING OF THE TWO MURDERED WITNESSES

AS TO Rev. xi. 13—the great earthquake, destroying the tenth part of the city and killing 7,000 persons, the remnant 'giving glory to the God of Heaven', i.e. admitting that the catastrophe was a divine chastisement for the murder of the 'two witnesses' —it is not an imitation of the earthquake following upon the crucifixion of Jesus in Matt. xxvii. 52, which does not kill the living, but awakens the saints sleeping in their rock-tombs. It is a close parallel to the story of the big earthquake of 31 B.C. 'killing 6,000 men', which Flavius Josephus represents in his *Capture of Jerusalem*—first published in A.D. 71—as the punishment of God following immediately upon Herod the Great's execution of the Messianist priests and teachers of the Law who had invoked against him the Deuteronomic prohibition of a foreigner's rule over Israel and tried to calculate the time when the Messiah was due to arrive.

As an earthquake taking a toll of thousands of lives had followed Herod the Great's murder of the Messianist priests and rabbis in 31 B.C., a similar catastrophe is supposed to have avenged Herod Agrippa's execution of the two Zebedaids. It is most interesting to note that the Latin text of Rev. xi. 13 as it was read by Primasius (d. after A.D. 554) has '70,000 men' (*numero LXX milia hominum*) for 7,000, just as we find the 6,000 corrected into 60,000 in the passage of Josephus.

Nothing remains to do but to explain the connexion of Rev. xi. 3–13 with the introductory lines Rev. xi. 1 f.—the precise date of which has been convincingly determined long ago by Wellhausen. The correct interpretation of these two lines will enable us to account at the same time for the result of Archdeacon Charles's keen and minute observations of the style and language of this chapter, which have established beyond the possibility of reasonable doubt that Rev. xi. 1–14 has not been composed by the author of our Apocalypse, but 'borrowed and revised by him to suit his own ideas'.

The angel's command to the seer to measure with a rod 'the Temple of God and the altar and those that worship therein' but to 'leave out and not to measure the court without the Temple, for it is given to the Gentiles', '(it) and the holy city they shall tread under foot for forty-two months' clearly presupposes: first, that the sanctuary is still existing and worship going on around the altar, and second that the outer court and the whole city of Jerusalem is in the hand of the Gentiles and 'trampled down' by the enemy. This is precisely the situation which existed in the last period of the siege of Jerusalem in A.D. 70, when the Zealots still held the sanctuary and the inner court around the altar on which the daily morning and evening sacrifices were offered until the 17th of Panemos.

Josephus has put it on record that in these last weeks a 'false prophet' had proclaimed an oracle promising salvation and final delivery in the last hour of supreme danger to the remnant crowded in the sanctuary which God would never abandon to the heathen. This inviolate asylum, with all there is in it, is to be measured now, so as to prove afterwards that not an inch of it has been abandoned by God to the enemy's attack.

It seems evident that Rev. xi. 1, 2 and the preceding chapter x about the swallowing of the 'little book' presented by the angel to the prophet—generally admitted to have been wedged in between ix. 21 and xi. 14, which are obviously the two last of the verses describing the 'second woe'—is an echo, if not the actual text of this unfortunate pseudo-prophet's oracle received in the sanctuary of Jerusalem in the last days before the suspension of the *tamid*-sacrifice in the month Panemos= Tamuz of A.D. 70. In this originally Jewish source, which the Christian apocalyptic writer has converted into a vision reflecting the passion of the two sons of Zebedee executed by Herod Agrippa in A.D. 42, the 'two witnesses' vanquished by 'the Beast' rising from the Abyss and warring against them were, of course, the two high priests Jesus and Annas murdered by the Idumean invaders of the city, the corpses of whom the

Zealots had thrown out unburied to the dogs and vultures (Rev. xi. 8 f.). According to Josephus the downfall of the city wall—which the Romans had been unable to batter down with their rams and pickaxes (our Pl. VII, Fig. 1), but which had spontaneously collapsed during the following night—the destruction of the city and the massacre of its inhabitants were the divine punishment for the killing of the two high-priests.

It is the name of the murdered high-priest Jesus (the son of Gamaliel) which reminded the original author of Rev. xi. 4 of the High-Priest Jesus (the son of Jehoṣadaq) and of Zerubbabel, the 'two anointed ones' 'standing before the Lord' in Zech. iv. 14, of the candlestick (Zech. iv. 2)—multiplied by two to suit the occasion—and of the 'two olive trees' (iv. 3). All these features would never have been suggested by the memory of the two sons of Zebedee, who were not anointed priests and had never stood in the presence of the Lord, and neither of whom was called Jesus. Yet it is from Zech. ii. 1, 5, that the essential introductory feature of measuring a circumference as a guarantee of protection is derived. It is in Zech. xi–xiv that the original author of this oracle found the destruction of Jerusalem, but also the destruction of her destroyers, the saving of a remnant and the future safety of the reconstructed wall-less city guarded by God, as it were by a wall of fire around her.

The identification of the two martyred high-priests with Moses and Elijah was certainly an essential part of the original oracle. Josephus has recorded the prodigy that until the arrival of Titus Jerusalem had been suffering from such a terrible drought that the Siloam and the other fountains had dried up and water was sold by the jug. A Jewish apocalypse, surviving in a Latin translation and in the Hebrew original, identifies the last of the high-priests, elected by lot under the pressure of the Zealots during the siege, Phaneas (Pinḥas) son of Samuel, with the Zealot Pinḥas b. 'Ele'azar of Num. xxv. 13, reborn as the prophet Elijah. This apocalypse 'foretells' that in the Last Days this Elijah *redivivus* will shut up the heavens, bring Elijah's drought (1 Kings xvii. 1) upon the earth, open the heavens again (1 Kings xviii. 49)—that is the free flow of the waters attributed by Josephus to the arrival of Titus—and finally be killed, resuscitated, and raised up into heaven.

The conclusion of this Jewish oracle issued by a visionary during the siege of A.D. 70 survives in Rev. xi. 19:

'and the temple of God was opened in heaven and there was seen in his temple the ark of the covenant.'

This line can hardly be anything else but a reminiscence of the impressive, unforgettable prodigy of clouds and sunset-light which happened immediately before the destruction of the sanctuary of which we have a description of matchless beauty in the words of Tacitus:

> '*visae per caelum concurrere acies, rutilantia arma et subito nubium igne conlucere templum.*'
> 'Armies were seen in heaven rushing against each other, shining armouries, and, of a sudden, amidst clouds, a temple shining in fire.'

XXV

THE 'APOCALYPSE OF JOHN', A PSEUDEPIGRAPHIC WRITING BY THE GNOSTIC CERINTHUS

ACCORDING TO the 11th-century sacramentary of Bergamo the lessons prescribed for St. James's and St. John's day were *'omnia de apostolis'*, 'all there is in the Scriptures about the(se) Apostles'. The lector of the primitive Church, who had to read on this day the original, uncensored wording of Acts xii. 2 (above, p. 74), and was, therefore, still aware of the fact recorded in the earliest martyrologies, that both sons of Zebedee had been executed in Jerusalem under King Herod Agrippa, could have no doubt about the meaning of Rev. xi. 3-10 (above, p. 86 ff., Pl. VII). He could not fail to understand that the seer described in Rev. x. 10 as feeling the bitter foretaste of death and the sweetness of ultimate triumph must be meant to be John, the son of Zebedee, one of the two 'Sons of Thunder.' But the same reader must have felt extremely puzzled when he tried to combine the history of the growth of the Christian Church described in the first eleven chapters of the canonical Acts, from the beginning of the book to the execution of James ⟨and John⟩ in ch. xii, v. 2, with Rev. i. 11–iii. 22, i.e. with the book of the seven divinely dictated epistles of 'John' to the messengers of the seven Churches of Asia.

Apart from the fact that the extant text of the Apocalypse of John does not explain who these 'messengers' or delegates are, where, when and why they came to John in order to receive his written messages to the Churches which had delegated them for this purpose, the earliest readers must have realized that —according to the extant text of the Apostles' Acts i–xii— until the time of the great famine under Claudius and Herod Agrippa I, the community of believers in Jesus as the Messiah had not spread beyond Galilee, Judaea, Samaria, Phenicia, Cyprus, and Antioch, and that during the lifetime of the two

Zebedaids the glad tidings of Jesus had not yet reached Asia Minor.

How then could John the son of Zebedee receive messengers from and dispatch through them letters to the seven Churches of Asia, which did not exist at the time and could not even know anything either of Jesus or of John?

It seems obvious that the chronology of Acts viii–xii excludes not only the possibility of John, the son of Zebedee, having written letters to the seven Churches of Asia, but equally so the supposition that any forger would ever have published such letters under the name of a martyr known to have died before any Christian Churches were founded in Asia Minor through the efforts of St. Paul and his companions Barnabas, John Mark, Silas, and Timothy.

Letters purporting to be written by a saint and prophet John to seven Churches in Asia Minor, the list of which is in no way identical with the series of place-names occurring in the itinerary of Paul in Acts xiii. 51–xiv. 24, could only have been attributed to one of two persons: either to John Mark—who departed from Paul and Barnabas 'from Pamphylia' (onwards), and might have been believed, in an emergency, to have founded these seven Churches in the course of a missionary expedition of his own—or to the Ephesian John, the son of Annas, the former high-priest of the Jews whom Polycrates of Ephesus mentions as buried in Ephesus. The Ephesian John might have been believed, as we see in Tertullian, Clement of Alexandria, and in Muratori's fragment, to have enjoyed a great authority among the faithful of the various Churches of Asia while residing in Ephesus—that is, after A.D. 70—and he might well have been identified with the Elder John, letters of whom were known to the Churches of Asia at the time of Papias, who quotes one of them.

This is the reason why I think Professor Emmanuel Hirsch is quite right when he points out the fact that the present text of Revelation has

A double beginning: (*a*) i. 1–3, 7; (*b*) i. 4–6, 10, 11 f.; and

A double ending: (*a*) xxii. 6–10, 18–19; (*b*) xxii. 11–17, 20, 21; and that the letters to the seven Churches and the apocalyptic visions were originally two different books, clumsily combined by a later awkward editor.

The paradoxical juxtaposition of two different titles: 'REVELATION OF JOHN (THE DIVINE)': 'Revelation of Jesus Christ, which God gave to him . . .' etc. is due to the conflation of two originally separate books, the one containing the seven epistles being entitled: 'REVELATION OF JOHN'; the other: 'REVELATION OF JESUS CHRIST which God gave unto him, to show his servants things which must shortly come to pass'—an indication of the contents which fits the visions, but not the seven epistles.

The attribution to the two different, albeit homonymous ostensible authors was, beyond doubt, made perfectly clear, if not in the original superscriptions themselves, in a short *lemma historicum* of the sort which introduces certain psalms and certain oracles of the major and minor prophets. As the visions of Ezekiel are introduced with the lines i. 2 f. (which ought to be printed before i. 1): 'In the fifth day of the (fourth) month, which was (in) the fifth year of King Jehoiakin's captivity, the word of the Lord came expressly to Ezekiel, the son of Buzi, in the land of the Chaldeans by the river Chebar, and the hand of the Lord was there upon him', so probably there were prefixed to the original edition of the 'Revelation of Jesus Christ' the words read by Apringius of Paca in the 'ecclesiastical reports': 'At the time of Caesar Claudius when the famine prevailed . . . Caesar ordained a persecution for the Church. At that time he ordered John, the apostle of our Lord J. Chr., (the son of Zebedee), to be deported to the island of Patmos,' etc. Equally so the Revelation of John must have had a preface explaining the coming of the 'messengers' (ἄγγελοι) of the seven Churches to John (the son of Annas in Ephesus), submitting to his decision some of their troubles, which is echoed in St. Jerome's preface '*plures fuerunt qui* . . .', where he speaks of 'nearly all the bishops of Asia and delegations of many Churches which had come to John'. Without some such *lemma historicum* the abrupt introduction of the 'messengers' of the various Churches in Rev. ii. 1, 8, 12, 18, etc., is unintelligible, and it has indeed actually been misunderstood by many readers as referring to 'angels'.

Such title-lines or prefaces are easily lost with the first leaf or cover of a codex, or mutilated through the rough handling of the top-end of a scroll. Once lost, the absence of these little prefaces would make it impossible to distinguish the two ostensible authors originally quite clearly characterized by their patronymics, titles, or historic connections.

It does not make much difference whether the reader is willing to accept this hypothesis or whether he prefers to believe that John the son of Zebedee, exiled to Patmos and executed in Jerusalem under Claudius and Herod Agrippa I, was represented by the author as having written seven inspired epistles to seven Churches of Asia, among them a letter to the Church of Smyrna—which did not even exist in the last year before the Neronian persecution!—and as having foretold not only his own and his brother's death, but also much later events such as the return of Nero *redivivus*, with such transparent clarity that even ancient writers like Irenaeus and Hippolytus saw that John's Apocalypse was written under Domitian. In both cases the modern critical historian cannot help considering Revelation as a pseudepigraphic book—or rather as a conflation of two pseudepigraphic books—however ready ancient Church Fathers like Hippolytus and modern fundamentalists of the same type of mind may be to attribute the miraculous foresight of the alleged author to the divine inspiration of the prophet.

As to the book of the Seven Epistles to the Seven Churches of Asia—which are very properly described in the *Canon Muratori* as a counterpart to and alleged model of the collection of the seven letters of Paul—the most plausible interpretation of their—imperfectly preserved—superscription would seem to be that they were issued as letters of the Ephesian John i.e. of John the Elder or Senator, the ostensible author of the three canonical Epistles of John (and of the Fourth Gospel), who was alive at the time of the publication and resented the forgery as much as Origen did, when the Valentinian heretic faked the record of a discussion with the Alexandrian Church Father which had never taken place.

The similarity of the very characteristic style and language—peculiar to the real author of both books—probably also of the visions and auditions (Rev. i. 13–20 and iv. 2–11), introducing

THE 'APOCALYPSE OF JOHN'—A PSEUDEPIGRAPHON

the two apocrypha, enabled an editor intent upon saving space and copyists' fees, to combine the two badly preserved texts into one book, as best he could.

It is not true and it never was true that 'there is not a shred of evidence, not even the shadow of a probability for the hypothesis that the Apocalypse is pseudonymous'. On the very page, xxxix, on which Archdeacon Charles printed these peremptory words he had to admit in a footnote that the authorship of the Apocalypse was attributed to the heretic Cerinthus by Gaius of Rome—A.D. 200–220—and by the *Alogoi* of Asia Minor in the course of their attacks against the Montanist heresy. It is the contrary of sound historical method to try to disqualify the testimony of an orthodox, very learned Roman Churchman of the 2nd century and of the whole conservative ecclesiastical opinion in Asia Minor round about A.D. 160, as 'an utterly baseless and gratuitous hypothesis', in order to substitute for it the really 'baseless and gratuitous' theory of a 'prophet John of Asia Minor' as the 'otherwise unknown' author of the Patmian 'Revelations', let alone the late B. W. Bacon's phantastic thesis that the 'Apocalypse of John' was written by one of the daughters of the Apostle Philip.

As a matter of fact, the pseudepigraphic character of John's Apocalypse is as well attested as that of the apocryphal 'Acts of Paul,' of which Tertullian, a contemporary of Gaius, and less orthodox than Gaius, indeed, in his later age a Montanist heretic, said that they were forged by a presbyter of Asia, 'for love of Paul and in his honour', who had to admit his guilt 'before John' (of Ephesus). Nobody has ever doubted Tertullian's assertion, although the same Hippolytus who defended the Apocalypse of John against the accusations of Gaius and of the Asiatic *Alogoi* accepted those Acts of Paul as a genuine source for the life of the Apostle. Nobody has ever expected Tertullian to produce proofs of his assertion that the forger had confessed his authorship, nobody has ever treated his statement as 'utterly baseless and gratuitous'.

If it should be urged that the 'Acts of Paul' are not part of the canonical Bible, the ready answer would have to be that, equally so, John's Apocalypse was rejected as spurious and uncanonical, since Dionysius of Alexandria proved to the hilt, in A.D. 262, that it could not possibly have been written by the author of the Fourth Gospel and the Johannine Epistles, by no less an authority than Eusebius, and that Cyril of Jerusalem (315–386) not only excluded it from the list of canonical books, but also forbade its use for public and private reading. Revelation does not appear in the list of canonical books in Canon 60 of the Synod of Laodicea (c. A.D. 360), nor in Canon 85 of the Apostolic Constitutions, nor in the list drawn up by Gregory of Nazianzus (d. A.D. 389). Amphilochius of Iconium (d. 394) states that the Apocalypse is rejected as spurious by most authorities. Chrysostom (d. A.D. 407) representing the school of Antioch in Constantinople, Theodore of Mopsuhestia in Cilicia (350–428), Theodoret of Cyrrhus (386–457) never so much as mention it. It is excluded from the so-called Synopsis of Chrysostom, from the List of Sixty Books and the stichometry of Nicephoros. The Apocalypse formed no part of the *Peshiṭtô* Version of the New Testament, published by Rabûla of Edessa (A.D. 411). Junilius wrote in A.D. 551: '*de Joannis apocalypsi apud Orientales admodum dubitatur*'. Bar Hebraya (d. A.D. 1208) still regards it as the work of Cerinthus or of 'the other John.' The Nestorian Syrians reject it to this day. In the Armenian Church it was not received until the 12th century. Even a westerner who had travelled extensively in the East, like St. Jerome, did not conceal his doubts about its canonicity, and the *Capitulare Aquisgranense* (A.D. 789) excluded it in its Canon 59 from the list of the canonical Scriptures.

There is, moreover, strong evidence for attributing the Apocalypse to a Gnostic of Egyptian education such as Cerinthus.

A few months before the outbreak of the world war the late Professor Franz Boll, of Heidelberg, then with Franz Cumont the greatest authority on ancient astrological texts, published a masterly demonstration proving conclusively that—just as the most important visions of Daniel—the 'Revelations' of Ps.-John were 'night-visions' of the prophet observing the constellations of heaven and interpreting them according to the current doctrines of Greco-Egyptian astral lore.

Boll has shown that the 'woman clothed with the sun who was with child and gives birth to a male son who shall break all the nations with a rod of iron' in Rev. xii. 1–6, is primarily the constellation of the Heavenly Virgin, described by the astrologer Teukros of Babylon in Egypt (1st century A.D.) as 'a goddess ... suckling a child, whom some call the goddess Isis suckling Horus', while the Persian translation (A.D. 542) surviving in an Arabic version, describes her as 'holding two ears' (i.e. the star Spica) 'and nursing a little boy whom certain nations call '*Isu*, i.e. Jesus'. In a Nabataean paraphrase (about A.D. 904), she is described as 'the pious virgin who has not seen a man and educated her child until it reached a grown-up man's age with 49,000 years'.

Space does not permit of our reproducing here in all its most instructive details Boll's demonstration that the essential features of Rev. xii. 1–6, 13–17 can all be paralleled from astral myths connected with the constellation Virgo interpreted as Isis with her son Horus, persecuted by the dragon Typhon. It will be sufficient to point out that Boll has been able to explain the curious tautological phrase: 'and she gave birth to a son, a man child' as a characteristic Egyptianism. A 'male son' for 'a son', *sꜣ ṯꜣsj* in the classical, *šrj ḥꜣwtj* in the younger vulgar form, is a regular and well-known Egyptian idiom.

The man who used it in his incredibly barbaric but rigidly systematic Greek full of Semiticisms, need not necessarily have spoken either the old classic or the younger vulgar Egyptian. But he must at least have used a Greek astrological text translated from an Egyptian original describing the Heavenly Virgin-Mother of Horus. It is inconceivable that an 'unlearned and illiterate' Galilean fisherman should have used Greco-Egyptian astrological texts and that he should have assimilated pagan, Hellenistic mythology to such an extent. But it is exactly what we should expect from a Gnostic heretic educated in Egypt and steeped in Greco-Egyptian astral-mysticism.

XXVI

THE 144,000 'VIRGINS' IN REV. XIV. 4 AND THE 'VIRGIN' JOHN OF THE 'LEUCIAN' ACTS

ARCHDEACON CHARLES himself has recognized with perfect clarity the heretical character of Rev. xiv. 3 f. about the 144,000 redeemed ones

'wh'ch were not defiled with women: for they are virgins. These are they which follow the Lamb. . . .'

He could not help seeing that, according to the teaching of these verses, 'marriage is a pollution' and 'neither St. Peter nor any other married Apostle, nor any woman whatever, would be allowed to follow the Lamb on Mount Zion'.

Nothing could, indeed, be more obvious than that the writer of these lines belonged to some ascetic 'encratite' community recruited through the aggregation of converted 'neophytes' and not through children being born into the fold.

Dr. Charles attributed the crucial verse to an editor, upon whom he heaped every possible abuse, calling him 'a monkish interpolator', 'a narrow ascetic', 'an arch-heretic of the 1st century, though probably an unconscious one', of 'abysmal stupidity', who 'introduces into Christianity ideas that had their origin in Pagan faiths of unquestionable impurity'.

I hold no brief for defending this or any other 'editor' against the rough treatment which this unfortunate class of writers is by now accustomed to suffer under the hand of the Higher Critic. But would Dr. Charles have said: 'To regard marriage as a pollution is impossible in our author who compares the covenant between Christ and the Church to a marriage (xix. 9) and calls the Church the Bride in xxi. 2, 9; xxii. 17', had the great connoisseur of Jewish and Christian apocryphal Scriptures remembered the Latin 'Epistle of Titus', discovered by Dom de Bruyne in a Würzburg 8th-century manuscript and

THE 'VIRGIN' JOHN OF THE 'LEUCIAN' ACTS

incorporated by Dr. M. R. James into his English version of the 'Acts of John'? This fragment says:

'Receive therefore in thy heart the admonition of the blessed John, who, when he was bidden to a marriage, came not save for the sake of chastity, and consider what he said: Little children, while yet your flesh is pure and ye have your body untouched and not destroyed, and are not defiled by Satan, the great enemy and shameless (foe) of chastity: know therefore more fully the mystery of the nuptial union: it is the experiment of the serpent, the ignorance of teaching, injury of the seed, the gift of death' (35 more clauses of abuse) 'the impediment which separateth from the Lord, the beginning of disobedience, the end of life, and death itself. Hearing this, little children, join yourselves together in an inseparable marriage, holy and true, waiting for the one true incomparable bridegroom from heaven, even Christ, the everlasting bridegroom.'

Have we not in this openly encratite, i.e. Marcionite passage exactly the same allegedly 'impossible' combination as in the Apocalypse of John of abuse heaped upon the sacrament or 'mystery of the nuptial union' with the most enthusiastic praise of the inseparable marriage, holy and true, with Christ the everlasting bridegroom in heaven?

Is not the vilification of all human marital relations, however sacred and legitimate, and the corresponding idealization of the mystic, 'spiritual' union between the worshipper and his divinity the particular characteristic of all the encratitic sects?

He was indeed a rather dull and unintelligent editor who combined the Patmian visions attributed to the exiled John, the son of Zebedee, with the Seven Epistles to the Seven Churches of Asia Minor attributed to the Ephesian John, for the purely practical purpose of facilitating the wider distribution of the single volume by reducing its bulk and the cost of copying it; yet it is most unlikely that he would have inserted a line which could not fail to antagonize all the married readers and—last but not least—all the female patrons of mystic literature.

Since the above quoted paragraph from the Marcionite 'Acts of John' proves that the alleged incompatibility between Rev. xix. 9, and xxi. 2, 9; xxii. 17 and xiv. 4 is entirely imaginary, there is no reason left for attributing the heretic doctrine underlying Rev. xiv. 4 to an editor or interpolator, indeed to anybody else but the author of the Apocalypse himself. As a matter of fact it is the most palpable proof that anybody could require for the truth of the assertion of the learned presbyter and faithful son of the Catholic Church, Gaius of Rome, that the Revelation of John is the work of a Gnostic heretic, Cerinthus.

Since we read in Epiphanius that Cerinthus was educated in Egypt, it is quite easy to determine the source of the particular convictions underlying Rev. xiv. 4.

It has often been supposed that some at least of the rich apocalyptic literature of late Judaism—e.g. Enoch cviii. 7 f.—was produced by the Essene community and belonged to the books which the order endeavoured to hide from the profane eyes of outsiders. Although it is not the fashion any more to trace Essene influences in the ascetic tendencies of early Christianity, it would be difficult to find a simpler explanation for an eschatology reserving the access to Mount Zion for an *élite* of male celibates and excluding the other sex entirely from the company of the Lamb, than to derive this confident hope for a 'paradise without woman' from the misogynic tenets of a confraternity, no member of which

'took to himself a wife, because woman is immoderately selfish and jealous and terribly clever in decoying a man's moral inclinations and exploiting them into subjection by persistent cajoleries. For the man who is either ensnared by the charms of a wife, or induced by natural affection to make his children his first care, is no longer the same towards others, but has unconsciously become changed from a free man to a slave.'

Starting from such premises, it would seem natural that a visionary who had come under the influence of the Essene *therapeutae* in the desert near Alexandria, described in Philo's book *De vita contemplativa*, should have wanted to exclude such a disturbing unsocial element from the New Jerusalem. It seems equally natural that the encratitic, heterodox bias of this one line should have been overlooked by a catholic editor as well as by generations of Catholic readers, accustomed to interpret these hundred and forty-four thousand as a mere privileged bodyguard surrounding the Lamb, as an *élite* of the *ecclesia militans*, which need no more exclude the rest of the faithful from disporting themselves in the gold-paved streets of the New Jerusalem at the feet of Mount Zion, than the earthly bodyguard of priests and Levites guarding the Temple had prevented the rest of the people from inhabiting and enjoying the Holy City surrounding the sanctuary. After all, women had been confined to an outer courtyard of the sanctuary in the earthly Jerusalem, and it was only natural that they should have had to wait until the feminist 20th century for a learned Anglican theologian to point out the heretical origin of the prophecy foretelling their exclusion from the immediate presence of the Lamb.

It is quite obvious that he who fathered these lines upon the Zebedaid John, exiled to the island of Patmos, did certainly not mean to exclude this Apostle himself from the bliss in store for the 'virgins undefiled by contact with women'—although he may well have meant to keep St. Peter, all the married Apostles and all women away from Mount Zion and out of the New Jerusalem. On the contrary, St. John, in the opinion of this writer, is evidently the teacher, the model, and the spiritual leader of all these 'virgin' ascetics selected from the twelve tribes of Israel. For the author of the Apocalypse, John the Divine, is himself, as Epiphanius calls him, the 'holy virgin', ὁ ἅγιος παρθένος, *virgo electus a Deo*, as the Monarchianist prologue to the Fourth Gospel puts it, specially beloved by his Master because of his 'virginity'.

This is certainly what the Marcionite encratitic author of the 'Acts of John' seems to have inferred from no other source than the crucial line Rev. xiv. 4, the only conceivable basis for a phantastic characterization which cannot have the slightest basis in any historic tradition about John the son of Zebedee, or for the matter of that, about the Ephesian John, who had been a rabbi and a high-priest.

There is complete unanimity among all the rabbinic teachers interpreting Gen. i. 28; ix. 7 as constituting a legally binding obligation for every Jewish father to see to it that his son is married at the customary age of eighteen, at the latest twenty years. 'Seven', says a *baraitha* in the Babylonian Talmud, 'is the number of those upon whom God has pronounced a ban, first among them he who has no wife'.

The school of Shammai used to quote Isa. xlv. 18, 'God hath not made the earth in vain. He formed it to be inhabited,' as a proof that 'the world was created only that men might be fruitful and multiply' and there is a rabbinic saying that 'an ascetic virgin (*bethulah sajjemanith*) disturbs the order of the world', that 'a man without a wife is no man', and 'one who does not procreate like a murderer'.

In view of all these unequivocal testimonies nothing could be more unlikely than that either of the sons of Zebedee lived and died as a bachelor. Most probably John and James were just as normally married as that other Galilean fisherman Peter, although we just do not happen to know anything about their wives and mothers-in-law.

The only Jews living as bachelors and practising sexual abstinence were the members of the Essene order. The only conceivable basis of a *bona fide* assertion that John had been a devotee and propagator of sexual asceticism would seem to be a confusion of the Ephesian John, the former high-priest and Governor of Gophna and Acrabetta, with his colleague John the Essene, Governor of Thamna, Lydda, and Emmaus, mentioned in the same paragraph of Josephus' *Jewish War*.

But there is no trace of an acquaintance with Josephus' *Jewish War* in the Marcionite 'Acts of John'—used as Scripture by the Encratite communities 'pullulating' at that time, according to Epiphanius 'in Pisidia and Phrygia Kekaumenē, in Isauria, Pamphylia, Cilicia, Galatia, in Antioch of Syria, and in the Roman parts of the world'. Nor has the mawkish 'virginity' of their sorry hero, thanking God for having bestowed upon him the saving grace of congenital impotence, any resemblance whatsoever with the soldierly vow of continence and celibacy observed by the strenuous Essene order, the pacifist character of which is a transparent fiction of the Jewish apologists Philo and Josephus.

Just as there is not the faintest possibility of any historic tradition underlying the identification of the Ephesian John with the Galilean fisherman of the same name in the Marcionite 'Acts of John', even so there cannot be the slightest factual basis behind the perverse characterization of the beloved disciple in this *vie romancée* of the imaginary composite Apostle, deservedly rejected with such indignation by the second Council of Nicaea (A.D. 787). If the Ps.-Leucius represents the John of his sickly imagination as thanking the Christ for having three times prevented him from marrying and for having 'kept me until this (last) hour for Thyself, untouched by contact with a woman', and the Christ as saying to his favourite: 'John, if thou hadst not been mine (!), I would have suffered thee to marry'; if this blasphemous romancer goes so far as to apply to the Saviour the well-known epithet ὁ καλός, 'the beautiful one', which the Greek ἐραστής was wont to use for his ἐρώμενος, this is, indeed, as Dr. Charles has suggested, due to the infection of early Asiatic Christianity by the contagion of the local pagan religion of the emasculated clergy of the Ephesian Artemis, the Phrygian Attis 'the Beautiful' and the Syrian Kombabos.

It is this syncretistic infiltration which is responsible for the strange distortion and confusion which has converted, almost beyond the possibility of recognition, the memory-images of two such disparate but equally virile figures as the former priestly ruler, army-commander, and senator John, the son of Annas and that Galilean firebrand, the illiterate fisherman John, the son of Zebedee, into the revolting composite caricature of Tertullian's 'eunuch of the Christ' (*spado Christi*) and Epiphanius' travesty of 'John, the holy virgin'.

XXVII

ST. JOHN GOING TO SLEEP IN HIS TOMB

THE SAME Asiatic influences which are responsible for the strange conversion of the Fourth Evangelist into a figure resembling nothing so much as one of the effeminate castrate priests of the Ephesian Mother-goddess, impersonating her youthful son and lover, have equally inspired the curious legend of St. John, sleeping until Doomsday in the underground vault under the altar of the Ephesian basilica.

The story must have been well known even in Rome about A.D. 200, when Hippolytus wrote his treatise *De Antichristo*. Otherwise he would not have apostrophized, in its 36th chapter, the 'blessed John, Apostle and disciple of the Lord', with the words: 'awake (γρηγόρησον) and tell us what thou sawest and heardst of Babylon, for it is she who sent thee into exile'. Hippolytus does not say where the Patmian exile is supposed to sleep, but since he called the evangelist John in his *Odes to all the Scriptures* (above, p. 55) the 'Ephesian high-priest' and since no rival burial-place of the saint is known, he must be thinking of Ephesus.

Anyhow there is the explicit testimony of St. Augustine who says in his 124th lecture on John xxi. 19–25 (A.D. 417), that, according to John xxi. 23, St. John is dead, but continues in this way: 'He, however, who wants to, may object (to this interpretation). While accepting as true what John said: that the Lord had not *said* "This disciple shall not die", he may assert that, nevertheless, this is the implicit meaning of such words as John attributes to the Lord. And he may say that the Apostle John is alive and may contend that he is only sleeping and not lying dead in that tomb which is at Ephesus. He may argue that there the earth is said noticeably (*sensim*) to bubble up (*scatere*) and, as it were, to boil over (*ebullire*) and he may assert that this happens through his breathing (*eius anhelitu*) constantly or persistently (*pertinaciter*). People cannot fail to believe it, since there is no dearth of men who will believe that Moses is alive, because it is written, that his grave was not found and because he appeared with the Lord on the mountain together with Elijah of whom it is written that he did not die, but was translated. . . . How much more will they believe of John, because of the words "Thus I will that he tarry until I come", that he sleeps alive under the earth. Of him too the story goes (which is found in some Scriptures albeit apocryphal) that he was present and alive when he had his tomb made, and that—when it had been dug and carefully prepared—he lay down in it, as it were in a bed and died immediately. Those, however, who understand the Lord's word in the way in question say that he did not die, but lay there like unto one dead and was buried sleeping because he was supposed to be dead. And until the Second Coming of the Christ he will remain so and show that he is alive by the welling up of the dust. Of this dust it is believed that it is raised by the breath of him who rests underneath so that it rises from the bottom to the surface of the tomb (*tumuli*). To combat this opinion I think superfluous. Those who know the place may look whether the earth actually does or suffers there what people say it does, and what we too have heard from men by no means frivolous. Let us give its due to an opinion which we cannot refute with sure arguments, so as not to raise that other question, why the earth should seem, as it were, to live and to breathe over one dead and buried. . . . If his body rests in his grave, inanimate like that of others who are dead, and if it really happens there what fame disseminates concerning the dust which increases again, in spite of its being repeatedly removed, then nothing remains but to say that this happens in order to glorify his "precious death" (Ps. cxv. 15), because martyrdom has not distinguished him (since the persecutor did not kill him for the sake of his faith in the Christ), or for some other reason which we ignore. But the question remains why the Lord said of a man, destined to die: "Thus I want him to remain until I come." '

This long chapter is well worth reproducing *in extenso* because it shows the incredible influence which the apocryphal 'Acts of John' exerted on the minds of the most prominent Catholic Church Fathers. Here is St. Augustine of Hippo asserting that 'martyrdom had not distinguished' the evangelist, in direct contradiction to the competent Catholic Bishop of Ephesus' letter to Victor of Rome, claiming that the John resting in Ephesus had been a martyr like Polycarp, Thraseas, and Sagaris. Since *Tract.* vii. 9 *In Joann.* proves conclusively that St. Augustine identified the Fourth Evangelist with John the son of Zebedee, called by the Lord 'from his boat', the above quoted lines are equally in manifest contradiction to the text of the old Martyrology of Carthage—i.e. of St. Augustine's own African Church province—commemorating, at least at the time of St. Cyprian (*c.* A.D. 250, above, p. 64), the martyrdom of the two sons of Zebedee on the 27th of December, the vigil of the real day of their glorious death. Evidently the interpolation of the epithet '*Baptistae*' after '*S. Joannis*' in this line of the African martyrology (above, p. 60) had been inserted in Africa and before the time of St. Augustine, who quotes as his only source of information for the particulars of John's death certain, admittedly 'apocryphal' i.e. heretical, scriptures.

The book to which he refers is of course no other than the notorious Ps.-Leucius (*c.* A.D. 160). Chs. 111–115 of our extant Marcionite 'Acts of John' actually describe how the Apostle ordered his disciples to dig a grave for him, pronounced a long prayer and, at the end of it, 'laid himself down in the trench where he had strewn his garments: and having said unto us "Peace be with you, brethren", he gave up his spirit rejoicing'.

Unfortunately, the great and learned Bishop of Hippo, the strenuous fighter against the Manichaean and Donatist heresies, has not noticed that the legend of the saint's voluntary self-burial, deservedly rejected by St. Jerome, is a most unorthodox, typically Gnostic story which was equally told of the Samaritan heretic Simon Magus and of his rival Dositheus.

Both Simon Magus and his disciple Menander of Kapparataea claimed to have immortal, incorruptible bodies. Now that is exactly what the Priscillianist Instantius, the author of the Monarchianist preface to the Fourth Gospel, claims for St. John: '*descendens in defossum sepulturae suae . . . tam extraneus a dolore mortis, quam a corruptione carnis invenitur alienus.*'

St. Augustine has not noticed either that the Ephesian legend of the Evangelist sleeping and breathing peacefully in his underground tomb is nothing but a very superficial and wholly transparent Christianization of the pagan myth describing the emasculated Attis, the beloved darling of the great Mother-goddess, as not really dead, but sleeping in his Pessinuntian grave, his hair continuing to grow and his *digitus* still able to stir. This curious story must have been well known to the Christians of Asia Minor since we happen to know it through the Christian apologist Arnobius.

These Gnostic legends and pagan myths and no historic evidence whatsoever are the basis of the Leucian *vie romancée* of John which has supplanted in 'ecclesiastical tradition' the various orthodox and perfectly reliable original testimonies concerning the martyrdom of both John the son of Zebedee and John the former high-priest buried near Ephesus.

XXVIII

ST. JOHN'S GRAVE AND THE DUST RISING OUT OF IT—ARCHAEOLOGICAL EVIDENCE FOR A MIRACLE LEGEND

ST. AUGUSTINE'S question whether and why the earth seemed to be alive and, as it were, to breathe over the tomb of

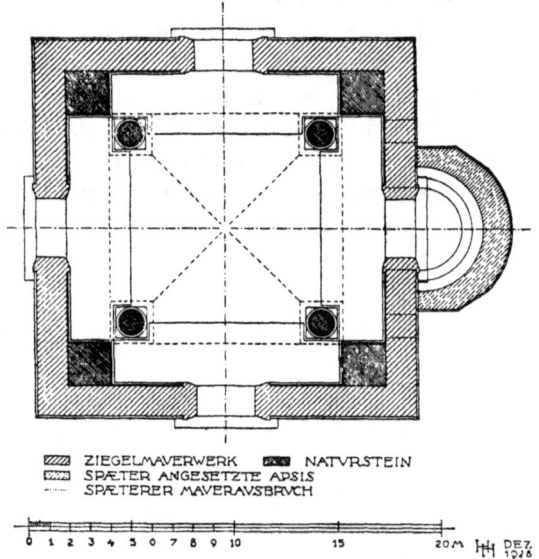

PLAN OF THE ORIGINAL LATE 3RD- OR EARLY 4TH-CENTURY MEMORIAL CHAPEL OF THE EVANGELIST JOHN IN EPHESUS
Jahreshefte des oesterreichischen archaeologischen Instituts, vol. xxv, Beibl. cols. 21-22, fig. 10. Courtesy of Profs. Rudolf Egger and Josef Keil

one who was dead, and buried, was answered ten years ago by the spade of the archaeologist.

The Austrian excavations on the site of the magnificent basilica which the Emperor Justinian built in honour of the

THE RUINS OF THE EPHESIAN BASILICA OF ST. JOHN THE DIVINE BUILT OVER THE TOMB OF THE FOURTH EVANGELIST
'Η ΜΕΓΑΛΗ ΕΚΚΛΗΣΙΑ (p. 126)
before the Austrian Excavations of 1927

PLATE VIII

Ephesian John (our Pl. VIII) have revealed the remarkable fact that the great church has been built around an earlier, small, square chapel (see our Plan, p. 120), the cross-vault of which rested on four slender columns, a building of the purest ancient style which may very well have been built, according to Professor Joseph Keil's expert judgement, in the 4th or even in the 3rd century A.D.

Underneath this chapel, Professor Joseph Keil has found a system of subterranean vaults approximately shaped like a cross (Pl. IX). One of these underground rooms was exactly below the altar. These very low catacombs were originally accessible from above through a steep and narrow passage provided with steps, which was completely walled up at a later date. Only an air-shaft was left open, the orifice of which was situated immediately beside the altar. Now the 'Wanderings of John' purporting to be written by Prochoros—in their present shape at least, a late post-Islamic text, but incorporating whole chapters of the early Leucian 'Acts'—conclude with the story that John ordered a tomb to be excavated for himself to lie down in it *in the shape of the cross.*

All this proves conclusively that Justinian's basilica was built around a chapel, constructed above what was then considered the tomb of the Ephesian John, at the latest under Constantine I, when the Church was permitted to build sanctuaries for communal worship, but possibly at a much earlier date, since there was no law prohibiting the building of a private funerary chapel over a martyr's tomb even in the periods of the worst persecution.

Immediately under the pavement of the church a big empty earthenware jar was found to have been built in with the lid tightly sealed upon it, a piece of leaden tube leading into it near the bottom and another piece of leaden tube leading out of it near the top. Professor Keil explains this strange contrivance tentatively as a container of consecrated water (ἁγίασμα). It is, however, difficult to imagine consecrated water to have been stored underground in such an earthen vessel and being conveyed to it and from it to a font or wherever it was finally used by means of a pipe-line. I cannot help thinking that the excavators have discovered the wind-box or air-vessel of a ventilator system for the low underground vaults into which air could be blown by letting water flow intermittently from a certain height into this container. The installation may have been analogous to the water-organ invented by Ctesibius of Alexandria, of which a section-drawing and explanation can be found in Albert Neuburger and Henry L. Brose's excellent book, *The Technical Arts and Sciences of the Ancient* (London, 1930, p. 230, fig. 300).

Greek technicians were perfectly well acquainted with the *siphon*—the manifold uses of which are described by Heron of Alexandria. If water flowed under pressure from a certain height—Ephesus had several aqueducts bringing water down from the mountains—into the said closed jar through the pipe at the bottom, air would escape under pressure through the pipe opening into it at the top, until the water reached the upper pipe. Then the water would begin to flow out again through it into a siphon. If the inflow of water was turned off by means of a tap shutting off the water and letting air flow into the tube, the siphon would empty the jar into some cistern or drain at a lower level and suck air into it. By means of another tap, disconnecting the upper pipe from the siphon and connecting it with an air-pipe leading into the underground vault, more air would be blown into the catacombs in alternating gusts.

The purpose of this primitive hydraulic air-blast must have been the *bona fide* desire to force fresh air into and to blow out the vitiated air from the mouldy underground caves through the air-shaft leading into the church, so as to make it possible for a small number of people to worship underground on the saint's day. The dust rising up out of the air-hole with the stale air, incense fumes and candle-smoke, seems to have been reverently collected by the pilgrims, who could probably feel the pavement vibrate over the wind-jar, found *in situ*, when the hydraulic ventilator was working. The intermittent gusts of dust-laden air coming out of the ventilator-hole would appear like the breathing of a giant, sleeping underneath. When the entrance to the tombs was walled up and underground services discontinued, officious beadles may still have continued to work the old ventilators in order to earn tips from credulous pilgrims to whom they related their silly cicerone's stories.

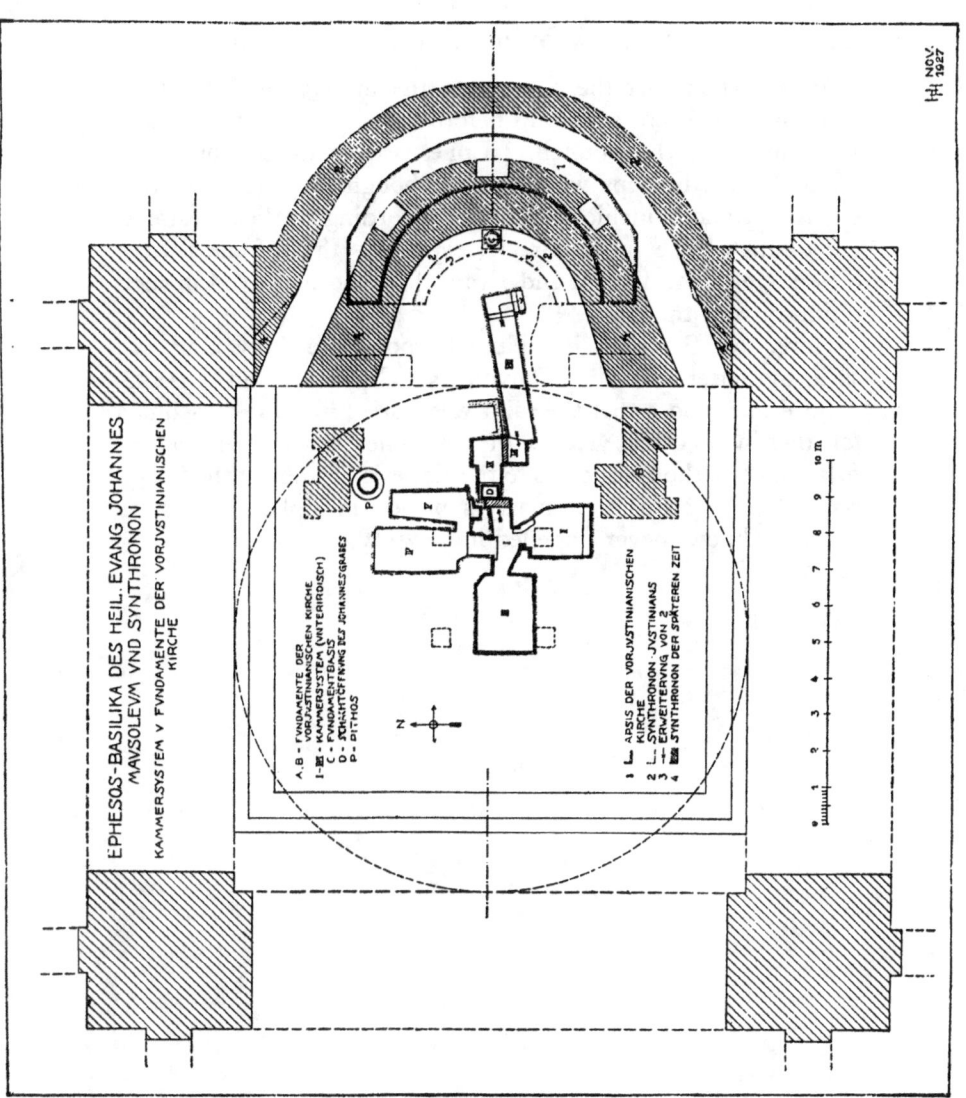

PLATE IX

THE CROSS-SHAPED GROUP OF CATACOMBS FOUND UNDER THE ALTAR OF THE BASILICA OF ST. JOHN THE DIVINE IN EPHESUS BY PROF. JOSEF KEIL IN 1927

Jahreshefte des oesterreichischen archaeologischen Instituts, vol. xxiv, *Beiblatt*, cols. 65–66, fig. 36. The circle in the upper right-hand corner of the inner square is the vessel (p. 121) found under the pavement. Courtesy of Profs. Rudolph Egger and Josef Keil

It is certain that the descent to the underground tomb of the saint had been walled up before A.D. 431, since we read in the minutes of the Council of Ephesus the pathetic complaint of the Syrian bishops who were, 'although they had travelled such a distance, unable to worship according to their desire at the tombs of the holy martyrs, especially that of the thrice-blessed John the Divine and Evangelist who had lived in such intimacy with the Lord.'

Here, too, St. John is included among the 'holy martyrs', as in the letter of Bishop Polycrates of Ephesus, and it seems natural to suppose that the saint was buried in these catacombs together with other victims of the same persecution (below, p. 209), since the free access to the Ephesian tombs of the Seven Sleepers, the only other martyrs buried in Ephesus, was, as far as we know, never impeded in any way.

XXIX

THE TWO TOMBS OF ST. JOHN IN EPHESUS

CURIOUSLY ENOUGH, the recent excavations of Justinian's and Constantine's basilica of St. John the Divine would seem to provide a *prima facie* confirmation of the alleged tradition concerning the two Ephesian tombs of John which was introduced into the discussion by Dionysius of Alexandria (A.D. 262). Quoting from this bishop's exemplary analysis of the difference in language, style, and ideology between the Fourth Gospel and the Johannine Epistles on the one hand, the Apocalypse attributed to John the Divine on the other hand, Eusebius says (*h.e.* vii. 25, 16; iii. 39, 6): 'But I think that there *was* a certain other (John) among those that were in Asia, since it is said both that there were two tombs at Ephesus, and that each of the two is said to be John's.'

The question whether or not this assertion was true is of course, of no consequence for the thesis advocated in this book. In no case is it conceivable that the body of John the son of Zebedee, thrown out unburied in Jerusalem on the 28th of December, A.D. 42, and—according to the legend recorded in Rev. xi. 12—resuscitated and wafted up into heaven, was buried in Ephesus. It is, however, quite possible that the Ephesian John, the former high-priest, was provisionally buried after his martyrdom in a certain grave, from which his mummified body or an ossuary with what remained of it, was transferred into the catacombs under the above-mentioned square chapel, as soon as the construction of this little memorial sanctuary was completed. It seems that a curiously confused and blurred, anachronistic echo of this transfer of the Saint's relics has survived in the Parisian Cod. Gr. 1468 of the Leucian 'Acts of John' which says that 'on the morning after' (John's inhumation) 'they all came with prayers to lift his body so that it should be put to rest in the big church (ἆραι τὸ σῶμα αὐτοῦ ἐν τῇ μεγάλῃ ἐκκλησίᾳ ὅπως κατατεθῇ). But when they opened the grave (τὸ ὄρυγμα) they found nothing'.

Quite possibly the idea was to bury him with those who had been martyred together with him and to collect the remains of all of these victims, originally buried in different places, so as to worship them in common on the anniversary day of their martyrdom—in all probability the 26th of September, the date at which a great religious feast and fair of world-wide renown was celebrated at Justinian's basilica of St. John until its destruction by the Seldjouk conquerors (A.D. 1090).

The translation of a martyrs' relics from a first burial-place —possibly in a family vault—to a specially constructed sanctuary must have been a frequent practice, leading finally to intolerable abuse, otherwise the emperor Theodosius would not have prohibited, in a special law (ix. 7) of A.D. 386 every removal of a dead body once buried. The assembling of several martyrs to be worshipped together is an occurrence for which hagiographic sources offer many parallels. The worship paid to pieces of cloth (*brandea*) which had been lowered into a saint's tomb and the special virtues attributed to anything that had come into contact with his body proves that the empty grave may well have continued to be revered after the removal of the body.

It is quite possible that the location of the first grave remained well known to the neighbourhood and that eucharistic worship was continued there, or resumed as soon as the access to the vault under the basilica was closed.

If this explanation is accepted, it would follow that the little square chapel at the centre of the later basilica was not only pre-Constantinian but anterior to Dionysius of Alexandria (A.D. 262).

In any case, it is interesting to find that the Greek inhabitants of Ajasoluk (i.e. Ἅγιος Θεολόγος), now Seldjouk, who (until the recent expulsion of all the Hellenic population from Asia Minor in 1920) dwelled amidst the ruins of Ephesus, used to worship, to decorate with wreaths and to light lamps before a simple arcosol-tomb cut into the rock, a little to the east of the ancient stadium, as being the grave of St. John (Pl. X). At that time the basilica of St. John had not been excavated; its site was

ROCK-TOMB
Worshipped by the former Greek population of Ephesus as the Grave of John the Evangelist
TO 'OPYΓMA
(p. 126)

PLATE X

not known with any degree of certainty. Therefore Professor Keil thinks that the pious belief of the local worshippers attached itself to the said rock-tomb in default of any other place to resort to.

I should be willing to accept this hypothesis if it were not for the existence of the Greek church of St. John, now used as a depot, on the hill of Ayasoluk, quite near the ruins of the ancient basilica, and for the little 6th or 7th century chapel of St. John on the highest point of this hill where St. John is said to have written his evangel, two places to which the uninformed devotion of local worshippers could easily have turned; if it could be supported by the evidence of a local aetiological legend of the well-known type, explaining the discovery (*inventio*) of a sacred place or relic, telling us, e.g. that at the time when the site of his tomb was wholly forgotten, St. John appeared in a dream to a shepherd or hermit or monk and revealed to him the place where his body had been hidden, etc. But in default of any such 'tradition' I think it is far simpler and methodically sounder to suppose that the rock-tomb in question (Pl. X) is indeed the other one of the two Ephesian graves of St. John mentioned by Dionysius the Great in A.D. 262.

XXX

THE CONFUSION OF THE TWO JOHNS

IT SEEMS that we have dug down to the rock-bottom of the problem, and can now try to group our various findings into an intelligible pattern.

It is wholly unlikely that anybody should have invented the curious anecdote of the Evangelist John leaving the Ephesian public bath in a hurry, to avoid meeting the Gnostic Cerinthus. This story, reported by Clement of Alexandria, rings true.

If it is true, it proves that John had a serious grievance against this heretic—probably a former *servus litteratus*, since his name 'Bee-bread' is only known as a slave's name—who had been educated in Egypt, but was teaching in the various provinces of Asia Minor in his mature years.

The simplest explanation of the incident is to accept as true the allegation of Gaius of Rome and of the so-called *Alogoi* of Asia Minor accusing Cerinthus of having fathered upon the former high-priest and senator of Jerusalem, living in Ephesus and enjoying throughout Christian Asia Minor the authority due to his rank, position and presumably also to his wealth, a pamphlet of seven letters of praise and censure to the seven Churches of Asia, claiming to be a trance-script directly inspired by the Holy Ghost. The same expert in the production of pseudepigraphic scriptures under spirit dictation published— probably under the reign of Domitian—a series of apocalyptic visions purporting to have been seen and recorded in writing by John the son of Zebedee, during his exile on the island of Patmos, in which the martyr was represented as having foreseen his own and his brother's execution, resurrection and ascension to heaven.

There is nothing unusual in the production of a pseudepigraphic Apocalypse. Archdeacon Charles admits (p. xxxviii) that 'in Jewish apocalyptic literature practically every book was pseudonymous'. The reasons which Dr. Charles gave for his assertion that there was no incentive to pseudepigraphic production any more after the advent of Christianity are refuted by the number of extant undeniably pseudepigraphic Christian apocalypses. With the same arguments, one could attempt to prove that the apocalypses attributed to Peter and Paul must be, if they were not written by the two Apostle-princes, at least the work of some otherwise unknown seers of the name of Peter or Paul.

Anyone familiar with the practice of mediumistic impersonation and the reception of spirit dictation—going on unceasingly in our own days—knows that it makes no difference whatsoever to a 'ghost-writer' whether his alleged 'control' is the spirit of a person recently departed or having died centuries ago. Nor is the evident use of identifiable literary sources an argument *a priori*, excluding *bona-fide* 'inspired' writing. On the contrary, it is typical for such 'inspiration' to be largely based on cryptomnestic reminiscences of what the 'ghost-writer' has read under strong emotional reaction. But the script is invariably adapted to what the writer knows about the historic circumstances of the alleged 'controlling' spirit's earthly life. Glaring improbabilities are avoided with the careful solicitude of a realistic poet composing an historic novel.

There is, therefore, not the slightest reason for supposing that Cerinthus meant to father the seven Epistles to the seven Churches—none of which existed during the lifetime of John the son of Zebedee—on the Galilean exile in Patmos, or that he ever thought of the Ephesian John as having been deported from Ephesus *in insulam* and seen there, in retrospective visions, the martyrdom of the 'two witnesses' in Jerusalem.

The only sensible explanation of the confusion of the two Johns is to attribute the muddle to the editor who combined into one book the two linguistically and ideologically very similar, indeed partly identical pseudepigrapha, originally fathered by Cerinthus upon two different but equally illustrious ostensible authors.

The activity of such an editor—intent upon shortening and thereby cheapening and popularizing the Scriptures he desired to circulate throughout the various provinces of the Church—

can be traced throughout the greater part of the canonical New Testament. It is this dull and reckless, but perfectly orthodox, hack who shortened—as the late Professor Albert C. Clark has definitely proved—the Bezan text of the Acts by deleting mechanically a certain number of lines and 'botching' clumsily the resulting gaps.

This procedure which we are able to trace with certainty in the case of Acts, thanks to the survival of the longer text in the Codex Bezae and its allies, must equally have been applied to the four canonical Gospels, since they all bear in an important group of manuscripts the candid superscription:

ἐκ τοῦ κατὰ Ματθαῖον (κατὰ Μᾶρκον, κατὰ Λουκᾶν, κατὰ Ἰωάννην) εὐαγγελίου.

Shortened and thereby cheapened editions of extensive works appealing to a wider circle of readers than the publisher could hope to reach with the original expensive edition were well-known to the ancient book trade. To the ancient publisher, who could not reduce the cost of production by increasing the number of copies issued, the process of producing a cheaper edition by shortening the text of a successful book had a much greater economic importance than to his modern colleagues. As we should therefore expect, *epitomae* of Livy, of Josephus, of Dio Cassius and other authors have survived, in some cases even after the longer original edition has been lost.

We can see now quite clearly how the necessity of shortening the Scriptures incorporated into what we call the canonical New Testament arose in the course, and as a consequence of, the fight against Marcion's heresy. Until this ancient 'Higher Critic run wild' put forward his preposterous claim to possess the one and only genuine evangel, it did not seem to matter a great deal which of the three, four or more existing gospels a given community possessed and used as its lectionary. It is certain, that the various gospels were still separately circulated when the first Latin versions were made in different Churches of the West, where the one or the other of them used to be read. But as soon as the necessity was felt to provide each Church with a given standard collection of authorized gospels, epistles, apocalypses, the question of the cost of such a whole *bibliothēkē* or 'chest of books' became a consideration of no mean importance. The lamentations about the high price of books abound in ancient literature and, although it is a mistake to exaggerate the poverty of the primitive Churches, consisting by no means exclusively of little artisans, slaves and other small fry, most of the Christian communities were certainly not wealthy. The length which the one and only Gospel of the primitive Churches might have, without making the acquisition of the book—as far as possible in more than one copy—too expensive, had to be reduced as soon as it became an imperative necessity for the smallest community to have Four Gospels, the Acts, the Epistles, and the Apocalypse. Most probably the process of shortening, by cutting out as many lines as possible and 'botching' the resulting gaps, was first applied to the Acts simply because Luke's work was a 'two-volume' publication and, therefore, too expensive for many would-be buyers. Since the price of books was necessarily a multiple of the standard price of a sense-line ($\sigma\tau\acute{\iota}\chi os$), publishers and non-commercial publishing institutions, such as the *scriptoria*, which metropolitan Churches may have organized very soon, must have more than once issued instructions to their chief-scribe—to him whom our modern 'Higher Critics' call 'the editor'—to shorten the text by so many lines. The crudity and irreverence inherent in the process must have been strongly felt by the more sensitive readers—otherwise the Codex Bezae would not have survived. Still, economic pressure was and is irresistible, and the Church authorities must have preferred to supply the greatest possible number of readers with a shortened edition rather than to produce a necessarily smaller number of copies of the uncut original texts.

It is by no means a mere coincidence that we find the Fourth Gospel and the Apocalypse emphatically attributed to one and the same author, 'John the Apostle (from among the Twelve)', by the interpolator (above, pp. 22; 35) of the anti-Marcionite prologue to Luke, which is frequently found as the only preface in Latin New Testament manuscripts because it deals with all four Gospels, the Acts and the Apocalypse. The interpolator of the preface *is* the 'editor', the scribe who shortened and 'botched' the two books fused into our one canonical 'Apocalypse' of John. It is he who deleted in the Gospel of

Luke the oracle of Jesus predicting the martyrdom of the two sons of Zebedee and, in Acts xii. 2, the mention of John beheaded simultaneously with his brother James, together with all the relevant details of their passion (above, pp. 74 f.). It is he who was the first naïvely to identify the Ephesian and the Zebedaid John, for no other reason than the obvious identity of the very peculiar style and ideology in the two pseudepigraphic spirit-dictated trance-scripts 'received' by Cerinthus.

The real authorship of the composite book was, however, inevitably well-known in those Churches of Asia Minor, where the man had lived or through which he had passed. These Churches of Asia Minor are the *Alogoi* who fought so desperately against its inclusion into the canonical New Testament. But it was, naturally, unknown in other centres further West, where the canon was just being delimitated by the authorities leading in the fight against Marcion, notably in Corinth and Rome.

Ever since Cerinthus' mediumistic impersonation of the exiled John in Patmos had transformed the notoriously illiterate and unlearned Galilean martyr, supposed to have risen from death in his body and still to survive in the company of Moses and Elijah, into a posthumous author, reluctantly 'forced to write' a book, the barbarous, but in all its solecisms obstinately consequent Greek of the half-educated slave or freed-man Cerinthus was scrupulously preserved, even in cases where it could have been most easily corrected and smoothed over, probably because it was considered as a mark of authenticity in the alleged *manu propria* script of an 'illiterate and untaught' fisherman, differing considerably, in this respect, from the style of the Fourth Gospel, which he was supposed to have produced with the help of a secretarial collaborator.

The very fact that Marcion—a native of Asia Minor and certainly as well-informed about Cerinthus as anybody could be—rejected the Apocalypse, must have incited all the orthodox anti-Marcionite apologists to stand up for its apostolic origin. Had Marcion accepted it, the same critics would have been more likely not only to recognize the unorthodox 'encratitic' character of Rev. xiv. 4, but also to see that the rapture of the Messianic child born by the heavenly Virgin in the Zodiac—symbolizing the Philonic Sophia, the bride of the Creator, giving birth to the Logos—being 'caught up to God and to His throne' (xii. 5), is the logical prelude to the story about Jesus' sudden dropping down from heaven as a grown-up man of thirty years into the synagogue of Caphernaum, as it is found in Marcion's evangel and in other heretic gospels. They might have seen how incompatible this astro-mythological revelation is with the simpler and homelier traditions about the infancy of Jesus in Matthew and Luke. They might have recognized that the flight of the woman clothed in a fairy robe of sunshine and pursued by a dragon 'into the wilderness', and her miraculous preservation (Rev. xii. 14), does not correspond to the flight to Egypt of Jesus' parents as much as to the legend about John the Baptist's mother Elisabeth escaping from the persecutions of Herod by hiding in a mountain cave in the desert and remaining there for some years.

Because Marcion rejected the Apocalypse, it seems to have been considered a proof of orthodoxy in the West to believe in its apostolic origins and to overlook even the heterodox 'encratitic' eschatology of Rev. xiv. 4.

In the face of those who contested the authenticity of the Apocalypse and the Fourth Gospel, the apostolic origin of the two *antilegomena* was strenuously defended. The argument of the Marcionite author of the 'Acts of John', that the untaught and illiterate Galilean fisherman had refused to put into writing the mysteries revealed to him by his Master, was accepted, together with Cerinthus' characterization of John as a 'virgin' ascetic, and together with the confusion of the two Johns, which the Marcionite romancer had readily taken over from the careless editor, who had combined into one book the alleged Patmian visions of the Zebedaid and the Seven Epistles fathered on the Ephesian John, the latest survivor of those who had seen the Christ.

What had been an ingeniously framed argument against the authenticity of the Revelation, as well as of the Fourth Evangel, was converted into an additional title to glory of the ostensible author of both books. The praiseworthy modesty of the Apostle who had refused to write anything and insisted on his literary incapacity was said to have been finally overcome by the entreaties of the delegates (or 'messengers') of the seven Churches—this is how the ἄγγελοι of Rev. ii. 1, 8, 12, 18; iii. 1, 7, 14 were, very properly, interpreted—and by the repeated, direct orders of the Holy Ghost to 'write down' the mysteries (Rev. i. 20) which the Son of Man had dictated. The humble saint's commendable resistance having been vanquished by the urgent prayers of 'his bishops' and the direct intervention of the divinity, the reluctant *auteur malgré lui* was supposed to have been finally persuaded to write a gospel, while still on the island of Patmos.

These are the elements out of which a preface to the Apocalypse and the Gospel of John was composed, which is frequently quoted as the '*ecclesiastica historia*'. Its author knew or thought to know from the Leucian 'Acts of John' that John the son of Zebedee, specially beloved by Jesus because of his ascetic virginity, had been exiled to Patmos after having travelled throughout Asia and founded the seven Churches mentioned in the Apocalypse. Among these was the Church of Ephesus, where he stayed until the day when he descended—at the hoary old age necessary for one who lived on until Trajan after having been 'one of the Twelve' Apostles selected by Jesus—into a grave dug at his own orders by His disciples.

He was, indeed, believed to have suffered martyrdom, to have duly undergone the 'baptism' predicted by Jesus—not, however, a baptism of blood, but a bath in a kettle of boiling oil—and to have drunk the lethal cup which his Master told him he would have to empty—a poison cup like the one of which Socrates had died—but to have survived both this torture and the hemlock draught, all this before his exile to Patmos.

Both these legends—grown out of the perfectly credible tradition that John the son of Zebedee had been sent to Rome and sentenced there to deportation, quite possibly after having undergone some sort of torture during his trial—are variants of the story in Rev. xi. 11-13, that the executed sons of Zebedee were miraculously raised again in their bodies and wafted up into heaven like Moses and Elijah before them. They are all transparent attempts to harmonize the genuine and trustworthy tradition of the early martyrdom of James and John the son of Zebedee, suffered in due and inevitable fulfilment of Jesus' prediction, with the words of Jesus concerning the survival of the beloved disciple until the second coming in John xxi. 22 f. and with the knowledge that John the high-priest had lived to an extreme old age in Ephesus, where he was buried.

In the edifying bio-bibliography of an immortal surviving his own executions by the sword, by poison and boiling in oil, not as a disembodied spirit, but in his reanimated flesh, the pious reader was not absolutely forced to notice, if he did not like to do so, the glaring chronological incompatibilities due to the conflation of two completely different personalities. Decapitated in Jerusalem with his brother James under Herod Agrippa I (d. A.D. 44), the resuscitated John could be believed by Tertullian and Clement of Alexandria to have ordained bishops and founded Churches in Asia, which did not yet exist during the lifetime of St. Paul (d. A.D. 64), to have been exiled to Patmos by Domitian (d. A.D. 96) or even by Trajan (d. A.D. 118).

As the proverbial sleep-addict Epimenides, the Cretan philosopher, quoted by St. Paul in his epistle to Titus (i. 12) was said to have reached the age of 154 or 157 or even 299 years, St. John was supposed to have lived for 120 years. As Plato had no difficulty in believing that the same Epimenides, who had purified Athens after the murder of Kylon's followers under Solon at the end of the 7th century, had returned to Athens in 500 B.C., miraculously to postpone the Persian war for ten years, even so we find the author of the 'Lucinian' preface to the Fourth Gospel reporting that John dictated his Gospel to Papias, a companion of the martyr Polycarp (d. A.D. 156), and that he reproved Marcion, the heretic expelled by the Roman Church in A.D. 144. More than that, there are Tertullian and St. Jerome telling us that the Asiatic forger of the 'Acts of Paul'—a book which the modern critic can easily see to be dependent on the *Martyrium Polycarpi* (A.D. 156)—was convicted of his imposture before the Ephesian John (*apud Johannem*).

XXXI

THE IDENTIFICATION OF JOHN THE SON OF ZEBEDEE WITH JOHN MARK AND WITH JOHN THE EVANGELIST IN PSEUDO-HIPPOLYTUS

TO MAKE the confusion created by the conflation of John the son of Zebedee with the high-priest John the son of Annas of Acts iv. 6 and of the Polycrates letter worse confounded, a presbyter of the church on Mount Zion in Jerusalem remodelled the Chronicle of Hippolytus (*c*. A.D. 220), which gave what the author believed to be the dates of the various gospels and of the Apocalypse, and was used as an introduction to the New Testament in certain old manuscripts of the episcopal library of Jerusalem, in such a way as to identify John the son of Zebedee with John Mark of Jerusalem, the son of Mary of Acts xii. 12.

In this faked Ps.-Hippolytean Chronicle, of which a very late still more interpolated version is used as an elaborate preface to the Apocalypse in a Paris manuscript (Codex Coislin, 224), and in the Greek 'Acts of James' surviving in a 12th-century manuscript (Gr. 1534) of the Paris National Library published by Mr. J. Ebersolt, the two sons of Zebedee are described as rich young men of noble birth, their father Zebedee as a Judaean, a big ship-owner, employing numerous craft on the Lake of Tiberias, one of the first citizens of Galilee. John and James are said to have been the two disciples in John i. 34 f. to whom the Baptist said: 'Behold the Lamb of God', the first to follow Jesus, but obliged to separate from Him when He retired to the desert. They return to Galilee, where Jesus meets them again in Genesareth when they follow His call. The claim for them to sit on two thrones to the right and the left of the Saviour is raised by their mother (Salome) during a visit of Jesus to her house in Galilee. While the sons follow Jesus, their father Zebedee dies, his Galilean estate is sold and the sons acquire in Jerusalem one of the houses of the high-priest Caiaphas!

Because of this purely legal transaction, John is 'known to the high-priest' (John xviii. 16), without there being any friendship between the two. Under the cross, Jesus entrusts His mother Mary to John, who is to be, henceforth, the Virgin Mary's adopted son. Immediately after the Crucifixion, John takes Mary into his house in Jerusalem, where she remains until her death, and where the other Apostles are accustomed to meet. John's mother Mary mentioned in Acts xii. 12 is the Virgin Mary! The house in the upper room of which the Last Supper was celebrated, where the Holy Ghost descended on the Apostles at the first Pentecost, survived and was dedicated as the Church '*Hagia Sion*, the mother of all Churches'. This mother Church of all Churches is, however, unknown to the itinerary of the pilgrim from Bordeaux (A.D. 333) and to Eusebius of Caesarea (d. A.D. 340). It is first mentioned in A.D. 348 by Cyril of Jerusalem, without any reference either to St. John or Mary. To Antonius Martyr (*c*. A.D. 570) the house where the Virgin Mary lived was shown in the valley of Gethsemane or Josaphat. The first datable author to identify it with the Church *Hagia Sion* is the patriarch Sophronios of Jerusalem (A.D. 638). But even he does not believe that it belonged to the Evangelist John.

It would hardly be worth while mentioning these late ingenious combinations of an unknown Jerusalemite, intent upon attracting pilgrims to his church full of the most curious relics, were it not for the modern resuscitation of the equation between the Fourth Evangelist and John Mark by the Swedish theologian, Dr. Samuel A. Fries of Upsala (1898), the late Professor Johannes Weiss (b. 1863) of Heidelberg (1904, 1907, 1917) and by the Dutch scholar, Professor Daniel Voelter (b. 1855) of Amsterdam (1907).

XXXII

PAPIAS ON THE APOCALYPSE OF JOHN AND THE FOURTH GOSPEL

BEFORE WE BEGIN to analyse the quotation of Papias' views on the origin of the Fourth Gospel in the 'Lucinian' prologue and in Fortunatian's preface to the Evangel of John, we should like to know what the Hierapolitan exegete thought of the 'Apocalypse of John the Divine'. Unfortunately, Eusebius, who disliked the millenniarism of the Revelation and questioned its authenticity, does not explicitly quote Papias' opinion on this moot point, thus forcing us to resort to a preliminary searching analysis of the available indirect evidence.

We find it, first of all, in Andrew of Caesarea's commentary on the Apocalypse, who quotes two sayings of Papias about the two angels governing the earth and their fall in his chapter on Rev. xii, and thus seems to have had first-hand knowledge of the Hierapolitan's book. In the preface to this commentary, he enumerates Papias as the first among those who accepted the Apocalypse of John as 'trustworthy'.

This proves that Papias did quote the Patmian Visions as Scripture and that he did not consider them a pseudepigraphic forgery of the Gnostic heretic, Cerinthus. But it does not prove that he considered the Apocalypse as the work of John the son of Zebedee. He would not have thought the Patmian 'Revelation' less 'trustworthy' if he believed that it had been vouchsafed to the Elder John, whose hearer he himself had been, according to the perfectly credible testimony of Eusebius, and from whom he had received directly and indirectly, through the Elders, whenever he met and was able to question one of them, certain eschatological traditions about the Messianic reign of a thousand years and about the marvellous fertility of the vines and the stalks of wheat in the coming Kingdom, which pleased Eusebius no more than the Apocalypse itself, and which the historian of the Christian Church preferred to consider as more or less mythical.

PAPIAS ON THE APOCALYPSE OF JOHN

Having heard directly and indirectly from the Elder John such picturesque descriptions of the future bliss awaiting the faithful, Papias might have been quite willing to believe that the 'presbyter' or 'senator John' whom he had known, in other words the former high-priest Joḥanan Theophilus, living in Ephesus, was the author of the Apocalypse.

Just as the picturesque description of the birth of the Messianic child in Rev. xii must be interpreted as a retrospective vision of a past event, Papias may have been ready to interpret the vision of the martyrdom of the two witnesses in Rev. xi as a vision of the Elder John seeing 'in the spirit' what had happened in the past to the Zebedaid twins. After all, it was by no means impossible to understand the Elder John as feeling full of bitterness at the sight of such a painful spectacle and as tasting at the same time the sweetness inherent in the account of the glorious resurrection of the two martyrs.

It might have seemed quite plausible to Papias that the John buried in Ephesus—who was, according to Polycrates of Ephesus and Hippolytus, a former high-priest and Elder of Jerusalem—should have written letters of praise and blame to the seven churches of Asia, while he must have felt unable to imagine what connection could possibly have existed between the Christian communities of Asia Minor and a Galilean disciple of Jesus, exiled to Patmos and beheaded together with his brother in Jerusalem for illicit reversion to Palestine, long before there were any churches in Asia.

If Papias attributed the Apocalypse to the long-lived Ephesian John, whom he and Polycarp had heard and seen, it is easy to understand why Irenaeus (v. 30, 1), discussing the question whether the mystic number of the beast is 666 or 616, says that all the good and approved manuscripts have '666' and that 'those who have seen John face-to-face testify to this figure'. According to one of the next chapters (v. 33, 4), 'Papias, the hearer of John and companion of Polycarp', is one of those who have seen John 'face-to-face'. There would be no sense in quoting Papias, the hearer of the long-lived Ephesian John, as a competent witness to the correctness of a certain reading in the Apocalypse, unless it was clear to Irenaeus reading Papias' book that the Hierapolitan exegete considered this long-lived John and not John the Zebedaid as the author of the Apocalypse.

More important still is the passage in Irenaeus v. 30, 3, quoted by Eusebius *h.e.* iii. 18, 3, which says that the Apocalypse 'was not seen a long time ago, but almost in our own generation, towards the end of Domitian's reign'. Irenaeus, writing round about A.D. 180, cannot have called the reign of Domitian (A.D. 84–96)—very nearly a century, exactly three generations, before his own time—'almost his own generation'. But, if we suppose that he is, in this passage about the secret name of the Antichrist and the number 666, copying Papias who must have been born about A.D. 90 or 100—as St. Jerome copies again and again in his *De viris inlustribus* '*usque hodie*' ('unto this day') from Eusebius, without acknowledging it—and that the crucial words ought to have been, as it were, enclosed between inverted commas, everything is in perfect order.

If Papias believed, as Irenaeus (v. 30, 3) seems to prove, that the Apocalypse was 'seen' under Domitian—N.B. 'seen', not written, which might refer to a later record of much older visions—he cannot have believed that the Patmian visions were granted to John the Zebedaid, but must have attributed them to the Ephesian 'senator' and former high-priest, whom he had personally come to know after having collected what hear-say he could gather about his teaching from others who came his way after having called on John in Ephesus.

This is, obviously, the impression Eusebius had received from his perusal of Papias' book and which he conveys to the reader in the vexed chapter iii. 39, 1–7, the story being unfortunately obscured by the author's mixing up an attempt to tell us what he read in Papias with his mischievous attacks both on St. Irenaeus and on Papias, whom he calls 'a man of very little intelligence'. Having told us that this Papias clearly distinguishes two Johns, the one the brother of James the Apostle, the other the Elder (or 'senator') he goes on saying: 'this calls for attention: for it is probable that the second (if anyone does not want to admit that it was the former) saw the Revelation which passes under the name of John. The Papias whom we are now treating confesses that he had received the

PAPIAS ON THE APOCALYPSE OF JOHN 141

words of the Apostles from their followers, but says that he had actually heard Aristion and the Elder John.'

In spite of the cautious wording, these lines are clear enough. Eusebius does not say in so many words that his own thesis is the opinion of the 'unintelligent' Papias, but when he says that 'probably' the Apocalypse was seen by the Elder John, whom Papias had heard, he leaves us free to infer that this 'probable' supposition is derived from the source quoted,—but only for the particular fact that there were two Johns.

The very passages in Irenaeus which Eusebius attacks, are conclusive proof that Papias' views about the author of the Revelation of John was indeed what Eusebius propounds as his own opinion.

But, in the same chapter, almost in the same breath, the biased church historian manages entirely to misrepresent Papias' views about the Fourth Gospel. He says:

'It is worth noting here that he (the Hierapolitan) twice enumerates the name of John, counting the first John with Peter and James and Matthew and the other Apostles, *clearly* (σαφῶς) *meaning the evangelist*, but by punctuating (διαστείλας) his argument, he places the other outside the number of the (twelve) apostles, putting Aristion before him and clearly calling him an Elder.'

Authors who say 'clearly', 'obviously', 'evidently', 'surely,' say so—and this general principle applies with full force to the present writer and the present sentence—because they want to emphasize their own conviction in the face of the contradiction which they know their statement is sure to provoke.

The crucial passage of Eusebius is *the* classical example for the general rule of critical method, warning us to look twice as warily at a statement accompanied by an affirmation of its 'certainty'. Far from being 'certain', it is, indeed, strictly impossible that Papias attributed the Fourth Gospel to the John whom Eusebius considered as the Evangelist.

Nobody who knew and taught, as Papias did, that James and John the sons of Zebedee had suffered martyrdom long before Peter, could ever think of identifying John the son of Zebedee with the beloved disciple destined by Jesus, according to John xxi. 21 f., to outlive Peter for so many years that the legend arose he would not die at all until the second coming of Christ the Lord.

Papias cannot either have identified the Zebedaid John, martyred long before Peter, with the 'Elder John', who—again according to Papias—had criticized the lack of logical and chronological order in the Gospel of Mark, written by Peter's interpreter on the basis of 'what he remembered of the Apostle's teaching', i.e. after Peter's death.

All the known fragments of Papias point, on the contrary, to the perfectly plausible conclusion that the Hierapolitan, just as Irenaeus, believed John the Elder—ὁ πρεσβύτερος of the superscription to the Johannine Epistles—to have written the Apocalypse, the Fourth Gospel, and the Epistles of which Papias quoted the first one.

If this is the case, it follows, of course, immediately that Eusebius was completely wrong when he criticized Irenaeus for attributing to Papias the claim to have personally known and seen John the son of Zebedee. Papias made no such absurd pretence. He said that he had heard and seen John the Elder, whom he believed to have seen the Visions of Patmos and to have dictated the Fourth Gospel. Irenaeus, who believed the same, never meant to suggest that Papias and Polycarp had known John the Zebedaid martyr under Claudius, when he said that these men had seen the Evangelist and the alleged seer of the Patmian Visions. Nobody but Eusebius, blinded by a prejudice inherited from the school of Origen, is responsible for a muddle which has obscured the problem for sixteen centuries.

This almost inevitable conclusion raises, of course, immediately the problem how two educated Greek 2nd-century writers and orators like Papias and Irenaeus could possibly believe, in the face of the glaring difference of style and language, analysed with such consummate mastery by Dionysius of Alexandria (A.D. 262), that the Apocalypse on the one hand, and the Fourth Gospel and the three Epistles on the other hand, could ever have been written by the same author.

Such considerations are of considerable importance, because ancient readers were, as a consequence of their refined rhetorical education, very sensitive to differences of this kind and quite accustomed to find grammarians discussing problems of authenticity on the basis of such arguments in the bio-bibliographical prefaces to their books.

St. Jerome explaining to his pupil Hedibia, that the difference of 'style and character, construction and vocabulary' (*stilo inter se discrepant structuraque verborum*) between the two canonical Epistles of Peter is due to the fact that the Apostle was forced by circumstances to employ various interpreters (*ex quo intellegimus pro necessitate rerum diversis eum usum interpretibus*), did not do so in order to disturb his disciple by showing off his own critical acumen, but in order to assuage or to forestall legitimate doubts against the authenticity of one or of both these Epistles, which even an educated Roman laywoman of the 4th century was sure to raise in the face of divergences of Greek style, which are imperceptible to the most attentive modern reader of the English New Testament. Considering that the differences of language, style and character between the two Epistles of Peter are negligible in comparison with the abyss separating the 'style and language' of the Fourth Gospel from the barbarian Greek of the Revelation of John, and considering the decadence of ancient learning among 4th century Romans as compared with Greek scholars of the 2nd century, it may be taken for granted that Irenaeus and Papias could not have overlooked discrepancies much more glaring than those which Hedibia submitted to St. Jerome.

Observing such patent linguistic and stylistic differences, they were exactly in the same position as the modern scholar who discovers by painstaking analysis and statistic tabulation what they felt by immediate intuition: they could either rashly attribute the stylistically and linguistically differing books to different authors—as Professor A. C. Clark began to doubt Luke's authorship of the Acts as soon as he had ascertained certain essential differences of diction between the Acts and the Third Gospel—or they could attribute these discrepancies to the well-established fact that ancient authors, notably SS. Peter and Paul, often employed secretaries. Starting from this plausible assumption, they could trace the hands of their different συνεργοί, as St. Jerome (or his source) has done in the two Epistles of Peter and as, in our days, the late Dr. H. St. J. Thackeray has done with such signal success in the various books of Flavius Josephus, where the style changes sometimes within the limits of one book, nay in the middle of a chapter.

If Irenaeus attributed—as he most obviously did—the whole *instrumentum Johanneum* to one and the same author, i.e. to the Ephesian long-lived John and not to the Zebedaid, the conclusion is inevitable, that he must have done it, because he knew and trusted the two anti-Marcionite prefaces to Luke and to John, in other words, on the strength of the argument that the Apocalypse was written by John himself, while the Fourth Gospel was composed by a secretarial collaborator, a native of Asia Minor, and, therefore, able to write better Greek.

This proves definitely, first that the apposition 'one from among the Twelve' after the words 'John the apostle' in the Greek anti-Marcionite preface to Luke, not to be found in Fortunatian's Latin translation, must have been added after Irenaeus (A.D. 180), although possibly before Fortunatian (A.D. 313), who seems to have deliberately omitted them in his translation; secondly, that the anti-Marcionite preface to John was known to Irenaeus—a fact which cannot be demonstrated on the strength of particular phrases borrowed by the Bishop of Lyons from this prologue, while such points of contact have been established by Dom de Bruyne and Harnack between Irenaeus and the prologues to Luke and Mark.

The same reasoning can be applied to Papias. If Papias believed that the Apocalypse and the Fourth Gospel, and the First Epistle of John were the work of John the Elder—the John who calls himself ὁ πρεσβύτερος in the superscriptions of the Second and Third Epistles of John—he must have believed that the Apocalypse was an autograph of John—as stated eight times by the author of Rev. i. 19; ii. 1, 8, 12, 18; iii. 1, 7, 14—while the Fourth Gospel was written by a secretarial collaborator of John, writing a better Greek than the Palestinian Jew living in Ephesus could muster. This enables us, as we shall see in the next chapter, definitely to determine the in itself uncertain extension of the quotation from Papias, which the 'Lucinian' prologues and Fortunatian's prefaces submit to the reader in support of their own assertions.

XXXIII

THE QUOTATION FROM PAPIAS IN FORTUNATIAN'S PREFACE TO THE GOSPEL OF JOHN

WE ARE NOW at last prepared to deal with the testimony of Papias quoted by Fortunatian the African, without being nonplussed by what Dom de Bruyne could not avoid stigmatizing as 'violent anachronisms', simply because he thought that the 'John' mentioned in this preface must be the son of Zebedee. If he is not meant, and cannot be meant, Dom de Bruyne's question (p. 208), 'Who can have believed that John was still alive at the time of Marcion?' is easily answered by a simple reference to Irenaeus who certainly did believe and who taught that both Polycarp—who had rebuked Marcion as 'the firstborn son of Satan'—and his 'companion Papias' had heard and seen the Ephesian John, the ostensible author of the Apocalypse, the Gospel and the Epistles.

Both Fortunatian's and the 'Lucinian' prologues (Folder 1) agree in quoting from Papias the extremely important statement that John's Gospel was published during his lifetime, evidently in contradistinction to the evangel preached by Peter which, according to Papias, was committed to writing by his dragoman Mark from memory after the Apostle's death. We shall have to come back in our ch. XL to the far-reaching consequences of this statement.

For the moment we have to observe that in Fortunatian's preface—i.e. in the original source of the 'Lucinian' prologue—the statement quoted from Papias seems to end with the quotation of the title of his book.

This title has obviously suffered corruption. The Greek name of Papias' book *In Exegeticis*, quoted as the source of what the preface has to say about the Fourth Gospel, must have been difficult to read in the archetype of our manuscripts: the second and third ε must have been so heavily inked as to be mistaken for an o—hence the v.l. *exotoricis* for *exotericis*—the ɢ so cramped as to be mistaken for an 'uncial' τ—in this script the vertical stroke did not rise above the line—and the τ after the third ε so misformed or disfigured by some fortuitous spot on the papyrus as to be mistaken for an r. A glossator wanting to translate into Latin the resulting conjectural reading '*in exotericis*'—probably supplied by an editor remembering the λόγοι ἐξωτερικοί of Aristotle or Plutarch's ἐξωτερικοὶ διάλογοι —inserted '*id est in externis*' or '*in extraneis*'. This gloss was further misread '*in extremis*' and understood to mean 'in the last five books' of Papias. '*Id est*' is, of course, the well-known, regular formula for introducing a gloss.

'*Manifestatum est*' stands for Greek ἐφανερώθη, as may be seen from the Vulgate Latin version of Tim. iii. 16, cp. John ii. 11 and xvii. 6. The above-mentioned Ps.-Hippolytean preface to the Apocalypse of John in the Cod. Coislin 224 says that some time elapsed from the moment when the visions were seen (θέα) until the year when they were recorded in writing (συγγραφή, cp. the verb *conscripsit* in the 'Lucinian' prologue) and finally 'until the publication and edition' (μέχρι φανερώσεως καὶ ἐκδόσεως).

We should expect for the 'giving out' of the book to the Churches the composite verb *editum* instead of *datum*. But we have in von Soden's collection a little preface to Matthew which says that 'having written' (συγγράψας) the evangel in Hebrew, 'he gave it' (ἔδωκεν) 'in Jerusalem'. Here, too, the simple verb διδόναι is used instead of the more usual ἐκδιδόναι to be found in all the other short prefaces of this type. This shows how literal and exact a translation Fortunatian provided of what he found in his source.

It is very characteristic that the title 'bishop' is not given to Papias in Fortunatian's preface, although we find him promoted to this rank in the 'Lucinian' prologue, probably through an act of grace on the part of St. Jerome who calls Papias '*Hierapolitanus in Asia episcopus*' in his *De viris inlustribus* 18, copying Eusebius' *Ecclesiastical History*. III. 36, 2.

XXXIV

PAPIAS, 'THE BELOVED DISCIPLE OF JOHN'

A VERY CURIOUS epithet for Papias is the '*discipulus Johannis carus*' in Fortunatian's preface. The 'Lucinian' preface has dotted the i's and crossed the t's in this line by adding *et* between *discipulus* and *carus*, the meaning being now 'the disciple of John and his beloved' (ἠγαπημένος).

That Papias had heard John, we know from Irenaeus. Eusebius too found in Papias' book that the author claimed to have been a hearer of John the Elder. But it goes without saying that Papias cannot have been so ridiculously conceited as to claim in his own book to have been 'John's beloved disciple', however limited his intelligence may have been.

It is easy to see that the words in question are inspired by the Fourth Gospel, calling John the Beloved Disciple of Jesus, and by the Third Epistle of John addressed to his disciple 'the beloved Gaius whom I truly love'.

Nevertheless the idea itself of constructing, as it were, a chain (διαδοχή) of 'favourite disciples' handing on the knowledge of the most intimate mysteries to the reader, is typically Hellenistic and essentially un-Jewish. Nowhere in any early or late Rabbinic tradition is there any mention of any teacher having a 'preferred' or 'favourite' or 'beloved disciple'. On the contrary, the *Ascension of Moses*—a book written soon after the year A.D. 6—mentions among the horrors which are to appear immediately before the end of the world 'teachers who will favour those among their disciples for whom they lust and who will accept bribes' (v. 5). The Socratic or Platonic ἔρως παιδαγωγικός has never played any role whatever as a connecting link in the Jewish 'chain of tradition'.

On the contrary, it is a commonplace of the Greek bio-bibliographical notes in Callimachus' and similar library-catalogues to tell the reader whose 'pupil and sweetheart' this or that famous poet or philosopher was said to have been.

Thus we read, e.g., in Suidas' dictionary of the poet Olympus, son of Maion, a legendary 'composer of songs and elegies', that he was 'the disciple and beloved of Marsyas' (μαθητὴς καὶ ἐρώμενος Μαρσύου, corresponding exactly to the *Johannis discipulus et carus* in the Lucinian prologue). Or we find in Diogenes of Laerte's *Lives of Philosophers* (VIII. 8, §86), that

'Eudoxus, the son of Aeschines was an astronomer, a geometer, a physician, and a legislator. He learned geometry from Archytas and medicine from Philistus the Sicilian, as Callimachus tells us in his Tables.'

(N.B.—the direct quotation of the official library catalogue of Alexandria!)

'When he was twenty-three years . . . he set sail for Athens with Theomedon the physician who provided for his wants. Some even say that he was Theomedon's beloved (παιδικὰ ὄντα).

Or in the same author, a little further on (IX. 5, 25) about Zeno of Elea:

'Zeno was a constant hearer (διακήκοε) of Parmenides and became his beloved (γέγονεν αὐτοῦ παιδικά).

It is this literary commonplace of the contemporary Greek bio-bibliographical preface which the bookseller publishing Papias' *Exegesis of the Lord's Sayings* seems to have utilized in all innocence for his 'blurb', advertising a book in which the Sayings of the Lord were said to be authentically interpreted by the man who had been the beloved disciple of the Beloved Disciple of the Master. If that did not fetch the reader, nothing ever would!

What the author of the anti-Marcionite preface to John's Gospel cannot have found in Papias' book itself, he can very well have found in the usual biographical introductory note to Papias' *Exegetica* added by his publisher.

XXXV

WHO WROTE THE GOSPEL DICTATED BY JOHN?

THE MOST striking feature about Fortunatian's preface to the Fourth Gospel is the assertion—differing from the statement in the anti-Marcionite prologue to Luke—that John did not write his Gospel as he was supposed to have penned the Apocalypse, but dictated it to a secretary.

We have seen at the end of our chapter xxviii that this important fact must have been known to Irenaeus and before him to Papias, otherwise neither of the two could have believed for one moment that the two books, so different linguistically and stylistically, were the work of one and the same author. It follows, that the prologue-writer's quotation from Papias does not end with the assertion that John's gospel was published during his lifetime, but extends at least over the sentence which tells the reader that the Evangelist had dictated the book to a clerical assistant. Being derived from Papias, who had known John, the information is *prima facie* worthy of the most serious consideration, much more so than the obviously baseless assertions of a certain Greek preface to the Tetraevangel pretending for the transparent purpose of exaggerating the direct apostolic authority of the two subapostolic Gospels that Mark's and Luke's evangels had been 'dictated by St. Peter and St. Paul' to these writers.

To offer some information about the secretary who took the author's dictation is in itself by no means an unusual or unheard-of feature in Greek bio-bibliographical notices. The public seems to have manifested a certain interest in these humble collaborators of famous men, and critics have sometimes not refrained from circulating malicious stories about the more than clerical assistance given by the secretary to his master.

The *vita Ciceronis* would have recorded the help he received from his faithful clerk Tiro, even if it had not been written by this efficient secretary-stenographer of the great orator himself. We happen to know from Diogenes of Laerte that the philosopher Lykon's secretary was a certain Chares. The anonymous

Life of Euripides attached to the manuscripts of his tragedies has a good deal to say about 'ink-blackened Kephisophon,' suspected of being more than a mere secretary, indeed an unavowed collaborator of the dramatist and a paramour of his wife. The philosopher Epicure throws it into the face of the famous and, in his later life, very rich and conceited sophist Protagoras, that he was once a humble secretary of the philosopher Democritus. The *Rhapsodies* of Orpheus the Divine—the θεολόγος of the foremost Greek mystery-religion—were believed to have been dictated by the severed head of the martyred prophet to his disciple Musaeus.

In view of these and other parallels it is not at all surprising that we should be told who it was that penned the Evangel dictated by John. But is it possible that the author of the Greek anti-Marcionite preface to John translated by Fortunatian can have read either in Papias' books or anywhere else that it was Papias himself who had been John's secretary? Yet this is what we find quite clearly and unambiguously stated both in the 'Lucinian' preface and—in Greek—in the prologue to a patristic chain-commentary on the Fourth Gospel, which Balthasar Cordier published in Antwerp in 1630 from a manuscript in possession of Queen Christina of Sweden, formerly in possession of Cardinal Nicolaus Cusanus, written in the monastery of St. John Prodromos in Constantinople. This preface, too, said:

'As the last (of the Evangelists) . . . at that time, when terrible heresies had developed, John dictated his Evangel to his disciple Papias.'

The parallelism of this text, not so much with Fortunatian's prologue mentioning only the one heretic Marcion as with the 'Lucinian' prologue, representing the Evangel as John's reply to the heresies of Cerinthus and the Ebionites, is quite unmistakable.

Ever since the main part of the 'Lucinian' prologue had been printed in Wordsworth and White's edition of the Latin New Testament, this statement—accepted as true by Zahn—was contemptuously discarded as fantastic by the more critical theologians, in spite of the Greek text supporting it and

WHO WROTE THE GOSPEL DICTATED BY JOHN? 151

although nobody has ever been able to explain how it could have originated and why anybody should have invented such a story.

For this sceptic attitude there was, indeed, a very good reason. Harnack was obviously right when he said: 'Eusebius could hardly have omitted to quote these words, if he had read them in Papias.'

This argument is irrefutable. It is absolutely impossible that Eusebius or Irenaeus read anywhere in Papias' five volumes anything suggesting that the author had written the Fourth Gospel under John's dictation. Had Eusebius found such an assertion in Papias, he could not possibly have been so blind as to say that Papias 'surely meant the Evangelist', where he speaks of the John, enumerated with 'James, Matthew and the other disciples of the Lord'. Having demonstrated on the basis of Papias' own words to his own and to his reader's satisfaction, that John had not known personally the Apostle John from among the Twelve, but had been a hearer of John the Elder only, he could not have failed to notice, that Papias 'surely meant the Evangelist', not where he speaks of John the Zebedaid, the brother of James, but where he speaks of the *Elder John*—if he had found anywhere in Papias' books the plain statement that 'John dictated his Gospel to Papias'. If he had noticed such a most important assertion, he could not possibly have passed over in silence a passage, which gave the lie direct to his own words concerning the Apostle whom Papias believed to have written the Gospel of John, without exposing himself to the most crushing refutation.

Even if it were permissible to suppose that Eusebius chose to suppress a statement of Papias about the clerical assistance which the Hierapolitan had been privileged to render to his master John, because he wanted to belittle the simple-minded champion of primitive millenniarism, who on earth would be prepared to believe that Irenaeus, bent on emphasizing the close personal contact between the Evangelist John and his disciples Papias and Polycarp, could have failed to mention the proud claim of Papias to have been John's secretary, if such a claim had ever been made anywhere by the honest collector and interpreter of the Lord's sayings?

This is the reason why Bousset and others after him have

branded the quotation from Papias in our preface as 'fraudulent'. They have not, however, been able to point out what conceivable purpose anybody could have hoped to attain by invoking the authority of Papias for an assertion, which the Hierapolitan exegete himself had never put forward. Moreover, it created a very serious chronological difficulty for all those who believed and taught, on the basis of John xxi. 24, that the Fourth Evangelist had been an eyewitness of the Crucifixion and a partaker of the Last Supper, not to speak of those who identified the Fourth Evangelist with John the son of Zebedee, martyred according to the same Papias, together with his brother James, long before the lifetime of this witness Papias, known to have been 'a companion of Polycarp' (d. A.D. 156).

There is also a further point which militates against the supposition that anybody would have invented a statement of Papias to the effect that the Hierapolitan himself had been the scribe who took down the Fourth Gospel from John's dictation. A close comparison of the two different versions of the anti-Marcionite preface to the Fourth Gospel on our Folder 1 or 3 shows that the longer version has been obliged, for a very cogent reason, to drop an essential feature of the shorter, namely, the statement that John dictated the Gospel 'correctly' (*evangelium dictante iohanne recte*). Seeing that Marcion had accused the Evangelists of having falsified the true Gospel of Jesus, it was clearly of the utmost importance to assert that 'John dictated the Gospel correctly'. This, however, could not be proved by appealing to the testimony of Papias, even if Papias had himself been the scribe who took down the text at John's dictation. All that the scribe could attest would be that John had dictated the Gospel to him and that he had taken it down correctly. He would not be in a position to say whether or not John had 'dictated correctly' the words which Jesus had actually uttered. If the scribe was only supposed to testify to his own painstaking care in 'writing exactly' what the Evangelist dictated, we should expect the preface to say: '*descripsit vero recte evangelium dictante iohanne*' instead of our present '*descripsit vero evangelium dictante iohanne recte*'.

Moreover, an assertion of this kind would have carried very little weight. For what could it matter whether or not the scribe

WHO WROTE THE GOSPEL DICTATED BY JOHN? 153

had 'correctly written down' what John dictated, when the whole point at issue was whether or not John had 'dictated correctly' the evangel of Jesus? Besides, it stands to reason that the followers of Marcion would not have attached any great importance to the testimony of a scribe whom they would naturally have suspected as an aider and abetter in the alleged crime of falsifying the authentic gospel of Jesus. In their eyes, such a witness would have deserved no more consideration than an unsupported statement of the accused in his own defence.

All that Papias could be expected to have witnessed was the identity of the author who dictated the Fourth Gospel. He could testify that it was John, and nobody else. That might have been useful evidence in the discussion against Epiphanius' *Alogoi* of Asia Minor or against the Roman presbyter Gaius who asserted that this Gospel had been written by the Gnostic Cerinthus. But Fortunatian's preface does not mention Cerinthus or Gaius or the *Alogoi*. It speaks of Marcion, who did not, as far as we know, deny that it was John who wrote the Gospel circulated under his name, but who did, on the contrary, accuse the evangelist John of having written yet falsified the evangel taught by Jesus.

The scribe of John, however, could not possibly know whether or not the Gospel dictated by John had correctly reproduced the sayings of Jesus. He could testify that he, the scribe, had taken down the dictation correctly (*recte*), but this would be utterly irrelevant from the point of view of the dispute between the Marcionite sect and the anti-Marcionite orthodox church.

Why then, should any anti-Marcionite preface-writer go to the trouble of inventing a testimonial which could not possibly help his cause, but could only create the obvious and serious chronological difficulties for the defender of the contested apostolic authority and authenticity of the Fourth Gospel which have shocked every modern interpreter of these lines?

All these arguments seem to make it extremely unlikely that Fortunatian's preface really meant to tell the reader that it was Papias who wrote the Gospel of John under the dictation of the Evangelist. As a matter of fact it does not say so directly. The sentence '*Descripsit vero evangelium dictante Johanne recte*' has no subject, although it would have been so easy to say: '*Descrip-*

sit ipse' or '*Descripsit iste*' or '*ille evangelium dictante Johanne*'. It is left to the reader to infer from the context who wrote what John dictated. The crucial phrase 'He wrote, however, the evangel, John dictating it correctly' appears to be one of those sentences which everyone happens to write occasionally only to find out afterwards that some correction or addition is necessary to make it clear to the reader to whom the pronoun 'he' refers.

This correction has, indeed, been applied to our clause by the editor, who expanded Fortunatian's preface before he inserted it into the Hispanic Bible-manuscripts.

There must have been a good reason for altering.

'*Descripsit vero evangelium
dictante Johanne recte*'

to

'*qui hoc evangelium Johanne
sibi dictante conscripsit.*'

It is plain that the editor who inserted the relative *qui* wanted to get rid, first of all, of the adversative conjunction *vero*, which he did not understand and which is, indeed, difficult to understand, although we can guess that the original writer wanted to say: 'the book was published in the author's lifetime, not by somebody else after his death. It is true (*vero*) that it was not written *manu propria*, but dictated to a secretary'.

He wanted further to delete the full stop dividing the subjectless sentence '*Descripsit vero* . . .' from the preceding mention of Papias, the author from whose book all this information is alleged to have been derived. By linking the clause with the preceding one, a subject is given to it which it did not have from the start. The question is, whether the corrector who tried to better what St. Jerome called Fortunatian's 'rustic style' did not make an egregious mistake by removing the full stop before the sentence without subject and thus linking the phrase to what precedes, instead of cancelling the full stop at the end of the sentence after '*dictante Johanne recte*' and joining the line to what follows.

If we have to agree with Harnack and Bousset and Walter Bauer that Papias cannot possibly have pretended to have been the scribe who wrote the Gospel of John under his dictation, the conclusion is simply that the editor who corrected and expanded Fortunatian's 'rustic speech' cannot have been right and that the whole trouble is somehow due to the punctuation of the text.

A corruption of that sort—suspected long ago, but unfortunately not emended with any plausibility by B. W. Bacon—is easy to heal. Even if there were no imperative material reasons for disregarding the *cola et commata* of our manuscripts, all the justification we need for this attitude could be found in Alcuin's letter to Charlemagne explaining to the great king that 'although the divisions and subdivisions by punctuation may be a most beautiful ornament (!) of the sentences, their use has been almost entirely abandoned by the writers, because of their boorish lack of education'. This means that Visigothic and Merovingian scribes did not habitually use the signs introduced by the learned Greek grammarians and rhetoricians for the purpose of facilitating intelligent reading and proper elocution, and that, as a rule, the lost punctuation of the text was restored by Carolingian revisers, possibly after a punctuated model manuscript, which may have been considerably older.

The stops and full stops which one of them inserted into Fortunatian's *sermo rusticus*, written after the manner of his time without any division of the words, let alone of the sentences, are no more binding upon the modern editor than his rather unfortunate correction '*id est in extremis*' for the corrupt '*id est in extrenis*', itself a transposition of '*in externis*' or a misreading of '*in extraneis*'. On the contrary, the only proper course to take is to print the text in undivided uncial capitals, as if we had the papyrus autograph of Fortunatian, and then divide it ourselves so as to make sense of it:

> EVANGELIUMJOANNISMANIFESTA
> TUMETDATUMESTECCLESIISAIO
> ANNEADHUCINCORPORECONSTITU
> TOSICUTPAPIASHIERAPOLITANUS
> DISCIPULUSIOANNISCARUSINEXE
> GETICISQUINQELIBRISRETULIT
> DESCRIPSITVEROEVANGELIUM
> DICTANTEIOANNERECTEVERUM
> MARCIONHERETICUSCUMABEO
> FUISSETIMPROBATUSEOQUOD

156   THE ENIGMA OF THE FOURTH GOSPEL

    CONTRARIASENTIEBATABIECTUS
    ESTABIOANNEISVEROSCRIPTA
    VELEPISTULASADEUMPERTULERAT
    AFRATRIBUSQUIINPONTOFUERUNT

No modern epigraphist or papyrologist, unaware of or unconcerned about the peril of scandalizing our 'weaker brethren', would ever have divided the text as it has been done by the 'most holy and blessed' reviser, whom we shall introduce to our readers in the next chapter.

This text simply does not say that Papias was John's secretary. On the contrary, it says with perfect clearness why Marcion had to be mentioned in a preface to the Fourth Gospel.

Neither is this preface composed of two logically disconnected halves, nor does it quote from Papias what Irenaeus and Eusebius could not have omitted to reproduce had they found it in the five exegetical books of the Hierapolitan.

All these difficulties are entirely imaginary, purely caused by wrong punctuation, and disappear like last year's snow in the spring sun as soon as we read what Fortunatian meant to write:

  '*Evangelium Iohannis manifestatum et datum*
  est ecclesiis ab Iohanne adhuc in corpore constituto
  sicut Papias nomine hieropolitanus,
  discipulus Iohannis carus
  in exegeticis quinque libris retulit.
  Descripsit vero evangelium, dictante Iohanne recte verum,
  Marcion haereticus. Cum ab eo fuisset improbatus, eo quod
  contraria sentiebat, abiectus est ab Iohanne.
  Is vero scripta vel epistulas ad eum
  pertulerat a fratribus qui in Ponto fuerunt.'

'The Gospel of John was revealed and given
to the Churches by John whilst he was still alive in his body,
as Papias, called the Hierapolitan,
the beloved disciple of John,
has reported in his five books of "Exegetics".
But (he who) wrote down the Gospel, John dictating correctly
  the true (evangel), (was)
Marcion the heretic. Having been disapproved by him for
holding contrary views, he was expelled by John.
He had, however, brought him writings, or letters,
from the brethren who were in the Pontus.' (*Plates XI–XIII*.)

XXXVI

THE PUNCTUATOR AND EMENDATOR OF FORTUNATIAN'S PROLOGUE—THE PRESBYTER PATRICIUS OF RAVENNA INSTRUCTED BY BISHOP ECCLESIUS

IT IS BY an exceptional piece of good luck that we seem to know even the name of the corrector who placed the full stop in the middle of Fortunatian's preface into the wrong line. In the *Codex Latinus Monacensis* 6212 (N)—one of the two MSS. which contain the summaries by Fortunatian and all the three earliest Latin Gospel prologues, among them the preface to John in the older and shorter form—the following note is to be found at the top of the prologue to Luke (f°, 40):

'*Evangelium secundum Marcum explicit. Incipit secundum Lucam.*'†
'*Precipiente sanctissimo ac beatissimo Ecclesio preposito meo ego Patricius, licet indignus, Christi famulus, emendavi et distinxi.*'†

End of the Gospel of Marc. Beginning of the Gospel of Luke.†

'According to the instructions of my most holy and blessed provost Ecclesius, I Patricius, albeit an unworthy servant of Christ have emended and punctuated (this).'†

'The name of Patricius', says Dom de Bruyne, 'is not rare and cannot offer us any guidance. But who is this *praepositus Ecclesius*?'

The question to which even Dom de Bruyne could not suggest a reply, has just been answered by the erudition of Dr. Bernhard Bischof, discussing the problem with Dom

Germain Morin, who kindly called my attention to a '*Patricius presbyter*' going to Rome at the head of the clergy of Ravenna together with their Archbishop Ecclesius (d. July 22, 532) in order to defend him against the accusations of the discontented among his flock (*Monumenta Germaniae, Scriptores Rerum Langobardorum*, p. 321, 15).

The connexion of the two names—one of them so rare—in this passage and in the above-quoted note cannot possibly be a mere coincidence. There is no doubt, that the presbyter Patricius of Ravenna, acting under the instructions of Archbishop Ecclesius of Ravenna, is the man who punctuated the Ravenna manuscript of the African text of the Latin New Testament to which the African summaries discovered by Dom de Bruyne in *Codex Latinus Monacensis* 6212 and in the *Barberinus Vaticanus* 637 were prefixed.

The title *sanctissimus et beatissimus*, from which the present writer concluded in 1930 that the 'most holy and blessed provost' had died when Patricius, complying with his instructions, revised and punctuated the parent manuscript of C.L.M. 6212, is nothing but an example of 'Byzantinism' such as one would expect in Ravenna. Dom Germain Morin refers me to the record of a donation made by a Gothic lady Hildevara, during the lifetime of Ecclesius, dedicated to '*beatissimo et apostolico viro* . . . (*Ecclesio*) *urbis episcopo*'. Dom Morin thinks, on the contrary, that Ecclesius had not even ascended the episcopal throne of Ravenna, but was still a mere *praepositus* of the church or convent of which Patricius was a presbyter, when the latter revised the manuscript in question under his instructions.

This copy had no punctuation and needed emendation rather badly—as we could see from the corruption of *in exegeticis* to *in exotericis* and even of the gloss *in externis* to *in extrenis* and finally to *in extremis*. This corruption—which proves that the Ravenna manuscript, corrected by Patricius under the reign of Theoderic the Great, the king of the Ostrogots, was at least four stages removed from the original text of Fortunatian (*c*. A.D. 313)—occurs in exactly the same form also in the Spanish so-called Visigothic Bibles.

If we suppose that Fortunatian the African brought his

African text of the Tetraevangel with his *Breves*—prefaces and summaries—prefixed to it to Italy, when he became patriarch of Aquileia; that the Church of Ravenna got a copy of this edition from Aquileia and that the subsequent corruptions of the text of the preface to John happened in Ravenna, we should have to conclude that the expanded version of the anti-Marcionite prefaces found in the Spanish so-called Visigothic Bibles, which show the same corruption '*exotoricis, id est in extremis*' as the Munich C.L.M. 6212 derived from a Ravenna parent MS. and which interpret Fortunatian's text in the same way as Patricius punctuated it, so as to put the orthodox Papias into the place of John's secretary from which the heretic Marcion is ousted, came to Spain from Italy via southern France. As a matter of fact, the expanded form of the prologues *is* found in a French manuscript (Perpignan 1, saec. XII) and in two Italian ones (Vatic. 6083, saec. XI, our Pls. IVf., and Vatic. 1, saec. XV). But they are decidedly younger than the Spanish Bibles, the oldest of which—the famous Toletanus of Sevilla—is an 8th-century codex.

Therefore, Dom de Bruyne, very plausibly, considered the French and Italian copies of this type to be dependent on a Spanish archetype, not vice versa.

If this is the case we must suppose that the Church of Ravenna did not obtain its African text of the Latin New Testament from Aquileia and that the above-mentioned characteristic corruption did not occur in Italy, but already in Africa, before the edition with Fortunatian's *Breves* prefixed to it was imported into Spain and into Italy.

Anyhow, the reverend Patricius was a rather indifferent corrector, and certainly a very poor Greek scholar, since the *Monacensis* 6212 has the very worst form of this corruption '*in exotoricis*', which could so easily have been emended '*in exotericis*'.

As to his punctuation, it was actuated in the crucial line discussed above (p. 154 ff.) not so much by an impartial desire to find out the real meaning of the sentence, as by a conscious anxiety to hide or a subconscious reluctance to admit such an embarrassing fact as the unfortunate secretarial collaboration of the heretic Marcion with the Fourth Evangelist.

But we must not criticize Patricius of Ravenna too severely. If the Spanish manuscripts are independent of the Ravenna copy, the same interpretation of Fortunatian's text to which he gave expression by inserting that fatal full stop in the wrong place was put upon the admittedly difficult text by the Hispanic author of the expanded version (above, pp. 9 and 13 ff.), who altered the text, instead of merely punctuating it (Folders 1 and 2).

In any case, it is certain that St. Jerome, who knew and used Fortunatian's *Breves*, who calls Papias 'a hearer of John' (*Johannis auditor*) and who would have been only too pleased to repeat the story of the Hierapolitan 'bishop' having taken John's dictation, did not understand the text as it was punctuated by Patricius of Ravenna or as it was 'interpreted' by the editor of the 'Lucinian' text of the Vulgate New Testament in Spain.

XXXVII

THE RESTORED WITNESS OF PAPIAS AND THE INTERNAL EVIDENCE OF THE FOURTH GOSPEL

THREE NEW and most important facts, each one entirely unexpected and impossible to invent, are revealed by the quotation from Papias which has now been recovered in its pristine, authentic form from Fortunatian's preface to the Evangel of John:

First that it is not a posthumous publication, but was 'issued during the lifetime of John', that is to say, revised by the author and 'given to the Churches' with his full authorization and approbation, in contradistinction to Mark's Evangel, written after Peter's, and Luke's Gospel written after Paul's martyrdom.

Second, that it was dictated to Marcion, the heretic, who had to be 'reproved'—evidently as an unfaithful, unreliable scribe, *improbare* meaning literally to declare someone '*improbum*', 'not *probus*', 'not faithful'. When the Evangelist revised the script which he had dictated, as every author who dictates to a secretary must do—this revision being the principal reason why the preface insists on the Evangel having been published during the Apostle's lifetime—it turned out to be influenced by the scribe's 'contrary views' or 'feelings' (*quod contraria sentiebat*). (Pl. XIII).

Since it is obvious that the author of the preface wanted to recommend the book to which he introduces the reader and not to discredit it as tainted with the heresy of the scribe who penned it, the text to which this preface was attached is to b understood as the revised edition of a preceding draft, to which the author had taken objection, but which might nevertheless have been circulated by the *improbus* and *improbatus scriba*.

Thirdly that it was this scribe—whose heresy and bad faith was discovered only after he had written down or 'copied' (*descripsit*, Pl. XIV) incorrectly the 'true Gospel' which John had dictated 'correctly'—who had brought to John from the brethren in his (native) province of Pontus γράμματα, 'writings' —Fortunatian was not sure whether that might not mean 'letters', presumably of introduction (γράμματα συστατικά), rather than 'Scriptures' of a literary, historical or religious character (Pls. XI and XII).

If Fortunatian hesitated to decide which of the two alternatives may have been meant by the Greek original, the modern historian knows that Marcion had been excommunicated by his own father. Being expelled from the Church of his native city, he could not bring 'letters of introduction' from his brethren, at least not from those who kept to the true faith, '*qui fideles in Christo erant*', as the very significant addition in the Lucinian prologue has it. If the γράμματα in question were not 'letters of introduction', mentioned in this connexion as an excuse for John's error in having employed such a dishonest secretary, they can only be 'writings' mentioned because they had something to do with the Evangel to which the reader is introduced. In other words, they are the presumable sources or at least some of the sources of the Evangel, which had to be mentioned because they still existed at that time, were accessible to the reader and probably used to be pointed out as the sources of the Gospel by its critics and by the adversaries of John, i.e. the Marcionites and the *Alogoi* of Asia Minor.

Therefore the author of the preface considered it wiser freely to admit what could not be denied. That is why he mentions the disagreeable incident with Marcion—the explanation for the existence and circulation of unauthorized copies tainted with Marcionism—as well as the sources supplied by the secretary.

It is as plain as it could be that the preface tries to deal as diplomatically as possible with a rather embarrassing situation. It is this embarrassing situation which has been successfully concealed in the West by one Patricius punctuating the text according to the instructions of Ecclesius the superior of his Church (Ravenna), thereby substituting for the objectionable heretical secretary Marcion the trustworthy Hierapolitan Papias, specially promoted to the rank of a bishop by the grace of St. Jerome.

Since this correction by the insertion of a mere full stop was

JOHN THE EVANGELIST STANDING ON THE KATAPAUSIS MOUNTAIN AND
DICTATING HIS FOURTH GOSPEL TO THE DEACON PROCHOROS
Miniature of the Cod. Mosq. 41 (42 Matthej), fol. 106 of Ps.-Prochoros'
ΠΕΡΙΟΔΟΙ ΙΩΑΝΝΟΥ
(On this pseudepigraph see p. 168)

PLATE XV

not possible except in the Latin text, where '*verum*' may mean either 'in truth', 'indeed' or 'the true' (viz. evangel), it is certain that the Greek preface in Cordier's chain (p.150), which says that John dictated the evangel to his disciple Papias, must have been translated from the Latin text as punctuated by Patricius according to the instructions of Ecclesius, very possibly in Ravenna itself, which remained for centuries the seat of the Byzantine exarch and his Greek clergy, until it was captured by the Langobard Aistaulph in A.D. 751, and was a trilingual city even at the time of Theodoric the Goth.

In the East the correction of the original Greek anti-Marcionite preface to John was not effected by punctuating the text, but by inserting the name of a confidence-inspiring orthodox scribe—St. Timothy or St. Prochorus—into the sentence about John's secretary.

The tradition about Timothy, the first Bishop of Ephesus, acting as John's secretary, is preserved in a manuscript of Mount Athos, published by Usener in his edition of the 'Acts of Timothy'. This seems to have been the official Ephesian version of the anti-Marcionite preface of which, so far, no Greek text has been found.

When Ephesus had been sacked in A.D. 1090, and the alleged original copy of John's Gospel had perished with the famous basilica of St. John, the founder of the new monastery of St. John on the island of Patmos, St. Christodulus (A.D. 1088), who until the Seljouk invasion was abbot of a convent in Heraclea at the foot of Mount Latmos, seems to have supplanted the Ephesian tradition by another 'legend'. According to this new invention, popularized through the efforts to attract pilgrims to the new sanctuary, John dictated his Gospel 'standing' (ἑστώς) on the summit of a mountain—κατάπαυσις, near Karos on the island Patmos—to Prochorus (Pl. XV), one of the first deacons, mentioned in Acts vi. 5, who wrote it on papyrus and made a first clean copy on parchment which remained in Patmos while the original papyrus was taken by John and Prochoros to Ephesus.

The story is one of the many pious legends fabricated in order to authenticate a particular relic, in this case probably the famous Gospel manuscript (N) written with silver and gold on purple parchment, brought to Patmos by Christodulus, of which a part is still in Patmos, while others have been dispersed by the greed of relic-hunters and relic-mongers. We find it incorporated in a Catholicized version of the old Ps.-Leucian 'Wanderings of John' which contains almost unaltered a number of chapters from the old heretical 'Acts of John'.

The three essential facts which can thus be taken as attested by the witness of John's personal hearer Papias must now be confronted with the internal evidence offered by the text of the Fourth Gospel.

In this way a definite series of questions will have to receive a precise answer.

The first problem to be solved is this: if the Fourth Gospel was published during the lifetime of John, how does this fact agree with the indirect chronological indications contained in the text itself? In other words, when was the Fourth Gospel—and incidentally the Epistles of John—written and published?

The second question is: if Marcion collaborated as John's secretary in the production of the Fourth Gospel and incurred his employer's disapproval by leaving traces of his own objectionable views in the text, can this most surprising admission of the preface-writer be substantiated by an analysis of the extant text?

The third question is: how can the statement that 'John's Gospel was published during his lifetime' be harmonized with the unmistakable hint of John xxi. 23 that the beloved disciple of Jesus had died, after all, before the Gospel was published?

XXXVIII

THE DATE OF THE FOURTH GOSPEL AND OF THE EPISTLES OF JOHN

MANY MODERN commentators—the latest I know of being Walter Bauer—placed the Fourth Gospel on general considerations between A.D. 100 and A.D. 125. Albert Schweitzer estimates that it must have been written 'at the beginning of the 2nd century', Alfred Loisy said 'certainly before Valentinus (c. A.D. 125)'. Only P. W. Schmiedel (1903), Eduard Meyer (1921) and Julius Grill (1923) considered the evangel as written after A.D. 135, because they understood John iv. 22 f. 'the hour cometh and now is, when ye shall neither in this mountain nor yet at Jerusalem worship the Father' as an allusion to Hadrian's prohibition against the Jews entering Jerusalem or even the district around it, thus making it impossible for them to worship even among the ploughed-over ruins of the Temple.

Eduard Meyer has abandoned this idea in an additional note to his third volume (1923). It is certainly erroneous. John iv. 22 does not predict, *ex eventu*, that the Jews will ever cease to worship at Jerusalem. Jesus is talking of the Samaritans only, whom he does not expect to be converted to the Jewish cult on Mount Zion, but to a spiritual religion neither Jewish nor Samaritan, not connected with any local sanctuary—in other words to Christianity. No clue as to the date of the Gospel can be derived from this passage.

The Fourth Gospel is, however, clearly dated by an unmistakable reference to a particular Pseudo-Messiah: in John v. 43 we read: 'I am come in my Father's name, and ye receive me not: if another shall come in his own name, him ye will receive'.

This prophecy cannot allude to the 'Messiah' Theudas who appeared under the reign of the Emperor Claudius, since this pretender came forward as the reborn Joshua-Jesus of the Old Testament, promising to lead the Jews dryshod through the Jordan. It cannot either allude to that Egyptian 'Messiah' who arose in the time of the procurator Felix, and who promised to bring down the walls of Jerusalem by blasts of the sacred trumpets, since he too tried to assume the rôle of a Joshua-Jesus *redivivus*. Josephus does not even know 'his own name'. Lastly, the prophecy cannot allude to the 'Messiah' Menaḥem, the last surviving son of Judah the Galilean, who proclaimed himself the liberator-king of the Jews in Jerusalem in A.D. 66, because he was almost immediately murdered by his opponents. Nobody could say of him that he was 'received' (i.e. accepted) as the Messianic ruler by the Jews.

At the earliest, therefore, John v. 43 can have been written in the reign of the Emperor Trajan, at the time when the 'Messiah' Andreas Lukuas had started a 'world-wide revolution' of the Jews (A.D. 115), but had been vanquished by Lusus Quietus and Marcius Turbo (A.D. 117). Had the prophecy been committed to writing in the days of Bar Cochba (A.D. 132–135), of his son Rufus, the 'Red One', the Antichrist with 'fiery red hair' described in the Ethiopian 'Testament of Our Lord J. Chr.', and of his grandson Romulus—the Armillus of Jewish eschatology—who succeeded him within a few days in A.D. 135—as P. W. Schmiedel, Julius Grill, and, for a short time, Eduard Meyer, supposed—we should expect the prophecy to speak in the plural of 'others who shall come in their own names,' etc.

This characteristic plural is, indeed, found in the First Epistle of John ii. 18, 'even now there are many antichrists ($\dot{\alpha}\nu\tau i\chi\rho\iota\sigma\tau o\iota$ $\pi o\lambda\lambda o\iota$)'—i.e. several pseudo-Messiahs—'whereby we know that it is the last hour'. These words look, indeed, as if they had been written in A.D. 135, i.e. under the reign of Hadrian. To assume such a late date for an epistle purporting to be written by one who had seen, heard and touched with hands the incarnated Divine Word of Life (1 John i. 1) would force us to believe that John really reached the fabulous age of Moses or Simon, son of Clopas, i.e. 120 years, which a sermon printed in Montfaucon's edition of *John Chrysostomus* (vol. viii. 2, p. 131) and the article on John the Evangelist in Suidas's dictionary attribute to the saint, probably because the writer from whom this statement is derived, based his calculation on the identification of the 'many pseudo-Messiahs' mentioned in

THE DATE OF THE FOURTH GOSPEL

1 John ii. 18 with the three kings of the Jews succeeding each other in the course of the year A.D. 135. Even if we presuppose the Lucan date of the Crucifixion, A.D. 29 or 30, which is incompatible with the Pauline chronology as it is established by Gal. i. 19–ii. 9 (above, p. 85), and if we submit that the Ephesian John claiming to have been the boy whom Jesus held in His arm while rebuking the worldly ambitions of His other disciples may have been at that time no more than six or seven years old—the age at which a boy began to be taught the Scriptures and would begin to be interested in a wandering teacher—he would have had to dictate this Epistle at the age of 111 or 112 years, a span of life transcending the length which may be considered as possible on the basis of critically sifted historic or contemporary evidence. Nothing but the strongest, absolutely incontrovertible evidence could support such a contention. It goes without saying that proof of this kind is not to be found in 1 John ii. 18. We know, that while the Jewish revolutionaries in Egypt and Cyrene were led by Andrew the Lycian—who may also have been the Messianic king recognized by the rebels in Lycia—the Jews who rose in arms in Cyprus were commanded by one Artemion. Although we do not happen to know who led the Jewish rebels in Mesopotamia, it is certain that they had a commander and they may have had more than one. Since the various ringleaders are more likely to have been or become the heads of independent revolutionary uprisings than faithful lieutenants of the one Andrew whom we know to have assumed the style and title of a king, it is perfectly possible that the Evangelist, who knew of one pseudo-Messiah only when he wrote John v. 43, say in A.D. 115, had got, say in 116 or 117, news of other rival 'anointed kings' of the Jews in Cyprus and Mesopotamia.

In the last resort it would be quite plausible to assume that John wrote in A.D. 115, 116 or 117: 'Little children, it is the Last Time, and as ye have heard: the antichrist shall come whereby we know that it is the Last Time'—alluding to Andrew the Lycian only. After this 'last hour' had passed, without having been the very last, a contemporary of Bar Cochba, Rufus and Romulus may have brought the text up to date in A.D. 135 by adding: 'and now we have (even) many antichrists. They went out from among us'—i.e. from among the believers in the imminent arrival of the Messiah—'but they were not of us', i.e. not real faithful believers in the Messiah Jesus. 'If they had been of us, they would have remained in communion with us, but they went out', i.e. seceded from us, 'that they might be manifest that they all were not of us'.

All this fits Bar Cochba and his son and grandson, all of them claiming to be descendants of David, and their followers very well. But it may equally well have been said of a Messiah hailing from Asia Minor, like Andrew the Lycian, and of his rivals and followers.

Our own conclusion that the Fourth Gospel was written in the reign of the Emperor Trajan, in the years or soon after A.D. 115–117, accords perfectly with the fact that we have now a small fragment of a papyrus-codex containing this one Gospel, the script of which proves it to have been written in the first half of the 2nd century A.D. If it is true that the autograph of the Evangelist—or rather of his scribe—survived in Ephesus (Folder 1, *verso*), that papyrus-codex must have been very similar to the one shown in Pl. XVI.

The date A.D. 115–117, supplied by internal evidence, agrees equally well with the tradition preserved by Irenaeus that the Evangelist John lived on until the time of Trajan (d. A.D. 117) and with the curious fact—for which there must be some good reason—that a number of manuscripts and the Slavonic version of Ps.-Prochoros 'Wanderings of John' exhibit a *lectio difficilior, ergo potior* which makes the Apostle live on until the age of Hadrian (A.D. 117–138). The Ps.-Prochoros is a late, certainly post-Islamic forgery, probably written shortly before A.D. 1088. But it incorporates large, otherwise lost portions from Ps.-Leucius's 'Acts of John', which the late Dr. M. R. James placed about A.D. 150, that is within living memory of Hadrian, when the allusion in 1 John ii. 18 to the three Messianic kings, succeeding each other within a short time, may still have been perfectly transparent to the readers.

The proposed date is, finally, in complete agreement with the tradition of the 'ecclesiastical history' quoted by various Latin authors and known to Eusebius that John did not write anything until the very end ($\tau\epsilon\lambda os$) of his life.

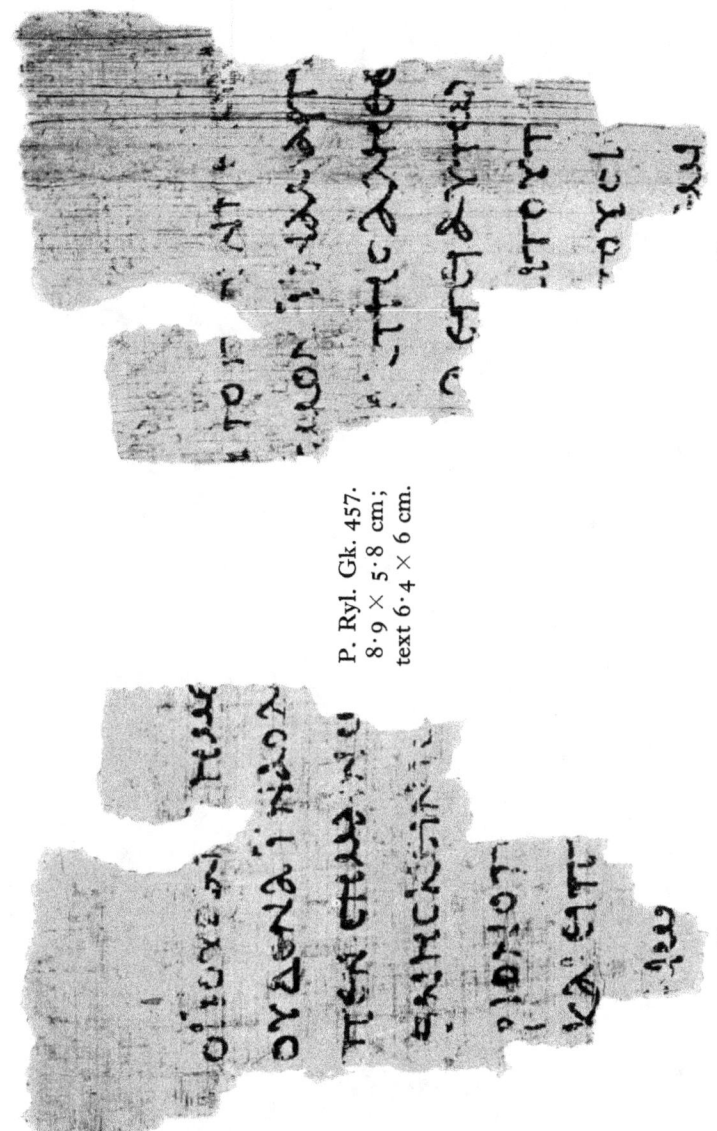

P. Ryl. Gk. 457.
8·9 × 5·8 cm;
text 6·4 × 6 cm.

Recto

Verso

THE PAPYRUS FRAGMENT OF THE FOURTH GOSPEL IN THE JOHN RYLANDS LIBRARY

PLATE XVI

If the First Epistle of John was written, as the Fourth Gospel itself, during the Jewish world-revolution of 115–17, under Trajan—as we believe it was—this would be the best explanation of its address, 'ad Parthos', credibly attested by certain manuscripts of the old Latin version, by St. Augustine (*Quaest. evang.* 2, 39) and Cassiodorus Senator (*instit.* c. 14), as well as in a corrupt passage of Clement of Alexandria, but dismissed as unworthy of serious consideration by our modern Higher Critics. The epistle—which first appears as an 'epistle general' (ἡ ἐπιστολὴ ἡ καθολική) in Dionysius of Alexandria (A.D. 262), and has obviously lost its original superscription in consequence of this easily understandable misinterpretation—has been very plausibly explained, from Grotius (1679) to Guericke, as intended for the Jewish Christians of Mesopotamia, i.e. in the Parthian Empire.

The case is absolutely analogous to the procedure of Flavius Josephus, who professes to have written a special edition of his *Jewish War* for the Jews in the Parthian realm, for the obvious purpose of discouraging them from joining in the Jewish rebellion against the Roman Empire. An epistle of John, warning the Christian addressees—i.e. the faithful believers in the imminent arrival of the Messiah—against the newly arisen pseudo-Messiahs, would be more appropriate in A.D. 115–117, when the Jews of Mesopotamia had risen in arms against Trajan's lines of communication, while he was fighting against the Parthians, than in A.D. 135, when we hear nothing about any support given by the Parthian Jews to Bar Cochba's rebellion against Hadrian, for the very good reason that Trajan's general, the Mauretanian prince, Lusus Quietus, had 'cleaned the Jews out of these provinces', murdering thousands of them, certainly without making any distinction between Jews and Jewish Christians.

Holtzmann has clearly seen that 1 John i. 3: 'what we have seen and heard, we declare unto you, that *ye also* may have communion with us' (i.e. with what we know), must be aimed at far distant addressees who would, without this written message despatched to them, be unlikely to share with the writer's community the knowledge offered to them. Since the letter itself does not convey the good tidings which it announces, but at best sums up the moral and religious conclusions resulting from it, it is reasonable to suppose that it is the covering letter of the announced message (1 John i. 5: 'this then is the message', ἀγγελία), in other words, of John's Gospel sent to the Parthians in the hour of tribulation through the appearance of 'the antichrist'—Andrew the Lycian—'who denieth that Jesus is the Christ' (1 John ii. 22), because he claims himself to be the expected Messiah. It is as irregular for an epistle to be dispatched without a proper address or superscription—i.e. in the state in which the First Epistle of John is found in the Greek New Testament manuscripts—as it is for an ancient book to be sent out without a dedicatory epistle—the '*epigramma quod extra ordinem paginarum est*', mentioned in Martial (IXth epist.).

That the First Epistle of John is the covering letter or epistolary foreword of the author, addressed to the readers named in the Latin superscription, would never have been forgotten or doubted had it not been for the absurd theory of Eusebius and St. Jerome, or rather of their sources, Origen and Dionysius of Alexandria, attributing the Gospel to John the Zebedaid, but the minor letters to 'another author of the same name; possibly John the Elder'. It has, nevertheless, been clearly perceived by a number of modern theologians like Hug, Fromman, Thiersch, Hausrath, Ebrard, Haupt, ever since Bretschneider (Pl. I) in 1820. Now that the person of the Evangelist is definitely identified with the Ephesian Elder and former high-priest John, and the minor linguistic, Christological and ideological differences between the Gospel and the Epistles can easily be explained as due to Marcion's collaboration and the use of the sources supplied by him to John, this simple explanation cannot be gainsaid any more.

The present writer sees no reason why the same interpretation should not apply to the shorter Second Epistle. If the First is the dedication prefaced to the edition sent 'to the Parthians', the Second is the Elder's dedication 'to the chosen Lady (ἐκλεκτῇ κυρίᾳ) and her children', that is to the Church of Palestine, the diocese of Jerusalem and its faithful members. The cryptic address uses a well-known rabbinic symbolism based on that selfsame story of *Sarah*—the name meaning 'queen'—the mistress or lady (κύρια, *gebhirah*), and Hagar, the handmaiden, in

Gen. xvi. 8, from which St. Paul has derived his allegory in Gal. iv. 23 f., and on Isa. xlvii. 5, 7, applying the word 'lady' (*gebhirah*) to Babylon, which 'shall no more be called Lady of Kingdoms' (*gəbhērēth mamlakhoth*) although she said 'I shall be Lady for ever'—the counterpart to the later boast of *Roma Aeterna*!—the word being used without the article as in 2 John 1. When a plague had broken out in Palestine, Rabbi Naḥman—a Babylonian Amora of the third generation—ordained a fast for Babylonia, saying (*Ta'an.* 21 b): 'If (the) Lady—*gebhirah*, again without the article like ἐκλεκτῇ κυρίᾳ (2 John 1) —is punished, how much more has the handmaiden to fear!' meaning, 'If Palestine is chastised, how much more has Babylonia to fear.'

In the same way, John sent one edition of his Gospel with the covering letter addressed '*ad Parthos*' to Mesopotamia, 'the handmaiden', the other to Palestine, 'to (the) Lady, (the) chosen one and her children'. It is pathetic to read how the centenarian exiled high-priest, having dictated pages and pages, rambling on and on, 'to the Parthians', writes a short dedication only 'to the Chosen Lady', his mother-country, hoping still 'to come unto you and speak face to face, that our joy may be full!'

That the First and the Second Epistles of John—first quoted by Polycarp (vii. 1) and his companion Papias—are posterior to the first publication of the Fourth Gospel can be definitely proved by the comparison of John xiii. 34 with 2 John 5 and 1 John ii. 7.

We find the Marcionite heretic, Marcus, quoted in Adamantius' *Dialogue* (ii. 16, 20), citing with approval the two passages John xv. 19 and xiii. 34, and laying great stress on John xiii. 34:

'A new commandment I give unto you: that ye love one another.'

In view of this significant Marcionite quotation of a Johannine saying of Jesus, it is most instructive to read John's repeated retractations or rectifications of this particular line of his Evangel in his Second Epistle (5):

'And now I beseech thee, Lady, not as though I wrote a new commandment unto thee, but that which we had from the beginning, that we love one another. And this is love, that we walk after His commandments. This is the commandment as ye have heard from the beginning.'

Still more emphatically, John writes in the First Epistle 'to the Parthians' (ii. 7 ff.):

'Brethren, I write no new commandment unto you, but an old commandment which ye had from the beginning. The old commandment is the word which ye have heard from the beginning. Again (πάλιν) a *new* commandment I write unto you, because the darkness is past and the true light now shineth . . . he that loveth his brother, abideth in the light. . . .'

The tiresome, repetitious iteration of the main idea in all these lines will immediately remind the reader of the famous picturesque description, which St. Jerome—probably after his source, Origen—has given, in his notes to Gal. vi. 2, of the time when John was 'still in his body and remained in Ephesus until his extreme old age, when he had to be carried to church by his disciples and could not talk coherently any more, but said in every assembly always the same words, "Children, love each other." Finally, the brethren and disciples attending the meetings, getting tired of hearing always the same words, asked their old master, 'Why do you always say but this?' and got the answer, 'because it is the Lord's command and because it is sufficient, if it is done.'

The necessity felt by John to rectify in the covering letters an essential passage, very dear to him, instead of correcting it in the gospel-text itself, proves that a previous edition of the gospel had already gone out and scandalized the readers, because it seemed to support Marcion's attack on the Jewish law as devoid of the spirit of love by ignoring the 'old commandment' to 'love one's neighbour as one's self'. The gospel having once been published in this shape, John could not alter what he believed to be and had presented as a saying of the Lord, but only try to explain away its heretical implications.

Clear evidence of the opposition which the Fourth Gospel aroused from the start is offered by John's Third Epistle to Gaius v. 10:

'I wrote unto the Church but Diotrephēs who loveth to have the first place among them receiveth us not, prating against us with

THE DATE OF THE FOURTH GOSPEL

malicious words: and not content therewith, neither doth he himself receive (us) but he even forbiddeth the brethren that are willing to and casteth them out of the Church.'

There is no reason to assume that John sent any instructions to another Church which an elder of that community refused to obey, excommunicating those who would accept such orders. It is a baseless, late deduction from this letter and the forged epistles of John in the Apocalypse that he was in the position of a monarchical archbishop—'a bishop of the bishops' (Tertullian)—able to ordain and to depose bishops and to lay down the law for the Churches of Asia.

But he could and did write to the various Churches such letters as the First and Second Epistles, and these Churches could 'receive' or 'not receive him', i.e. the evangel he was sending them by special messengers, accompanying the gift with dedicatory letters. There is no reason why any Church should refuse to 'receive' or 'not receive' such letters, but—as the controversy between Gaius of Rome and Hippolytus shows—there are a great many reasons why a community should 'receive' or 'not receive' the Evangel of John, and why a Diotrephēs—the first of the *Alogoi* rejecting the Fourth Gospel!—should go so far as to excommunicate 'those who are willing to receive' John and, incidentally, the 'new' and 'foreign commandments' (Papias) of Marcion.

All this fits very well together. Nobody will deny that the constantly recurring mannerism of the writer of the First Epistle, addressing all his readers as 'my little children' ($\tau\acute{\epsilon}\kappa\nu\iota\alpha$ μou, $\pi\alpha\iota\delta\iota\alpha$), unconsciously introduced by the author even into a speech of Jesus (John xiii. 33; xxi. 5), has an unmistakably senile ring, even if we refuse to accept as convincing evidence all the features in the Fourth Gospel which German theologians, E. Stange and Gerh. Hoffmann, have collected in order to prove that the book must have been the work of a very old man.

Nor is there any contradiction between these symptoms of extreme old age and the letter of Bishop Polycrates of Ephesus, which says that the former high-priest John, buried in Ephesus, was a martyr. There is the exactly analogous case reported by the Judeo-Christian traveller Hegesippus of 'the Lord's uncle Simon the son of Clopas, who, having survived until the reign of the Emperor Trajan' was 'accused before Atticus the Consular, tortured for many days and gave his witness, so that all, even the Consular, were extremely surprised how, at the age of a hundred and twenty (!) he endured, and he was commanded to be crucified'.

The Roman government, which seized and mercilessly executed under Trajan—obviously during the terrible war against the revolutionary Messianists under Lusus Quietus (A.D. 117)—an uncommonly old and entirely harmless man because he was betrayed to them as a descendant of David and as the presiding Elder of the Christian, i.e. of a Messianist community in Jerusalem, was not likely to leave free and unmolested an exiled former Jewish high-priest living in Ephesus, addressing special messages to the Parthians, to the Messianists of Jerusalem (and to all the seven Churches in Asia), merely because he was equally old and pacifist. On the contrary, the popular belief that these wonderfully strenuous oldsters were immortals, destined to live until the return in glory of the Messiah crucified under Pilate, was probably the chief motive which decided the cold and heartless *raison d'état* of the Empire. Thus it would be demonstrated to the credulous mob by a *demonstratio ad oculos* that the last descendant of the Kings of Judah and the last survivor of their high-priestly family could be subjected by the Roman rulers of the world to the vilest cruelty without provoking the hated nation's invisible deity, believed to have dwelt in the empty *adyton* of the thrice sacked and burnt Temple of Jerusalem, into destroying the Eternal City on the Seven Hills with the floods of water, wind and fire threatened by the Jewish Sibylline Oracles and Apocalypses.

The deplorable success of the Marcionite forger of the 'Acts of John', who concluded his phantastic *vie romancée* of the Ephesian John with the story of the saint's voluntary self-entombment, demonstrably borrowed—for reasons discussed in our vol. II—from the legends of Simon Magus and Dositheus, may have deprived us of the true tradition about the particulars of St. John's undoubtedly historical martyrdom. But it is more probable, that the real truth has survived in the legend of the Evangelist John being given the poison-cup. That he survived this treatment, unharmed like another Mithridates, is obviously a pious invention, but it may be true that he was sentenced to drink the hemlock-potion by a humane provincial governor wanting to preserve the venerable old man from a worse fate.

The above-suggested explanation of John v. 43 and 1 John ii. 18 proves conclusively that John wrote at a time of intense politico-revolutionary Messianist activity among the Jews, repressed by the Romans with the utmost energy, in a period in which the quietist, Paulinist Christian communities were forced to steer a narrow course between Scylla and Charybdis. On the one hand, the Roman government persecuted them as partisans of a Jewish king expected to come from heaven, to overthrow the Empire of the Caesar, whom their Apocalypses called 'the Beast', and to burn the City on the Seven Hills with fire proceeding from his mouth; on the other hand, the Jewish political Messiahs ferociously pursued them because they would not accept any one of those new self-styled liberator-kings as the true Anointed of the Lord.

It is in this period that the passionate desire of the Paulinist Christians, belonging to the wealthy conservative classes of society, to dissociate themselves definitely from the revolutionary activism of the proletarian Messianic Jews engendered in the rich shipowner Marcion the desperate idea, radically to cut the umbilical cord which still connected the millenniarist Jewish Christianity, represented by the Ps.-Johannine Apocalypse, with the political Messianism of the Jewish Zealots among the primitive followers of Jesus.

The same tendency would seem to account for the often observed paradoxical attitude taken by the Fourth Gospel towards the Jewish nation as a whole. While the synoptic writers show a clear consciousness of the fact that Jesus was opposed by certain sections of the Jewish people—the scribes, the Pharisees, the Sadducean high-priests, the Herodians—but acclaimed with enthusiasm by the masses—the Fourth Gospel opposes the Jews as a whole to the small circle of Jesus and his followers.

The wish to hide or to minimize the political aspects of Jesus' Messianic aspirations is clearly discernible in the Fourth Gospel. In John vi. 15 Jesus is pictured as 'escaping into the mountains when he perceived that the Jews would come and take him by force to make him a king'. Only in the Fourth Gospel (xviii. 36) is Jesus represented as telling Pilate that 'his reign was not of this world', just as, according to Hegesippus, the grandsons of Jesus' brother Judas told the Emperor Domitian, who had them arrested as descendants of King David, that 'the kingdom of the Messiah was neither of the world (κοσμική) nor earthly ἐπίγειος), but in heaven above (ἐπουράνιος)'.

The paradoxical transposition of the so-called 'cleansing of the Temple' from its natural and logical place in ch. xii in the account of Jesus' triumphal entry into Jerusalem to the very beginning of his career in John ii. 13–22—duly noticed by Roland Schütz (1907) and G. P. Lewis (1929)—serves a very obvious purpose. It is meant to conceal the connection of cause and effect between the proclamation of Jesus as King of the Jews, His inciting the multitude to 'destroy this temple', His forceful eviction of the cattledealers, and the bankers from the sanctuary on the one hand and, on the other hand, the penalty to which the Naṣōrean king of the Jews was sentenced by the Roman governor for this usurpation of sovereign power. That Jesus was allowed to go about and to preach for years on end, after having been the cause of the fatal riot in the Temple, is offered as proof that the authorities did not take such a grave view of the incident as to persecute Jesus for sedition and high treason.

It is, of course, this most important, wholly arbitrary, change in the chronological order of events in the life of Jesus, which made it necessary for John the Elder, i.e. the Ephesian John the Evangelist, to turn the tables on his critics and to say—in the hearing of Papias—that 'Mark, Peter's interpreter, wrote accurately all that he remembered, but not in the proper order (οὐ μέντοι τάξει) of the things said or done by the Lord. For he had not heard the Lord . . . but followed Peter, who used to impart his teaching as the occasion demanded, but not making as it were a systematic arrangement (ὥσπερ σύνταξιν) of the Lord's sayings . . .' etc.

Equally so the suppression of Jesus' sojourn in the desert 'with the beasts' of the wild (Mark i. 13) after His baptism by John, which gave such offence to the *Alogoi* rejecting the Fourth Gospel, is intended to obviate the comparison with the Maccabean Zealots, withdrawing into the wilderness to lead there, as Josephus says of the so-called 'bandits' of the Trachonitis, 'a life in common with the animals' (δίαιτα κοινὴ μετὰ τῶν βοσκημάτων). It was obviously undesirable to provoke a comparison with all the outcasts taking their refuge in the desert from the power ruling the cultivated and inhabited country.

Marcion, according to Tertullian, rejected the Messiah foretold by the prophets of the Old Testament as a 'militant fighter and armed war-lord' (*militaris et armatus bellator*, iv. 20; *bellipotens*, iii. 21) and substituted for this Jewish ideal of the victorious liberator-king the gnostic figure of a saviour of souls, sent down by the extramundane, transcendent, 'foreign' or 'good God' from the realm of Light into this wicked world, created and enslaved by the 'Just' Demiurge, who gave the law to the Jews. In this Marcion has either developed ideas which he had learned from his master John, or managed to introduce some of his own conceptions into the Evangel which he wrote for the old and wizened high-priest, who had himself been compelled by bitter experience to bow to the invincible power of the Roman emperors, fifty years before he was persuaded to write a new account of the life and Passion of Jesus.

XXXIX

TRACES OF MARCIONISM IN THE GOSPEL OF JOHN

THE UNCOMMON importance of the information derived from Papias by the author of the anti-Marcionite preface about Marcion's collaboration with the Evangelist John in the production of the Fourth Gospel and about the resulting quarrel will be clear to the reader who remembers von Harnack's observations (1920) about the historic position of John's Evangel 'on the line leading from St. Paul to Marcion'. As God is, for Marcion, a *spiritus salutaris*, so 'God is a Spirit' for St. John (iv. 26a). As for Marcion, 'God is love' for John (1 John iv. 8, 16), nay, 'the perfect love' which 'casteth out fear' (1 John. iv. 18).

'When the Christ cometh', according to John viii. 27, the Jews say that 'no man knoweth whence he is'. This agrees entirely with the teaching of Marcion, that the Redeemer will come from a transcendent, unknowable world outside into the creation, as the messenger of the 'strange God'—in contradistinction to the Jewish expectation of a human Messiah who would spring from the House of David and be born in Bethlehem, the city of David.

According to John x. 18, the Son himself has the power to 'give up his life' as an offering and to 'take it back again'. In order to introduce the same modalistic conception into the text of the Pauline epistles, Marcion altered Gal. i, 1: 'Paul, an Apostle by Jesus Christ and God the Father who raised Him from the dead' by deleting the words 'God the Father' and changing 'Him' (αὐτόν) into 'Himself' (αὑτόν). The same impudent forger has altered in 1 Cor. xv. 20: 'now the Christ has been awakened (ἐγήγερται) from the dead' into: 'now the Christ is proclaimed as having stood up from among the dead' (ἀναστάναι κηρύσσεται).

Marcion's deliberate substitution of ἀναστάναι, 'to stand up' (by His own power and will), for ἐγήγερται, 'was raised' or

ADOLPH VON HARNACK
(1851–1929)

His last portrait (1929)

'We write . . . for an ideal public, that is to say for ourselves and, perhaps, for posterity. . . .'—Letter to Holl, 1902 (p. 264 of the biography)

PLATE XVII

'awakened', explains perfectly the contrast between John ii. 22 ὅτε ἐγέρθη ἐκ νεκρῶν 'when He was raised' or 'awakened from the dead' and John xxi. 14, ἐγερθεὶς ἐκ νεκρῶν 'having been raised' or 'awakened from the dead' on the one hand; on the other hand xx. 9, ὅτι δεῖ αὐτόν ἐκ νεκρῶν ἀναστῆναι, 'that he must rise' or 'stand up from the dead' and xi. 25, ἐγώ εἰμι ἡ ἀνάστασις, 'I am the Resurrection,' lit. 'the standing up', a difference which prompted the Dutch critic, J. H. Scholten (1864) to question the authenticity of John ii. 21 f.

We can see now clearly that the active 'rising' or 'standing up from the dead' is the term employed by Marcion, which corresponds to his heretical Christology, while the passive 'raised up', 'awakened' (by God) is the orthodox expression, substituted by John revising Marcion's script, with the faltering attention of an old, weary scholar as badly served by his own failing eyesight as by the attention of the dismissed secretary's successor, thanks to whose incompetence we are still able to detect the traces of Marcion's 'contrary opinions' in the Gospel of John.

As in Marcion, so in John it is not God who judges the world. Rather is it the Son whom God has appointed as judge over the living and the dead. Yet the Son says (John xii. 47) that he has 'not come to judge the world, but to save it', because he is, according to Marcion, the son and messenger of the Good and not of the 'Just God'.

In John's Evangel, as in the system of Marcion, 'the World' (ὁ κόσμος) is a power of darkness which is alien to God and stands in hostile opposition to Him. 'The whole world lieth in wickedness' (1 John v. 19). Mankind, with the exception of the few Chosen Ones, who are 'of God', belongs to this world of evil and must be redeemed from it.

The marked hostility of John's Gospel towards 'the Jews' as such, i.e. towards the whole nation, is perfectly understandable, if not equally excusable, on the part of a former Jewish high-priest who had lived through the Jewish revolution of A.D. 66 and witnessed the atrocities committed by the fanatical masses against the priestly nobility and the ruling class in general, as they are described by Flavius Josephus, an author of the same antecedents—a Hellenised Paulinist, who had to hear again, in his extreme old age, the terrible news of the even worse atrocities committed by the revolutionaries under Andrew the Lycian in North Africa and Egypt and under Artemion in Cyprus, and who had probably severed all relations with those of his family who had clung to their ancestral Sadducean Judaism and would repudiate him as an apostate. But it is not the ineradicable Jewish anti-Semitism of all ages, but unmistakable Marcionism to say that 'the father'—i.e. 'the father(-god) of the Jews is the devil' (John viii. 44), 'the murderer from the beginning', i.e. the Demiurge who introduced death into his own creation, 'a liar and the father of all lies'.

The correction of the Marcionite passage John xiii. 34 about the 'new law' of love in John's Epistles has already been discussed (above, p. 171 f.) as proving that the Fourth Gospel must be older than the First and Second Johannine Epistles. John's rectification is obviously intended to obviate the use of this passage by those who 'memorize foreign commandments' (ἀλλοτρίας ἐντολὰς μνημονεύουσιν) as Papias says, i.e. by the Marcionites who substitute for the decalogue and the Law given by the 'just' Creator a series of commandments of the 'foreign' god, brought down by Jesus from outside the created world.

2 John 7, about the 'many deceivers' 'who confess not that Jesus Christ is come in the flesh', is a thrust aimed at the docetism of Marcion and his disciples, such as Megethius and Marcus, the *dramatis personae* of Adamantius' first and second dialogues.

In some cases it is possible to lay one's finger on one or another passage where the anti-Marcionite revision of the original draft is clearly visible. Thus in Origen's commentary to the Fourth Gospel (vol. iii, p. 598*a*), the words 'and the world was made by him' (sc. the Logos) are missing in the so-called prologue of the Evangel (John i. 10). The words which the Alexandrian exegete read, suggested, in contradistinction to our own *textus receptus*, the Marcionite doctrine that the Logos has not created the world and has not 'entered into his own' creation, but into a world to which he had until his descent been entirely 'foreign'. The clause 'and the world came into being through Him' καὶ ὁ κόσμος δι' αὐτοῦ ἐγένετο is, therefore, demonstrably one of the corrections inserted by St. John into the Gospel which he had dictated to Marcion. The importance of the correction can be judged from Irenaeus who devotes almost a page of his third book (III. 11, 1 f.) to the argument that 'According to Marcion and those of his kith and kin the world has not been made by Him and He came not "into his own" but into another's property'. 'John, however, has excluded this misinterpretation by beginning his Gospel with the words "In the beginning was the Word" . . . "all things were made by Him and without Him was not anything made that was made".'

A still more patent instance of John's anti-Marcionite revision of Marcion's script can be found in the one of the two oldest extant vellum MSS., the great Vaticanus Graecus 1209, known as the Codex B. This most important witness exhibits in John i. 4 'and the life was the light of men' the words 'of men' (τῶν ἀνθρώπων) in the margin only, but added by the hand of the same scribe as wrote the whole text. It is evident that the crucial words were missing in the manuscript copied by this *librarius* and had been found by him in another codex which he collated afterwards. At least, it is very difficult to believe that the scribe accidentally jumped and then inserted precisely the two words which made all the difference between the Marcionite and the orthodox cosmogony. According to Marcion, the primeval divine Light is by no means inborn in men, it is not dwelling in man ever since he was created by the Just God, the Demiurge and Lawgiver. On the contrary, it has to be brought to men by the Christ, the messenger of the hitherto wholly unknown 'foreign' Good God dwelling outside the created world in the transcendent realm of Light. Men dwell in darkness, the light 'which enlightens man' is given to them, not at their natural birth, but only when they are 'reborn from above' and made into 'children of Light'. On the contrary, John's own orthodox theory is expressed in John i. 9: 'the true light enlighteneth every man coming into the world'. Being born as a creature of the God of Light, man is enlightened from the start and nothing but his own sins can obscure this inborn true Light. The Logos-Light came 'into his own' creation, therefore the primeval Light is indeed 'the light of men'. What the correction in the Vaticanus B shows in a most instructive example is the almost insurmountable difficulty of securing an absolutely complete orthodox revision of a text tainted at the source with Marcionism, and the additional difficulty of securing the constant transmission of the completely revised text, after unrevised or incompletely corrected copies had once got into circulation.

Another example of John's efforts to revise an original, patently heretical line in Marcion's script is easily detected in John iv. 22, where Jesus is made to say to the Samaritan woman, 'ye worship ye know not what; we know what we worship', the following words 'for salvation is of the Jews' being a patent and not very happy addition to the original *logion*, intended to prevent the saying from being understood as an expression of the Marcionite thesis that the Good God is unknown and unknowable to Jews and Samaritans alike, because He has not been revealed to men before Jesus came, the Son who alone knows the Father, whom Moses and all those who came before Jesus completely ignored. Only Jesus and His disciples worship 'Him whom they know', Jews and Samaritans worship they 'know not what'; they worship, without knowing it, the inferior god who created this evil world and gave it an evil law.

The insertion about 'salvation being of the Jews' looks rather forlorn and weak in an Evangel in which (John viii. 10) Jesus is made to describe all his predecessors—without a word exempting Moses and the prophets from this sweeping condemnation—as 'thieves and robbers', in contrast to the one shepherd, and in which, contrary to everything told in the books of Moses about the revelation on Mount Sinai, especially in contradiction to Deut. v. 4: 'the Lord talked with you face to face out of the midst of the fire,' Jesus is made to assert (John v. 37): 'ye have never heard the Father's voice at any time.'

A further striking instance of John's revision is found in John xvii. 20 in the long sermon to which David Chytraeus (d. 1600) gave the now usual title of 'Jesus' high-priestly prayer'. In this long oration, the Christ addresses 'the true God' (John xvii. 3), the Father whom 'the world has not known', but Jesus has (John xvii. 25)—in other words, Marcion's unknown 'foreign' 'Good God', the *'el 'aḥer* whom the Jews are forbidden to serve according to the law of their God (Exod.

JOSEPH TURMEL
(December 1929)

PLATE XVIII

xxxiv. 14)—suddenly and quite inconsistently 'O Righteous Father' (John xxvii. 25). This is clearly a correction, identifying Jesus' Father with the Jewish 'Righteous Creator', the Lawgiver who is by no means 'unknown' to 'the world', since He Has revealed Himself to Moses and the Jews on Mount Sinai. Here, too, Marcion's script must have had 'O good Father' and John must have corrected the epithet into 'O righteous Father'.

On the one hand, Harnack has very well observed that—in spite of the doctrine of incarnation set forth in the prologue—the Fourth Gospel has 'left the human nature of the Christ in a spectral twilight'. Jesus takes no other 'meat but to do the will of Him who sent' Him (John iv. 32, 34). Like a ghost, He cannot be caught unless He allows Himself to be held (John vii. 30, 40; viii. 59; x. 31; xi. 57; xii. 36).

On the other hand, F. C. Burkitt has pointed out that nowhere else is such emphasis laid upon the human traits of Jesus as in this very Gospel, where the dogma of 'the Word became flesh' is first enunciated. Jesus is here portrayed as tired and thirsty, desiring water to drink (iv. 6, 7). He weeps at the grave of Lazarus (xi. 35) and has to work Himself into a state of excitement ($\dot{\epsilon}\nu\epsilon\beta\rho\iota\mu\acute{\eta}\sigma\alpha\tau o$) whenever He wishes to perform a miracle. When His body is pierced by the soldier's lance, blood and water stream out of it (xix. 34).

The clear perception of two conflicting tendencies in a number of passages of the Fourth Gospel has been the basis on which one of the most learned scholars among the Roman Catholic Modernists, the former Abbé Joseph Turmel (Pl. XVIII)—writing under the pseudonym Henri Delafosse—has built up his theory that the Fourth Gospel is a Marcionite evangel which has been subjected to a Catholic revision. The element of truth contained in this slightly exaggerated thesis is completely confirmed by the newly recovered statement of Papias, who could not help admitting and discussing the fact that Marcion had had a hand in the production of John's Gospel and had been ignominiously dismissed by John, when his master's revision of Marcion's script had revealed the surreptitious introduction of his peculiar heretical views into John's Evangel.

Neither Harnack (1920) nor Turmel (1925) was the first to notice and to discuss the unmistakable points of contact

184 THE ENIGMA OF THE FOURTH GOSPEL

between the Fourth Gospel and the heresies of Marcion. Hilgenfeld had, in various publications (1849, 1854, 1855, 1863 and 1875) maintained that John's Evangel is based on a dualistic gnosis, a kind of halfway house between the Valentinian and the Marcionite systems—the two heresies which John is supposed by Irenaeus to have 'refuted'. Volkmar (1857, 1858, 1870 and 1876) taught that John—whom he dated about A.D. 155—had started from Marcion's anti-Jewish gnosis and surmounted the dualism of this heresy by means of the 'monistic Logos-doctrine' of Justin the Martyr. The truth is, that Justin is dependent, as we shall see, on one of John's main sources and that the traces of Marcionite heresy are due to Marcion's personal collaboration, which need not have had such a menial, purely clerical character as the apologetic preface would want the reader to believe.

The case of a young, energetic secretary using an eminent but old and tired employer as a screen for his own ambitions, incidentally creating a lot of trouble for his master, and finally getting the sack as soon as he has got himself deep enough into hot water, has occurred more than once in the course of history.

In a now almost forgotten book the Swiss theologian Corrodi wrote: 'In the Gospel of John, Marcion would have found many things that seemed to favour his own views. Here he had a Saviour suddenly descended from heaven, here he found no antecedents, no genealogies, no birth of the Christ, which he would have had to delete. Here there were no objectionable passages about paradise, the banquet of the patriarchs, or the Jewish passover to cut out; here he found such a saying as the word that the Law had been given by Moses, but that Grace and Truth had come into the world through Jesus the Christ; here he found very few quotations from the Old Testament, little, if anything, favouring Jewish Christianity.'

Considering all these features, it seemed a difficult problem to Corrodi why Marcion should have decided to use the curtailed Gospel of Luke for his purpose. This problem has disappeared; we can see now that the characteristic features of the Fourth Gospel which seemed to predestinate it to be used as the Gospel of the Marcionite Church, owe their existence to the collaboration of Marcion with John. When the ascetic young heretic came from Sinope to Ephesus, where his excommunication by his own father may not have been known—just as later on the Roman Church does not seem to have been aware of his second excommunication in Ephesus through John—he must have hoped to be able to use the venerable elder as a mouthpiece for the gradual propagation of his own ideas. A wealthy shipowner, who was able to offer 200,000 sesterces as a gift to the Church of Rome in A.D. 139, is not likely to have served as a secretary to John for the sake of his board and wages. Nor was Marcion in A.D. 115–117 such a modest little young 'disciple' as we see him pictured on the Leningrad miniature (Pl. XIV), but rather a man in his prime as he is represented in the Pierpont Morgan evangeliary from Keiroussis (Pl. XIII). We cannot, finally, overlook the fact that Fortunatian's preface uses the verb *descripsit* for his collaboration—which may stand for a Greek ἀπέγραψεν 'he copied' as well as for κατέγραψεν 'wrote down', 'took down', while the 'Lucinian' prologue has deliberately altered the verb into *conscripsit*, which means συνέγραψεν, he 'composed', 'wrote together'. The Leningrad miniature (Pl. XIV) shows John dictating to a copyist from an autographic draft—an interpretation which is obviously designed—just as the schoolboyish appearance given to Marcion—to belittle the amount and the character of Marcion's secretarial collaboration.

A shipowner landing in his own cargo-boat, ostensibly in the course of his worldly business avocations, in the most flourishing harbour-town of Asia Minor, as he arrived later on in Rome; gaining the confidence of the grand old man who had worn in his time a high-priest's diadem, by presenting to him certain 'writings' or 'scriptures' which he had brought from the brethren in the Pontus; offering to take the venerable elder's dictation, if he could but be prevailed upon to write down a life and Passion of the Messiah, whom he was known to have seen and heard and even touched in his early youth (1 John i. 1); obtaining this honorary job and finally abusing his confidential position by producing 'untrue' copies of what the elder had dictated—all that does not look like an ordinary secretary, but much more like a would-be publisher or editor 'stooping to conquer' an unusually precious manuscript from an unwilling, illustrious author and anxious to use it as an instrument for reforming the Church of his age.

Or are we to picture Marcion as not only excommunicated, but disinherited by his father, the Bishop of Sinope, 'cut off with a penny', a poor adventurer, who made in Ephesus the fortune which he certainly had when he arrived in Rome, and who started his career as a paid secretary to the Elder John? A penniless man could as well make a fortune in those days in Ephesus, as he could do it in the 19th century in London or in New York, and the position as secretary to the presiding elder of the Asiatic Church may have enabled him to form very valuable business connections. The combination of remarkable commercial capacities with a speculative, sectarian trend of an ascetic mind (the *inquieta semper curiositas* blamed by Tertullian) is a typical phenomenon, well known to sociologists interested in the history of religions—since Troeltzsch, Max Weber and Tawney. But we should expect it to have been thrown into the teeth of a man who made so many enemies and concentrated the *furor theologicus* of two generations upon his austere personality, if he had been an upstart and a *nouveau riche*. Since Tertullian suggests mischievously that he may have transported stolen or prohibited goods in his cargo-boats (*in acatos tuos recepisti*), directed cargoes to false destinations (*onus avertisti*) and adulterated the goods he carried—quite a nice collection of hypothetical insinuations!—but does not accuse him of that most unpardonable crime of having been poor and become rich, I think we have to discount the possibility that he was ever employed as a paid clerk by John and to stick to the above-proposed explanation of his extraordinary venture.

XL

THE GOSPEL 'PUBLISHED DURING THE LIFETIME OF JOHN' AND THE AUTHOR'S SUPER- AND SUBSCRIPTION

SO FAR, the external evidence supplied by John's personal hearer Papias and the internal evidence derived from the analysis of the extant Gospel-text are in the most perfect accordance. But as soon as we compare Papias' statement that 'John's Gospel was published during his lifetime' with our present text of John xxi. 23 f., a glaring contradiction seems to appear, which cannot be overlooked.

John xxi. 23 has always been understood as an apologetic explanation—a very lame and unsatisfactory explanation indeed, but still an explanation—of the fact that the beloved disciple of Jesus had died after all, although Jesus was believed to have promised his favourite that he would 'tarry' until the second coming of the Messiah in glory.

The following verse: 'This is the disciple which testifieth of these things and we know that his testimony is true,' has been explained as meaning two things: first, that he 'who wrote these things', ὁ γράψας ταῦτα is 'the disciple which testifieth of these things', i.e. the beloved disciple of Jesus, and secondly, that 'these things' are our present Gospel of John; in other words, that John is revealed in this subscription, colophon, or author's 'signature' and 'seal' (σφραγίς) as being the anonymous 'beloved disciple' of the Lord.

As to the 'we' who testify for the truth of this disciple's witness, the story in the so-called Canon Muratori (*c.* A.D. 200) about John writing 'in the name' of all the Apostles, the others 'acknowledging' his account as true (*cunctis recognoscentibus*) proves that the 'we' was interpreted as referring to John's fellow-disciples and to 'his bishops' (*cohortantibus condiscipuli et episcopis suis*) i.e. to the bishops whom—according to Tertullian and Clement of Alexandria—he had ordained in Asia, the same 'bishops' whom St. Jerome and the various prefaces to the Apocalypse identified with the 'messengers' of the seven Churches of Asia, to whom John was supposed to have addressed the seven apocalyptic letters. The paraphrase of our anti-Marcionite preface to John in Philastrius of Brescia (Folder 1, col. 1 n.**) attributing the excommunication of Marcion not to John alone, but to 'the blessed John the Evangelist and the elders of Ephesus' shows that some early interpreter understood the 'we' in John xxi. 24 to be the presbyters of Ephesus—co-presbyters of John the presbyter, as St. Peter speaks in 1 Pet. v. 1 of himself as the 'fellow-elder' ($\sigma\upsilon\mu\pi\rho\epsilon\sigma$-$\beta\upsilon\tau\epsilon\rho\sigma$) of the 'elders who are among you'.

If this very early and in itself plausible explanation is accepted, these anonymous authorities who stand up before the reader as witnesses for the truthfulness of 'the witness who wrote this'—whoever they may be—are clearly the editors who issue, with their authoritative approbation and with the seal of their own authority, the testimony ($\dot{o}\ \mu\alpha\theta\eta\tau\dot{\eta}s\ \dot{o}\ \mu\alpha\rho\tau\upsilon\rho\hat{\omega}\nu\ \pi\epsilon\rho\dot{\iota}$ $\tau\omicron\acute{\upsilon}\tau\omega\nu$) and the writing ($\dot{o}\ \gamma\rho\acute{\alpha}\psi\alpha s\ \tau\alpha\hat{\upsilon}\tau\alpha$) of the beloved disciple, who was dead at the time when John xxi. 23 was written, in order to explain how this could happen, in spite of the prevailing belief that Jesus had promised that he would live until this doomed world came to an end.

This old and apparently convincing explanation—accepted, e.g., by Harnack in 1885—now stands definitely condemned by the witness of Papias and the anti-Marcionite preface. Indeed, we might say that Papias and the preface-writer meant to exclude this very interpretation. Dom de Bruyne saw this quite clearly, when he said: 'John xxi. 23 and 24 suggested the idea of a posthumous publication, but the preface reports that this suggestion is contradicted by Papias in his *Exegetica*.' Equally so Harnack who wrote (1928): 'Contrary to the opinion based on John xxi. 23, 24, that the Gospel was published after John's death by others, Papias said that John himself had given his Gospel to the Churches while still in his body.'

If John was alive when the Gospel before us was published, then John cannot be the beloved disciple, whose unexpected death this Evangel tries—in vain—to harmonize with Jesus' promise that he would pass directly into the deathless bliss of the Messianic world to come.

It is certain that Papias wrote the proem to his first book—and forewords are generally written when the book is completed and not before it is begun—under the reign of Trajan, while John was alive, since he makes a deliberate distinction between 'what Aristion and John the elder *are* saying' (λέγουσιν) and what 'Andrew or Peter or Philip . . . or John or Matthew *had* said' (εἶπεν) where he recounts his endeavours to collect whatever he could from occasional visitors of the reminiscences of the several 'disciples of the Lord'.

It is equally certain from what the anti-Marcionite preface quotes out of the five Exegetic books, that he knew the Fourth Gospel when he wrote them. Eusebius read in these same books—and the great historian, Theodor Mommsen, has said, very properly, that an author like Eusebius has to be believed when he says so—that Papias had personally heard John the Elder (not, of course, the Zebedaid John!). It cannot, therefore, be doubted that Papias had every chance of knowing and every reason for saying that the Fourth Gospel was 'published during John's lifetime' and that Harnack showed an exaggerated scepticism when he said, there is no reason for doubting that Papias really said what the preface quotes, although 'it need not be true'.

After the analysis of the texts reviewed in the two preceding chapters we feel satisfied that Papias' statement is proved to be absolutely correct. But, of course, we have, so far, no means to ascertain whether his edition of John's Evangel contained the appendix, ch. xxi, and if so, whether it contained the crucial verse xxi. 23.

There is, however, a fundamental rule of sound philological and historical method which decrees that we have to try to understand our documents, first of all, as they are handed down to us by the manuscript tradition, before we resort to any conjectural alterations of the text, such as the excision of alleged interpolations, additions, emendations, etc.

In our case it is sufficient to read our Evangel with open eyes and a free and unprejudiced mind from the beginning to the end in order to see at one glance that the apparent contradiction between Papias and John xxi. 23 f. is wholly imaginary.

It is a complete illusion caused by nothing but the traditional belief that the beloved disciple of Jo. xiii. 23; xviii, 15; xxi. 20, 23, 24 must be John the Evangelist, who dictated the Fourth Gospel.

It is universally admitted that this is nowhere said in the text of the Gospel, and that, as a matter of fact, no other John but the Baptist is ever mentioned in the Fourth Gospel.

But it is not so universally recognized that, on the contrary, John's Evangel says with the greatest clarity who the beloved disciple was: the supposedly anonymous disciple 'whom Jesus loved' is plainly and unambiguously named in John xi. 3 by the man's own sisters who 'sent unto Jesus, saying: Lord, behold, *he whom thou lovest*, is sick.' The two sisters have no doubt that the Master will understand this urgent message without any further explanation, in other words, they presuppose that *there is but one man 'whom Jesus loved'—Lazarus of Bethany*. The beloved disciple is Lazarus, whom He raised from the dead. The author who tells his story in this effective way could have no doubt that his readers would understand him. He could not know that a time would come when he himself would be identified by the Ephesians cherishing his memory, foremost among them their bishop, Polycrates, with the disciple who had rested his head against Jesus' breast, with the ἐπιστήθιος μαθητής, the 'bosom-friend' of the Master, simply because he used to claim to have been—as we read in the preface to John erroneously attributed to Hilary of Poitiers (above, p. 47 ff.)—the boy that Jesus had taken fondly into his arm, while he rebuked His disciples for discussing who was greatest among them.

The present writer is by no means the first or the only reader to have understood John xi. 3 as it must have been meant by the author. This equation was first proposed by Dr. Johannes Kreyenbühl of Lucerne (Pl. XIX), at that time *Privat-dozent* for Philosophy at the University of Zürich, in his book *Das Evangelium der Wahrheit, eine neue Lösung der Johannesfrage*, Berlin 1900 (vol. I, p. 158).

The late Dr. Rudolf Steiner of Vienna, the founder of the Anthroposophic movement, taught the same interpretation of John xi. 3—independently of Kreyenbühl, whose work he does not seem to have known—in 1903 in his book *Das Chris-*

Painted by Albert Welti

DR. JOHANNES KREYENBÜHL
(1846–1929)

PLATE XIX

tentum als mystische Thatsache. In his lectures on the Fourth Gospel delivered in 1908 in Hamburg (Nr. IV, pp. 2-5) he added to it the typical compromise with the conventional theory, that Lazarus assumed the name John after his resurrection—a combination which is not quite so far-fetched as it sounds, since it is an ancient Jewish custom, well known to folklorists, to give, as a last desperate attempt to save them, a new name to persons about to die, which they naturally keep if they happen to recover.

Without knowing either Kreyenbühl's or Steiner's theses the late Rev. William Kaye Fleming (d. 17th of October, 1937) has tried to convince what he called, resignedly, 'the impervious circle of theologians'—in an article contributed first to *The Guardian* in 1906 and, again, to *The Spectator* of August the 7th, 1926, that Lazarus of Bethany was the 'beloved disciple' and the source of some of the later chapters of the Fourth Gospel, while the aged John was the author of the Evangel who uses, in Jo. XXI. 24, 'the Apostolic we' with reference to his own attestation to the truth of the eyewitness beloved by the Master.

No less an authority on textual criticism than the late Dr. H.B. Swete of Cambridge (Pl. XX) said in 1916: 'of specializing love for individuals who are named in the Gospels we have only two examples, (*a*) John xi. 3, ibid. 5 . . . (*b*) the rich young ruler, Mark x. 21 . . . Could the beloved disciple of the Fourth Gospel have been one of these?

'Some of the conditions are satisfied by Lazarus. He lived within two miles of Jerusalem; his family were in good circumstances (so we may gather from John xii. 1 ff.); it is not impossible that he was acquainted with the High Priest; and his house at Bethany would have formed a suitable home for the Mother of Jesus. But it is difficult to believe that, if the Beloved Disciple had been the subject of our Lord's greatest miracle, the fact would have been passed by without notice either in the Fourth Gospel or in early Christian tradition. The other disciple whom Jesus loved answers better to the requirements of the case. The man was rich, even very rich (ἔχων κτήματα πολλά, Mt. Mk.; πλούσιος σφόδρα, Lk.); he was an ἄρχων (Lk.) i.e. probably a member of the Sanhedrin (cf. Lk. xxiii. 13; xxiv. 20; John iii. 1; xii. 42), and in A.D. 29 was still relatively young (νεανίσκος Mt. xix. 20), though he had passed his first youth (ἐκ νεότητος Mk.). He ran up to our Lord as Jesus started afresh on His journey to Jerusalem (ἐκπορευομένου αὐτοῦ εἰς ὁδὸν (cf. x. 1, 32) προσδραμών), hastening to seize the opportunity of putting to the Master the most vital of all questions. The Lord's answer disappointed him, at least for the moment; he went away with a clouded brow, a sadder man. But who shall say that Christ's love did not avail to bring him back? or that on his return he may not have attached himself to Jesus with a fervour and wholeheartedness which justified the Lord's immediate recognition of his worth?'

We shall see in vol. II that there is no need to decide between the two candidates for identification with him 'whom Jesus loved' and that Mark x. 21; Matt. xix. 16; Luke xviii. 18; John xi. 3; xiii. 23; xviii. 15; xxi. 20, 23, 24 all refer to one and the same person.

For the moment it is enough to say that it is hard to understand how Dr. Swete could say that the fact of the beloved disciple having been the subject of Jesus' greatest miracle has been 'passed by without notice in the Fourth Gospel and in early Christian literature'. The whole story *is* told in the Fourth Gospel as clearly as it could be done without immodesty by him 'who wrote that', i.e. by Lazarus himself whose account the Evangelist professes to 'know to be true'. As to early Christian literature, did not the Christian apologist Quadratus write to the Emperor Hadrian that some of those who were cured or *raised from the dead* by our Saviour survived 'even till our own time'? Whom can Quadratus mean to have been raised from the dead and to have survived until the time of the men who were alive under Hadrian, if not Lazarus the beloved disciple whose death the Fourth Gospel tries to explain in an appendix, the signature of which we have every reason to consider as contemporary with the introductory letter to the second edition, the First Epistle of John?

XLI

ST. JOHN WITNESSING THE TESTIMONY OF THE BELOVED DISCIPLE

IF WE START from the clear identification of the beloved disciple with Lazarus in John xi. 3, 5, no contradiction is left any more between John xxi. 23 and Papias. It is Lazarus who has died again, after all, although he had already gone through the agony of death once before, and although he claimed that the Lord said he was to 'tarry' here until the Second Coming. It is Lazarus, now at long last departed for ever, 'who testifieth to all that and who wrote that'. What did he testify to (περὶ τούτων), and what is the 'that' (ταῦτα) which he wrote? Why, all that for which he is quoted by John: first of all the story of the appearance of the risen Lord and all he said and did, and the account of what happened at the empty tomb, at and under the cross, and in the courtyard, and in the house of the high-priest Annas, and during the Last Supper in the upper room, and what the Baptist said about Jesus being the Lamb of God spoken of by the prophet Isaiah (liii. 7) before two of his disciples, one of them the later favourite of Jesus, followed their newly found greater Master; in short, all that John found in the source which he believed to have been written by Lazarus, and to the truthfulness of which he testifies.

Lazarus is dead, but John is very much alive. It is he who adds his witness to the testimony of the dead man, whose witness 'he knows to be true'. How could we all be so blind, as not to see that the 'we' is nothing but the *pluralis auctoris*, the *pluralis modestatis*, the 'we' which we too have used all the time in this book, the age-old rhetorical device for 'roping in' the reader into the team of the writer's willing adherents, the old threadbare *captatio benevolentiae* trying to win the reader's or the hearer's assent by making him believe that he, too, has, of course, discovered all these things simultaneously with the writer or orator, that he, too, would say or write the same things, if he happened to be in the author's or speaker's chair! Is not this 'we know' and this peculiar piling up of one witness over the other the most characteristic idiom of the author of the Johannine epistles? Does not the first of them end (1 John v. 18–20) with the twice repeated '*We know* (οἴδαμεν) that whosoever is born of God sinneth not', '*We know* that we are of God . . .', '*We know* that the Son of God is come that *we may know Him that is true*'?

Is it not 'the Elder' John (3 John 1) who, in a prosaic letter to one Gaius, instead of saying simply that 'brethren and strangers' have told him of the addressee's charity, pathetically and as if he were a judge summing up writes: 'they have borne witness of thy charity' (3 John 6: ἐμαρτύρησαν σοῦ τῇ ἀγαπῇ)? It is John who, in this simple little letter of introduction, instead of recommending Demetrius as a fellow believed to be honest by him and others—which is all a man can mean when he introduces another to a friend—constructs a whole three-decker of testimonials (3 John 13): 'To Demetrius all bear witness (μεμαρτύρηται ὑπὸ πάντων) and even Truth itself' (nothing less!) 'and we too bear witness (καὶ ἡμεῖς μαρτυροῦμεν) *and thou knowest that our witness is true*'.

What more proof than this striking parallelism between John xxi. 24 and 3 John 12—noted in the margin of Nestlé's Greek New Testament in both places—could anybody want for the fact that this legalistic super-witnessing is an idiom, that it is the very signature of John, who must have sat all his life as a judge in court, alone and with concurring colleagues—as he had sat in the Synedrion judging Peter and John of Zebedee (Acts iv. 6), hearing and witnessing testimonies, examining and approving written dispositions (μαρτυρογράφια), until he could not write any more without using this public notary's legalistic phraseology?

Nor can anybody say that this idiom occurs only in the appendix, ch. xxi, which may have been added to the original book by the hypothetical 'editor'.

There is the testimony of the beloved disciple, who saw the soldier's spear-thrust and the blood and water coming out of the side of the crucified Jesus, again super-witnessed by John in xix. 35:

'And he that saw (it) bare record (ὁ ἑωρακὼς μεμαρτύρηκεν) and true is his testimony (καὶ ἀληθινὴ αὐτοῦ ἐστιν ἡ μαρτυρία) and that one (καὶ ἐκεῖνος) knows that it is true.'

The correct explanation of this much discussed line has been given by Dr. Charles Cutler Torrey, Professor of Semitic Languages in Yale, who says in the notes to his new translation of the Four Gospels:

'It seems to me quite certain that in the mysterious ἐκεῖνος of this verse we are to see the personal testimony of the author of the Gospel. It is quite idiomatic, and there is no other way of explaining it. When, either through modesty or for some other reason, there is a wish to avoid the use of 'I,' the circumlocution *hahu gabra*, "that man", "that one", "a certain person", is used in Jewish Aramaic not infrequently. Margolis, *Gramm. of the Babyl. Talmud*, p. 70, speaks of the use of this phrase "in a mysterious sense", and gives examples. Dalman, *Gramm.*, 2nd ed., p. 108, mentions it as a feature of "the Galilean popular speech"; and in his *Worte Jesu*, pp. 204 f., he gives a rather long list of illustrative passages. Thus "*that one* must go and find out about himself" (i.e. *I* must go), Dalman, *Dialektproben*, 18, line 9. "Did not *that woman* (*hahi 'ittətha*) do right to commit adultery and bring you into the world?" (i.e. "did not *I* do right?), *ibid.*, lines 12 f. Similarly in Arabic, the pronoun *hadha*, "this" (with no noun appended) is used occasionally as a modest substitute for the first person singular. *G'bar* in the indefinite sense, "person", is ordinarily rendered in the Gospels (as Heb. *'ish* is rendered in the LXX) by τις, and it is plain that the Aramaean phrase in this passage could only have been rendered by ἐκεῖνος.'

The author of the Gospel here represents himself as holder of the tradition, not of John the son of Zebedee, as Professor Torrey says, misled by the current prejudice, but of the beloved disciple, Lazarus of Bethany.

XLII

JOHN THE EVANGELIST—AN EYEWITNESS OF THE ARREST OF JESUS. 'THE HIGH-PRIESTS' PRESENT AT THE CRUCIFIXION

THE ONLY REMAINING question how John could know that the beloved disciple's witness was true, is fully answered by the perfectly plausible explanation given by a number of Church Fathers for a most touching and most striking incident, which happened at the end of the dramatic nocturnal scene in the garden of Gethsemane. The only evangelist to report it is Mark xiv. 50, 52:

'And they all forsook him and fled. But (καί, the *vav adversativum* of the Aramaean source!) a certain little lad (νεανίσκος τις) wanted to follow him (συνηκολούθει, the *imperfectum de conatu!*) who had (only) a linen wrap cast about his naked body, and they laid hold of him, but he left the linen wrap (in their hands) and fled naked from them.'

'The incident', says Professor Erich Klostermann, in the most recent commentary to Mark, 'is enigmatic'. But it was by no means enigmatic to the ancient Church, which knew full well who the 'little lad' was.

He was certainly not the Evangelist Mark, as two anonymous ancient commentators guessed—demonstrably misunderstanding their source!—and as Theodor Zahn and Francis C. Burkitt used to teach in our days. This explanation is wholly excluded now that we know, from Fortunatian's prologue to Mark, i.e. from Marcion (above, p. 11), that the Second Gospel is the work of one Mark with the nickname 'Stump-fingers', the dragoman of Peter, writing in Italy, and not of the Jerusalemite John Mark, the acolyte of Paul.

Leaving aside these two visibly confused and worthless anonymous commentators, there remains the concordant testimony of St. Ambrose of Milan (*c.* 390), St. Epiphanius of Salamis (*c.* 400), and Peter Chrysologus of Ravenna (*c.* 450),

JOHN THE EVANGELIST—AN EYEWITNESS TOO

all of whom take it as a well-known fact that the little lad in the linen wrap was the Evangelist John.

As we should expect it from commentators of the fourth and fifth century they all naïvely combine this invaluable little bit of information with the current opinion—universally believed since the second century—that the Evangelist John was no other than the Beloved Disciple of the Last Supper.

One anonymous Greek writer only has clearly noticed the absolute incompatibility of the two equations: The Fourth Evangelist, he says, cannot have been both the elusive little lad of Mark xiv. 50 f. and the Beloved Disciple of John's Gospel: 'for John himself says that he (the Beloved Disciple) went with Peter into the palace of the high-priest. But if he was John, it is not probable that he went there merely in a linen wrap, but otherwise naked. That would hardly have been consistent with his dignity'.

This argument is conclusive: he who fled away naked leaving his only garment in the hands of his pursuers and the man of some consequence who obtained entrance into the high-priest's house because he was one of his 'familiars', while Peter had to wait in the courtyard, cannot have been one and the same person.

But the correct conclusion is not—as the anonymous Greek annotator thought—that the Beloved Disciple was John and the elusive little lad 'somebody from among the crowd, whom they tried to catch as if he belonged to the Lord's following and who escaped, leaving his wrap'. Quite on the contrary, the tradition that the young fugitive was John the Evangelist in his earliest youth is correct. Its incompatibility with John xviii. 15 proves only what we have already deduced from John xxi. 23 f., from the Papian quotation in the anti-Marcionite prologue (above, p. 156) and from John xi. 3: to wit, that the Beloved Disciple who went into the high-priest's house was not John the Evangelist, but the high-priest's 'familiar' or kinsman—Lazarus of Bethany.

The legitimate question, where the Fathers of the fourth and fifth century could find a tradition which corresponds as perfectly with our inevitable deduction from the statement of Papias quoted in the anti-Marcionite preface, as it is incom-

Sti. Ambrosii Enarratio in Ps. 36	Sti. Ambrosii Offic. II, 20, 101	Hieronymus in Jov. I 26	Tractatus Hilarii episcopi in Johannem (above, p. 47)
...Novit Scriptura adolescentem Paulum ... novit et Joannem adolescentem, qui in Christi pectore recumbentem, qui tam fortis fuit, ut persecutionem non timeret, malum vinceret. *Hic est puer qui patrem genitalem reliquit*, secutus Patrem eum quem cognovit aeternum; *adolescens amictus sindone Dominum sequebatur tempore passionis; qui sua omnia dereliquerat* (cp. Math. xix. 20 f. above, p. 192); maturior, Deum verbum in principio ipso semper fuisse atque esse cognovit et manere in se probavit.	Nam *adulescentem legimus in evangelio Johannem et sua voce*, licet meritis et sapientia nulli seniorum secundus.	Joannes unus ex discipulis (= Canon Muratori!) qui minimus traditur fuisse inter apostolos ... ut autem sciamus Joannem tunc fuisse puerum manifestissime docent ecclesiasticae historiae.	Joannes ... evangelista inter omnes apostolos iunior fuit. *Hunc*, cum disquirerent apostoli quis nam eorum maior esset, *tenuit Dominus* dicens: quicumque non conversus fuit sicut puer hic ... *Ipse est qui super pectus Domini recumbebat. Ipse est quem prae ceteris diligebat Jesus*, etc.

patible with the conventional identification of the fourth evangelist and the Beloved Disciple, is easily answered by a comparison of the crucial passage in St. Ambrose with that other one quoted above, p. 47, with the analogous statement of St. Jerome and with the parallel lines found in Ps.-Hilarius Africanus (see opposite page).

Nobody who is moderately familiar with the literary form of the bio-bibliographical notices dealt with in our ch. II can overlook for one moment that both St. Ambrose and the African Ps.-Hilary are entirely dependent on such a preface or several such prefaces. The recurrent *'hic est puer'*, 'this is the boy who left the father who sired him to follow Him whom he recognized as his eternal Father', 'this is he whom the Lord held in his arm when . . . etc.,' 'this is he whom the Lord loved more than the others . . . etc.,' is the typical feature of the bio-bibliographical note intended to distinguish a certain author from other *homonymous* persons by giving the essential dates of his biography which are needed for locating the man in time and space and in the chain of masters and disciples (above, p. 147 f.). Exactly the same sort of sentences occur e.g. in the Monarchianist prologue to the Fourth Gospel beginning with: '*Hic est Johannes evangelista unus ex discipulis dei, qui virgo electus a deo est . . . . Et hic est Johannes qui sciens supervenisse diem recessus sui. . . . .* "This is John the evangelist, one of the disciples of God, who has been chosen by God as a virgin' . . . . 'And this is John who knowing that the day of his withdrawal had come' . . . etc.

Considering the fact that St. Ambrose professes (above, p. 50) to have read in a gospel—in the record of St. John's 'own voice', albeit obviously not in our Fourth Gospel, but probably in our Matthew, believed to have been translated into Greek by the Fourth Evangelist—that St. John was a mere youth (*adolescens*); considering further, that a Greek preface quoted by Ps.-Hilarius Africanus identifies St. John with the child mentioned in Mark ix. 36, Matt. xviii. 2, and Luke ix. 48, it seems legitimate to suppose that all three above-quoted witnesses are simply alluding to an old Greek preface to John—possibly the selfsame preface which Ps.-Hilarius quotes (not necessarily *in extenso*)— which said of St. John, '*ipse est adolescens qui sequebatur dominum amictus sindone super nudo'*—οὗτός ἐστι ὁ νεανίσκος ὃς συνηκολούθει τῷ 'Ιησοῦ περιβεβλημένος σινδόνα ἐπὶ γυμνοῦ.

If such a statement was made 'without any justification' being adduced from any text—and that is exactly what modern critics have always objected to!—and if it was, nevertheless, widely believed, the only conceivable explanation is that it was contained in the original preface to the Fourth Gospel and that the two identifications quoted by Ps.-Hilary and the above-named Church Fathers represent nothing more nor less than the claims of the Fourth Evangelist himself.

Just as there is every reason to believe that the Gospel of Luke was published with all the regular paraphernalia of a Greek book of this period—dedication to the publisher and publisher's note introducing the author to the reader, surviving in the Bodleian Codex, Misc. Gr. 141—even so it is most probable that the Gospel of John was published with a proper dedication (above, p. 170 f.) and with a preface telling the reader who this John was and what were his credentials.

It is in this original preface—replaced by the various extant prologues to John, for reasons fully discussed in the preceding pages—that we should expect to find the source of all those in themselves consistent statements, which are so glaringly and irreconcilably incompatible with the later belief in the identity of John the Evangelist and John the son of Zebedee. It is this original preface which must have stated that John had been a high-priest, who had once worn the golden diadem on his forehead, that he had been the boy whom Jesus held in his arm while rebuking His ambitious disciples, and that he had been the lad trying to follow Jesus when all His followers had cowardly abandoned Him, the boy who left his linen wrap in the hands of those who arrested Jesus and managed a narrow escape.

If John the Evangelist was, as we have tried to show, the son of the high-priest Annas, then this explanation of Mark xiv. 51 f. has every claim to be accepted as true. *He* does not know what a precocious Jewish boy is like, who believes that Annas's son John—a lad of five, maybe of six or seven years in A.D. 22, destined to be himself a high-priest in A.D. 37—was sound asleep in the Passover night, when the Roman cohort and the high-priest's servants went out to the Mount of Olives to arrest the King, his King whom, but a few days before, 'the children in the temple' (Matt. xxi. 15), 'the flower-buds of the priesthood' (*pirḥêj kehunah*), John's elder cousins and comrades, the noble pages of the sanctuary, had hailed as the 'son of David'!

Since the costume described by Mark xiv. 51 is obviously that of a boy directly escaped from his bed, it is clear that the laddie is the child duly put to bed after the Passover meal in the high-priest's palace, the little boy who had managed to elude the vigilance of parents and servants, to follow 'the men of the high-priest' when they joined with their torches and staves the Roman soldiers, marching out to apprehend the beloved Master, the King of Israel, Him who had held this very little lad fondly in His arm, while He rebuked the sullen fellows around Him, quarrelling about precedence—the brave and agile little fellow, who left his night-wrap in the hands of those who tried to catch him, and who ran home, naked as the other little street arabs, to slip into the door of his father's house before the guard marched in with the royal prisoner.

We must imagine him being about the way when Jesus was brought to his father (John xviii. 13), and when the beloved disciple, known to Annas, came with Him 'into the palace of the high-priest'; wedging his way with the officers guarding Jesus into the room where Annas questioned the prisoner and where the captive King was struck by one of the officers, adding insult to injury.

The curious correspondence between Mark xiv. 51 and the prophecy of Amos ii. 16, 'he that is courageous among the mighty, shall flee away naked in that day, saith the Lord', is well known to ancient and modern commentators. But it is not sound method to suppose that any writer could or would have invented such an anecdotal feature to suit a certain prophecy— why this one rather than countless others?—if it is so much simpler to admit that the incident was recorded, *inter alia*, because it seemed to fit so marvellously a line in the prophets, which 'the witness who wrote this', steeped in Old Testament lore, remembered when he heard of this touching little exploit of the child 'that was courageous among the mighty'.

It is not Peter who would have observed and remembered an incident which happened while he ran for his life. It is not Peter who told this unforgettable detail to Mark. Nor can Mark 'Stump-fingers', writing in Italy, have heard it from old John in far away Ephesus, from John who did not like the limelight to be turned upon his own person in this connexion, from old John who did not even mention in his own Gospel the fact that Jesus had once put his arm around his shoulders. But Mark and Matthew and Luke could find both incidents concerning the young son of Annas in the book of Lazarus, the eyewitness who would be sure to know and to be interested in anything concerning the son of the high-priest Annas with whom he was 'familiar'.

If the Fourth Evangelist was, as we have tried to show, the 'John of the high-priests' kin' mentioned in Acts iv. 6, i.e. the John, son of Annas, mentioned in Flavius Josephus' *Jewish War*, then he may have been, more likely than not, an eye-witness, not only of the arrest, but equally so of the execution of the Messianic King of the Jews.

According to Mark xv. 31; Matt. xxvii, 41, 'the high-priests' were actually present at the Crucifixion.

Now there is on record a curious reminiscence of Rabbi 'Ele'azar, son of Ṣadoḳ, the elder, who saw, riding on his father's shoulders, the execution of the unfortunate daughter of a priest, burnt alive by order of the Sanhedrin for having had an illegitimate love-affair in the years of the great famine under Claudius and Herod Agrippa I. It proves that in those, as in much later times—indeed, until far into the 19th century—children were taken to see executions in order to be impressed at an early age by the terrible fate overtaking the evildoer. In view of this rabbinic testimony, nothing could be more likely than that the boy John was taken to Golgotha by his father, Annas I, to see the tragic end of the Messiah, 'who saved others, but could not save himself', the Redeemer of Israel in whom the child had believed with all the enthusiasm of his age, and whom he had followed about until his father's men got hold again of the runaway.

If he was present at the Crucifixion, he must have seen 'Ele'azar, the beloved disciple, who was 'known to the high-priest', standing near the cross and talking to the dying Naṣōrean, King of the Jews.

If the hoary old venerable exile in Ephesus could recognize in the 'scriptures' brought to him by Marcion but a few essential features tallying with the indelible impressions of those fatal days standing out among the dim recollections of his childhood, he could not fail to be deeply impressed, to accept all of them as genuine and gladly to testify to the truth of the witness of Jesus' beloved disciple—Lazarus of Bethany.

XLIII

THE FOURTH EVANGELIST IDENTIFIED

SO THIS IS, finally, the simple and straightforward solution of the Johannine problem, believed and proclaimed to be insoluble for more than a century by four generations of critics, unwilling or unable to undertake the laborious work of collecting, comparing, and analysing the mass of conflicting evidence available in the various prologues prefixed to the numerous extant manuscripts of our canonical Gospels.

It claims nothing more and nothing less than to account for the observable data: σώζειν τὰ φαινόμενα. It is not only a simple, but an extremely conservative solution, since it explains the subscription of the Gospel John xxi. 24, and the initial verse of the dedicatory Epistle, 1 John i. 1—the proud claims of an eyewitness writing about the Messiah, whom he has seen, heard, and touched with his own hands—without resorting to the strained, insincere, and sophistic explanations of the alleged 'collective we', supposed to have been used by the writer of John's First Epistle, or to the accusation of deliberate fraud against an author whose work has been a source of religious inspiration and aesthetic delight for generations of readers from the 2nd to the 20th century.

Hitherto, no one who perceived the impossibility of crediting the Fourth Gospel to John the son of Zebedee, nobody who felt inclined to attribute its authorship to the John known as 'the Elder' could avoid imputing an ample measure of pious fraud or—to use a more respectable term—of 'pseudepigraphic fiction' to the Ephesian presbyter, supposed to masquerade as the beloved disciple, whose head had rested against the shoulder of Jesus, who had stood in the shadow of the cross and looked down into the Master's empty tomb.

Besides, there was nowhere in the whole realm of history a more elusive ghost than this 'Elder John'—as long as he was but a name, a mere *flatus vocis* of Papias the Hierapolitan, echoed with doubt and hesitation by Dionysius of Alexandria, Eusebius of Caesarea, and all those who read and repeated their biased discussions.

Nothing more was needed in order to pour the blood of life into this empty shadow than the easy sacrifice of discarding an age-old prejudice—a false tradition, degenerated into an inveterate superstition without any foundation whatsoever in the text of any Johannine writing—nothing else but the cutting asunder of two perfectly different personalities, arbitrarily confused by readers blinded by their ignorance of Jewish history and a pardonable desire to exalt the glory of a local patron-saint: John, the former high-priest, the martyr buried in Ephesus, the author responsible for the Fourth Gospel, he who says 'we know' in John xxi. 24, and the beloved disciple—Lazarus of Bethany, he 'who testifieth of these things and wrote these things' into a book of his own, which was brought to John by Marcion of Sinope.

The intangible, empty shade of this John, entombed for centuries on end, not only in the inaccessible darkness of his grave, but under a mound of obsolete and useless books, has come to life again: 'very dry bones', long ago returned to the dust, have 'come together, bone to his bone, the sinews and the flesh have come upon them, the breath came into them from the four winds and they lived and stood upon their feet.'

We know more now of this John, the Fourth Evangelist, than of all the other three Evangelists together, and of St. Peter to boot.

Born as the son of Annas ben Sethi, the Sadducean, Boethusian high-priest of the years A.D. 6–15, probably in the last year of his father's reign over the priestly aristocracy of Jerusalem, one of five brothers, all of whom succeeded their father as acting high-priests in due time, the child heard, saw, and finally touched with his hands Jesus the Naṣōrean in the few days when He taught in the precincts of the Temple of Jerusalem 'as one in power', having been proclaimed as the Davidic King of Israel. The boy believed that this was the God-sent liberator, King of Israel, followed Him about and heard Him foretell how He would be handed over to his enemies and suffer death at their hands, but come back in glory, speedily, on the clouds of heaven to judge the quick and the dead and to reign over a pacified and splendidly renewed world for ever after.

The fairy-tale of the marvellous vine with its myriads of grapes, each berry holding barrels of sweet must, of the cornstalks growing heaven-high and raining down tons of flour on a blessed land flowing with milk and honey, which Papias heard repeated by old John as an authentic saying of Jesus, is just the kind of story which the kindest and wisest of teachers would tell to a child of seven asking what the Messianic Kingdom of God and the renewed earth would be like. The boy saw Jesus arrested and mishandled—as He had foretold that He would be. In all probability he saw Him crucified.

Having seen all His disciples desert Him in the fatal hour, when He had to drink the cup of suffering to the dregs, he had no reason to seek their company and to be taught by their ignorance what he had heard from the great Master and what he could read himself in the Scriptures which had been His only inspiration.

So he grew up, waiting for the King of Glory, the Prince of Peace to return at last, to 'restore again the kingdom of Israel' and to burn with the fiery breath of His mouth the insolent Roman oppressors of His nation, searching the Scriptures for more and more enlightenment about the future, discussing them with the other priests and nobles who had come to believe in Jesus, in spite of, nay because of, the ignominious end which the Servant of the Lord, the Lamb of God praised by Isaiah, had suffered. Having studied rabbinic lore and the wisdom of the Greek according to the traditions of his Boethusian family, he became in due time an assessor of the law court, known to the rabbis as 'the sons of the high-priests'. He sat in judgement on Peter and John the Zebedaid, casting his vote according to the opinion of Gamaliel, always anxiously waiting for the Kingdom to come.

In A.D. 37, Joḥanan, better known to the Hellenized Romanophile Jews under his Greek name Theophilos, was chosen by the Roman governor Vitellius to act as a high-priest. Four times he was allowed to enter the awe-inspiring innermost sanctuary of the God of Israel and to pray in the empty room harbouring the invisible presence of Ezekiel's *cherubim* and Isaiah's *seraphim* for his sinning nation on the Great Day of Atonement.

Deposed in A.D. 41 by Herod Agrippa I, he bided his time until the revolution of A.D. 66 brought to him—known to the Zealot party as a sympathizer with the Messianist revolutionaries—the command over one of the five armies occupying the provinces of Gophnitis and Acrabatene. He experienced the bitterness of defeat, tragic disenchantment, surrender to the Romans, who treated the high-priestly family fairly and even generously, and finally ate the bitter bread of exile in Ephesus for many a long and weary year. Disabused of all his youthful illusions about the possibility of armed resistance against the rulers of this world, he was now ready to enter into communion with the quietist, Paulinist believers, anxiously waiting for the Second Coming of the Christ, but willing to keep the *Pax Romana* for the short time that this condemned world of perdition could and would last. The old law, which he had helped to lay down and to interpret all his life, seemed but an empty shell now that the Temple in which he had officiated was burnt down, and the altar upon which he had sacrificed had been trampled by the heavy hobnailed shoes of the Roman legionaries. God had most evidently turned away from His chosen people, who had desecrated His holy city with unspeakable horrors even before the pagan army had sacked and burnt it.

He saw now that a new Israel of God had to be raised, reborn from above in the water of the saving baptism, which his older namesake, the martyr Johanan the Cleanser, had urged upon Jews and Gentiles alike. From all the nations of the earth the chosen ones would flock together to the banquet of Abraham. Nothing mattered any more but 'to love each other' and to wait for the promised Second Coming of the Redeemer.

His former high rank, the remains of previous wealth, an imposing personality, and the glory surrounding the last survivor of the generation who had heard, seen, and lovingly touched the Master, gave him a commanding position, not only in Ephesus. His fame spread over Asia Minor, a man like Papias in distant Hierapolis would question the wayfarers, what old John had said about the Christ when they heard him speak in the assembly of the Christians in Ephesus. Finally, he would go himself on a pilgrimage to see and hear the great old man while he was still alive.

St. Paul's follower, Luke the healer, would respectfully dedicate the two volumes of his Gospel and of the Acts to him, the 'high and mighty Theophilus'—this being the modest nucleus of truth at the bottom of the fantastic story told in Ps.-Polycrates' 'Acts of Timothy', that the three Evangelists came to John in Ephesus in order to submit their own notes, for him to arrange and to edit them 'under their own names'.

Finally, as a centenarian, he had the visit of a most impressive and most persuasive personality, the owner of a merchantman which had landed in the port of Ephesus, a very learned and serious young man, a trader from the shore of the Black Sea, who brought him 'scriptures' of arresting interest, among them the reminiscences of a man, well-known to John's family and to himself, Lazarus of Bethany, whom he had seen in those far distant unforgettable days.

This visitor, himself an ardent Paulinist, an ingenious student and critic of the law, to whom the old man liked to listen, kept on urging him to write a new evangel, a better and more enlightened one than the dull and more or less untaught disciples of Jesus—those who had betrayed Him and His ideas from start to finish—had so far been able to produce. The long resistance of the weary and modest old man, who did not feel able to do what he was asked to undertake, was finally overcome by the insistence, not of John's 'condisciples'—of whom he had never had any, nor of the 'bishops of Asia'—who had no need for a new gospel different from the three or more which they knew, but of Marcion, that powerful propagandist, who was to attract in the years to come such a host of converts to his doctrine all around the Mediterranean world.

Marcion's offer to act as the old man's secretary decided John, at last, to select what seemed acceptable from the scriptures brought by the Pontic merchant adventurer, to dictate a new pneumatic and logosophic Gospel such as would satisfy the aspirations of his strangely persuasive collaborator and to publish it under his own name and authority.

It is evident that he did not realize, before it was too late, how much and how subtly his thoughts and his words had been

HENRY BARCLAY SWETE, D.D.
(1835–1917)

PLATE XX

THE FOURTH EVANGELIST IDENTIFIED

influenced by his apparently most humble and obedient scribe. The storm, which the first edition must have aroused among the Jewish Christian members of the Ephesian and the other Asiatic Churches, broke the spell which the Pontic visitor had thrown upon an old man endowed with that kind of open and generous mind which is always liable to be swayed by the power of a stronger personality. The too efficient, too officious 'secretary' had to be dismissed now that his 'contrary views' had become manifest to John, who had to sit down and to revise as best he could the book that had gone out 'to the Parthians' and 'to the elect Lady' in Jerusalem, the Evangel which many a Diotrephēs in many a town had refused to accept, although it came under such an illustrious author's name.

But the quarrels with those Diotrepheis, in which John had been involved by his publication, were not the worst consequences of this belated enterprise of a centenarian's last days. In those terrible years, A.D. 115–117, when the Jews of North Africa, Cyprus, Lycia, and Mesopotamia had again risen in a desperate revolt against the Roman Empire, a former high-priest of Jerusalem, a former commander of a Jewish rebel army, spared and generously pardoned by Vespasian and Titus, had dared to address a book of his to those among the Parthians and to those in Jerusalem who waited for the King of the Jews, crucified under Tiberius, to come back from heaven and to set aflame, with the fiery breath of his mouth, the imperial city on the Seven Hills!

As soon as this became known to the vigilant *speculatores* of the government, the evident quietist, Paulinist character of his Evangel would be of little avail to an advocate defending John against the inevitable charge of high treason. Little would it help the accused of lèse-majesty to repudiate as a forgery the record of the apocalyptic visions and epistles which the Gnostic Cerinthus had circulated under his name and under that of his Palestinian namesake, the son of Zebedee. All those terrible anti-Roman ravings against the Beast rising from the Bottomless Abyss and the drunken Whore sitting on the Seven Hills would now unavoidably be laid to his door. Nothing could save him from a martyr's death. Probably at the end of the last year of Trajan, or in the beginning of the first of Hadrian, he had to drink the poison cup, which ended his long life of waiting and longing for the return of the Master to whom he had owned allegiance as a child, nearly a century ago.

Already, during the last years, especially since he had issued his Evangel, he had grown into a legendary figure. Those who did not read the new Gospel in a critical and carping spirit, questioning and censoring the orthodoxy of its theology and Christology, but with all the enthusiasm for the Redeemer and His God of Light and Love and Truth, which it was meant to arouse, very soon confused him who wrote or dictated the Evangel with the beloved disciple, whose writings John had quoted and approved. Of John too they believed that he would not die until the Second Coming. Even after he had drunk the hemlock-cup and been buried in his rock tomb, they were confident that the poison could not have harmed the saintly old man; that he was not dead, but had merely gone to sleep underground, and could still hear the prayers spoken by his humble brethren, breaking bread and blessing the loving-cup of remembrance before the entrance to his resting-place.

In the meantime, the errant skipper and spiritual adventurer who had tried to use the old man as a mouthpiece for his new radical Ultra-Paulinism was very much alive. Excommunicated by the Church of Ephesus, deprived of the possibility of using the gospel of John, which had been republished in a revised form and with a preface repudiating Marcion, he had lifted his anchor and set sail for the port of Ostia to conquer the Church by invading the capital of the world—this time with a gospel which he had patiently carved out of the Evangel of Luke. The strange fanatic who had been accused, rightly or wrongly, of having falsified the Gospel of John by interpolating words suggesting his own perverse views into the genuine text dictated by the Ephesian Evangelist, turned round now and pointed the same accusation with the fiercest, almost monomaniacal determination against his adversaries: not he, Marcion, had falsified the Gospel of John, but they—irredeemable Jews and Judaisers, sons of Satan—had falsified all four Gospels, perverting the true message of Jesus, which was known to none but Paul and to Paul's only true disciple, Marcion.

John, whom Marcion had tried to use as a mere tool, had

THE FOURTH EVANGELIST IDENTIFIED

lived long enough to turn against him and to thwart his carefully laid plans. Having failed in his attempt permanently to seduce the last living disciple of Jesus, the Pontic dreamer and schemer decided to pirate and to force into his service the Gospel of Luke, dedicated to 'mightiest Theophilus', and the Epistles of Paul—two Apostles who were dead and safely buried and thus unable to protest against the arbitrary proceedings of this fantastic patron-saint of the wildest 19th-century 'Higher Criticism'.

It is outside the scope of this book to follow Marcion's further career; to describe his second defeat in Rome, his subsequent sweeping conquest of a large portion of all the Christian communities around the Mediterranean and the powerful reaction of the Catholic Church against this invasion.

There is another task which confronts us, now that we have, at last, found out by whom, when, and where the Fourth Gospel was dictated, and by whom it was written. Our readers will now ask to be told all that can be known about the mysterious 'scriptures' which Marcion brought to John and which the anti-Marcionite preface to the Fourth Gospel would hardly have mentioned, unless it was common knowledge that they had been used by John as sources for his account of all those sayings and doings of Jesus which he himself could neither have heard nor seen. This is, indeed, a legitimate demand. There is a full and complete answer to it. But it is a long story, and will have to be told in another volume.

BIBLIOGRAPHY

THE ROMAN CATHOLIC view on the Johannine Problem may be studied in the Jesuit Father Donovan's book *The Authorship of St. John's Gospel* (1936).

The various opinions of Protestant scholars are conveniently summarized in:

Benjamin Wisner Bacon, *The Fourth Gospel in Research and Debate*, 2nd ed., New Haven, 1918, and in Wilbert Francis Howard, *The Fourth Gospel in Recent Criticism and Interpretation*, 2nd ed., London, 1935. The quotation on our p. 3 will be found on p. 234. The historical survey of 20th-century English, German and French literature pp. 33–84, and the bibliography pp. 272–282 do not mention the following items which the reader of this book might want to look up.

Dom Donatien de Bruyne—

Quelques documents nouveaux pour l'histoire du texte africain des Évangiles, Revue Bénédictine, XXVII, 1910, pp. 273–324, 433–446.

Les préfaces de la Bible Latine, Namur, Auguste Godenne, 1920. (A priceless, monumental work, $\kappa\tau\hat{\eta}\mu\alpha$ ϵis $\dot{\alpha}\epsilon \acute{\iota}$, 266 pp. in f° published anonymously and nowhere reviewed to this day, as far as I know.)

Les plus anciens prologues latins des Évangiles, Revue Bénédictine, 1928, pp. 193–214.

A. v. Harnack, *Die ältesten Evangelienprologe und die Bildung des Neuen Testaments*, Sitz.-Ber. d. preuss. Akad. d. Wiss., phil. hist. Kl, 1928, XXIV, pp. 323–241.

An admittedly incomplete collection and edition of extant Greek gospel-prefaces is offered in v. Soden's *Die Schriften des Neuen Testaments*, vol. I, Berlin, 1902, pp. 294–340.

The titles of Bretschneider's, Delff's, Turmel's and Kreyenbühl's books are given in connexion with their portraits.

BIBLIOGRAPHY

Readers who do not want to wait for the following volumes on the sources of the Fourth Evangelist *The Gospel of Lazarus* and *The Evangel of the Paraclete* and who do not want to turn to the author's German book mentioned in the Preface, p. x, will find a little series of articles 'The Paraclete Problem,' 'The Paraclete Claimant: Simon Magus' and 'The Evangel of Kerinthos,' 'The Book of Lazarus—the Beloved Disciple' in the Quarterly Review *The Quest*, vol. XXI, January, April and July 1930. They are, of course, in parts antiquated and superseded by subsequent research. So are the chapters on the anti-Marcionite prologue to the Fourth Gospel in the author's *Das Rätsel des Vierten Evangeliums*, Zürich, 1936, pp. 325–350, and his French article 'La ponctuation du Prologue Antimarcionite à l'Évangile selon Jean, *Revue de Philologie*, LVI, October 1930, pp. 350–371.

DIES DIEM DOCET

ANALYTIC INDEX

I.—AUTHORITIES

A.—Ancient

'Abdias' (Catholic Lat. version of 'Acts of John') 71
Agobard of Lyons 69
Alcuin, letter to Charlemagne on punctuation 155
Ambrose, St., of Milan 50, 51, 87, 196, 198 f.
Ambrosiastēr 81
Ammonius, Presbyter 52
Amphilochius of Iconium 108
Andrew St., of Caesarea, on Papias and Apocalypse 66, 138
Antonius Martyr 137
Aphraates the Syrian 64
Apollonius, anti-Montantist 96
Apringius of Paca (= Beja) 90, 91, 105
Arnobius, apologist 119
Augustine, St., on St. John in Ephesus 116–120, 169

Bar Hebraya 108

Cassiodorus Senator 169
Chrysostomus, John 26, 108, 166
Clement of Alexandria 56, 57, 67, 104, 128, 135, 169
Cyprian, Pseudo- 64
Cyril of Jerusalem 108, 137

Diogenes of Laertē 148, 150
Dionysius of Alexandria 21, 27, 28, 35, 48, 51, 57, 107, 125, 126, 142, 169, 170, 205
Dionysius of Corinth 12
Dorotheus of Tyre (Ps.-) 98

Epiphanius of Cyprus, *Panarion* (Folder 1) 14, 27, 28, 47, 56, 58, 91, 94, 115, 153, 196
Eusebius of Caesarea 9, 13, 21, 27, 28, 36, 48, 51, 56, 74, 82, 85, 125, 137, 138, 146, 170, 205
rejects Apocalypse 108
on epistles of John 170
on Irenaeus 140, 142
on Papias 140, 142, 146, 150, 156

Fortunatianus Afer, *Breves* of 8, 9, 11, 13, 22, 23, 35, 59, 144, 145, 146, 153, 156, 158 f., 160 f., 196
rustic style of 9, 154, 155

Gaius, Presbyter of Rome 47, 54, 57, 92, 94, 107, 112, 153, 173
Georgios Hamartolos 64
Gregory of Nazianz 108
Gregory of Nyssa 68

Hegesippus, Christian traveller 173
Heracleon, Gnostic 67
Hilarius, Ps.-, Africanus 46, 48 f., 51, 198 f.
Hilary, St., of Poitiers 49
Hippolytus of Rome 14, 47, 48, 49, 51, 54, 66, 92, 93, 98, 107, 173
'Odes on all Scriptures' 55, 59, 65, 116
Pseudo- 52 f., 136

Instantius, Priscillianist 6, 90, 118
Irenaeus, St., anti-Marcion. prefaces known to 7, 23, 25, 34 f., 54, 59, 66, 81, 82, 92, 97, 139, 140, 143, 144, 150, 151, 156, 180
alleged confusion in 81
criticised by Eusebius 142
on *instrumentum Johanneum* 143
on Marcion 181
Ishodad, Syrian 26
Isidor of Sevilla 21, 63

Jerome, St. 9, 13, 21, 23, 28, 48, 51, 81, 135, 140, 146, 154, 160, 170, 198 f.
anecdote of old John 172
on apostolic secretaries 143
on the boy John 198
on epistles of John 170
preface *plures fuerunt* 105
to Hedibia 143
Josephus, Flavius 39, 44, 50, 73, 92, 95, 99, 100, 101, 114
Josephus Tiberiensis 39
Junilius 108

ANALYTIC INDEX

Library notes, ancient bio-bibliograph 4, 24
'Lucinian' prefaces 21, 23, 24, 59, 135, 144, 145, 146, 148, 150, 160

Martyrology 59 ff.
  Armenian 60
  of Carthago 60, 63, 64, 118
  of Gellone 62
  Syrian 60
Muratori's Canon 25, 104, 106, 187

Origen 21, 27, 28, 74, 93, 142, 170
  eunuch 57

Papias—
  of Hierapolis 13, 56, 65 ff., 104, 140, 142–145, 152, 188, 193, 197, 204, 207
  bishop 146
  discipulus Johannis *carus* 147
  Exēgētica 145 f., 148
    see *Exegetica* and corruptions, Index II
  hearer of John 139, 160, 164, 187
  on Apocalypse 138 ff., 144
  on First Epistle of John 171
  on Marcion 180
  on Marcion, secretary of John 178
  milleniarist 151
  pilgrimage to John 207 f.
  secretary of John? 149 ff., 152, 156, 159
  'unintelligent'? 141
  witness to Fourth Gospel restored 161
  writing under Trajan 189
Peter Chrysologus of Ravenna 196
Philastrius of Brescia 188
  folder 1, col. 1**
Polycrates of Ephesus 36 f., 43, 46, 52, 53, 54, 55, 56, 57, 59, 67, 104, 124, 173
Prefaces (*see* Prologues, Proems) to *Christian Reader* 4, 6
Proem, *see* Prefaces
'Pro-evangel,' Marcion's 13
Prologues, *see* Prefaces and Anti-Marcionite Preface Index II

Solomon of Basra 23
Sophronios, Patriarch 137
Suidas' Lexicon 4, 47, 166
Syrian superscription of Fourth Gospel MS. 24

Tertullian 14, 57, 69, 81, 104, 107, 115, 135, 186

B.—Modern

Bacon, B. W. 86 ff., 107
  on punctuation of preface to John 155
Bauer, Walter 154, 165
Bell, I. H xx, 96
Bernard, J. H., Archbishop 66
Bischof, Bernhard 157
Boll, Franz 108 f.
Bousset, Wilh. 91, 151, 154
Bretschneider, C. G. xvi, 1, 170, Pl. I
Bruyne de, Donatien Dom xvi, xviii, xx, 3, 6, 7, 11, 12, 13, 34, 144 f., 157, 159, 188
Bultmann, Rud. 2
Burkitt, F. C. 183, 196
Burney, C. F. 25, 34

Charles, R. H., Archdeacon 82, 99, 107, 110, 115, 128 f.
Clark, A. C. 130, 143
Cordier, Balthasar 150, 163
Corrodi, W. 184

Dalman, Gust H. 195
Delafosse, Henri = Turmel, Jos. xxi, 183
Delff, Hugo xvi, 37, Pl. VI, 53

Ebersolt, Jean 136
Evanson, Edward 3

Fleming, W. K. xii, xxi, 191, Pl. XX
Fries of Upsala 137
Fromann 170

Gheyn, van den xviii
Goldschmidt, A. xviii
Grill, Julius 165 f.
Grotius 169
Guericke 169

Harnack, Ad. v. xx, 1, 6, 7, 12, 13, 24, 34, 144, 151, 154
  on John xxi 24–188
  on Marcionism of the Fourth Gospel 178, 183
  on Papias 189
Haupt 170
Hausrath 170
Hilgenfeld 184
Hirsch, Emmanuel 87, 104
Hoffmann, Gerh. 173

Holtzmann 169
Howard, W. F. 3, 52, 65, 66, 67
Hug 170
Huldreich, J. J. 69

James, M. R. 29, 111, 168

Keil, Joseph 121, 127
Kenyon, Sir Frederic xx
Koehler, Wilh. xviii
Krauss, Samuel 69
Kreyenbühl, Joh. xxi, 190, Pl. XIX

Lake, Kirsopp 38
Lampakis xvii
Langlois, Ch.-V. 1
Loisy, Alfred 165

MacGiffert, A. G. 79
Mai, Angelo Cardinal 46
Margolis 195
Meyer, Eduard 165 f.
Mingana, Dr., Peshiṭṭhô Codex of 24, 64
Morin, Dom Germain xi, 46, 76, 158

Nestlé's N.T. ed. 87, 194
Neuburger, Alb. 122

Puech, Aimé 2

Ramsay, W. M., Sir 79
Reinach, Salomon 96
Reinach, Théodore 45

Renan, Ernest 2
Réville, Jean 2
Roberts, C. H. xx

Schmiedel, P. W. 165 f.
Schubart, O. W. xx
Schwartz, Eduard 73, 75, 78 ff., 84
Schweitzer, Albert 2, 165
Seignobos, Ch. 1
Soden, H. v. 79
Spitta, Friedr. 79
Stange, E. 173
Steiner, Rudolf 190
Swete, H. B. xxi, 53, 191 f.

Tawney, R. H. 186
Thackeray, H. St. J. 143
Thiersch, Heinr. Wilh. Jos. 170
Torrey, Ch. C. 195
Troeltsch, Ernst 186
Tübingen School 78
Turmel, Joseph xx, 183

Voelter, Daniel 137
Volkmar, Gustav 184

Weber, Max 186
Weiss, Johannes of Heidelberg 137
Weitzmann-Fiedler, Josepha xviii
Wellhausen, Julius 73, 79, 99
Wendland, W. xx
White, Henry Julian, and Wordsworth, John, Bishop 150

Zahn, Theod. 65, 67, 150, 196

II.—SUBJECTS AND PERSONS DISCUSSED

Acrabatēnē and Gophnitis 41, 43
John, Governor of
Acts of Apostles—
 a posthumous edition 80
 iv. 6 39, 43, 46, 50, 52, 202
 xii. 2 71, 72 ff., 88
 xix. 14 42
 shortened text 130
 transposition of leaves in 80
'Acts of John', see Leucian Acts and Marcionite Acts 133, 174
Acts of Paul—
 forged 107
 forger convicted before John 135
Acts of Peter 96
Adamantius, Marcionite 32, 171, 180
African text of Gospels 5
African prologues 11
African summaries 5

ἀγράφως ἐκήρυξαν 32
Agrippa I (Herod) xvii, 66, 69, 73, 77, 97, 100, 103, 106, 202
 death of 95
 = Beast from the Abyss 100
Ajasoluk = Ἅγιος θεολόγος = Ephesus 126, 127
Alexander of high-priests' kin 39 f.
Alogoi reject Fourth Gospel 76, 107, 153, 162, 173
Alogoi object to its omissions 176
 see Diotrephes
Ambrosian liturgy 63
Amos ii. 16—Mark xiv. 51 f. 201
anachronisms, alleged 145
Ἀνανίου Ἰωάννης = St. John Ev. 40 f., 42
ἀναστάναι Marcionite corr. for ἐγήγερται

ANALYTIC INDEX

Anaxagoras 26
Anaximenes of Lampsacus 21
Andrew, St. 26, 30
Andrew, Lukuas, Messiah 167, 180
  See Lukuas
Annas b. Sethi, high-priest 39, 42, 104, 105, 200, 202
Annas II 41
anonymous figures in literature 26 f.
Antichrist 88, 165
Antichrists, several 166 ff.
anti-Marcionite—
  apologists 132
  arguments 83
  prefaces xx, xxi, 7, 12 f., 14, Pls. III–V, Folders, 34, 77, 131, 144, 148 ff., 150, 152, 153, 188, 192, 211
  Greek original of 12, 146, 150
  corrected 154
  corrected by Patricius of Ravenna 157 f.
Antisemitism (Jewish) in Fourth Gospel 175 f., 179 f.
Apocalypse—
  of John 11, 14, 22, 23, 34, 57, 66, 98 ff., 131, 139, 140, 145, 173
  barbaric language of 109, 143
  millenarism of 138
  prefaces to 90, 188
  pseudepigraphic 103, 106, 128 f.
  rejected by Marcion 133
  source of Rev. xi. 1–13 99 ff.
  spurious 107
Apostles' Council 79, 85
Apostolic Constitutions 23
ἀρχιερεύς 37
—Ἐφέσιος 54
Aristion, Presbyter 189
Armillus, Antichrist 166
Arsinous, Marcionite psalms by 30
Artemion, Jewish revolutionary leader 167, 180
Ascension of two witnesses 97, 125, 134
Asiatic influences on Acts of John 115 ff.
Assumptio S. Joannis 62, 88, 97, 134
astral mysticism 109
Astydamas, Older and Younger 24
Athanasius 9
Atticus, Consular 174
Attis, emasculated 115, 119
Austrian excavations at Ephesus 120 ff., 125

Autograph—
  of Apocalypse 144
  of St. John's Gospel xix, Folder IV° left, 163
  Methodios'—of prologue to Luke 22 f.

'Babel' banishing John 94
Bandit-chief, John the 70
barbaric language of Apocalypse 109, 143
Bar Cochba, Messiah 166 ff.
barjonîm = bandits 71
Basilica, Ephesian of St. John xvii, 121 ff., Pls. VIII, IX, 126
'Beast from the Abyss' 100, 209
Beatus of Liébana xvii, 88, 90
Beheading of Zebedaids xvii
  see Zebedaid brothers
bellipotens Judaeorum Christus rejected by Marcion 177
Beloved Disciple of Jesus, see bosom-friend and see Eleazar s. o.
  Deinaeus and Lazarus xxi, 26, 28, 30 f., 37, 48, 53 f., 59, 67, 83, 134, 141, 190
  death of 164, 187 f.
  familiar to high-priest 48, 201
  = John 197, 199, 209
  = Lazarus 190 ff., 195, 205
  of John 147
    see Papias
  of noble family 48
  Rich Young Man xxi, 191
  survival of 134, 196 ff., 193, 210
  un-Jewish concept 147 ff.
  —disciples of Greek teachers 148
Bergamo, sacramentary of 103
Bezan Codex—
  Acts iv. 6 40, 130 f.
  Gal. i. 9 81
bibliotheke = complete collection of Scriptures 130
Bio-bibliographical library-notes 4, 47, 147 f.
  ancient 149 f.
blood-baptism 134
Bobbio, Missal of 62, 75, 76
Boethusians 205 f.
Book swallowed by John 88, 100
bosom-friend of Jesus 54, 55, 59
  see ἐπιστήθιος and Beloved Disciple
'botching' of shortened texts 131
brother's name used instead of father's? 73 f.

Caiaphas, high-priest 39, 42, 136
Callimachus 4, 24, 47, 147

Capharnaum, Christ drops from Heaven into synagogue of 133
Carmona, inscription of 60 f.
carus, discipulus, see Beloved Disciple and Papias 147 f.
castrate priests of Artemis 116
Catacombs, Ephesian xvii, Pl. IX, 121 ff., 125
Cerinthus, Gnostic 14, 54, 128 f., 132, 138, 150
   forger of Apocalypse 128, 209
   St. John meets — in Ephesus 128
Charlemagne, Alcuin's letter to 155
   of John's Gospel, *see* autograph xix
'children, little,' idiom of old John 172
—in the Temple 201
Christodulos, St., of Patmos 164
chronological difficulty 152
   order of Marc altered and criticised by John 176
Chronology of—
   Acts xii. 3 96
   Acts xiii. 51–xiv. 21 104
   of Crucifixion 85
   Herod Agrippa's 95
   of Paul's conversion 84
   Pauline 167
   of St. John 135, 152, 164
Churches of Asia, letters to Seven 92, 102, 104, 106, 111, 129, 133, 139, 174, 209
Claudius, Emperor 90, 91–93, 94, 96, 106, 142, 165
   letter of 96
Comicus, liber, of Silos 63
Commandment, new (Marcionite) 171 f.
Congratulations, world-wide in Rev. xi. 10 95 ff.
Constantinian rescript of A.D. 312 8
Crucifixion—
   date of 85, 152
   Lucan — — 167
   John present at crucifixion 202, 206
Ctesibius of Alexandria 122
Cumanus, Governor 40
Cuspius Fadus 92
Cyprianic text 6, 8
Cyprus, Jewish revol. in 167, 180, 209
Cyrene, Jewish revol. in 167

Davidides 168, 174
Demetrius recommended by John 194

deportatio in insulam 91
descripsit = ἀπέγραψεν = copied 161, Pl. XIV, 185
desert sojourn of Jesus omitted by John 176
Devil, father of the Jews 180
Dexter Numerianus 9
Diadem of high-priest worn by John 36, 200
διαστέλλειν, διαστολή = punctuation 141
dictated gospel 11 f., 149 ff.
dies imperii 95
Diocletian's *edictum libr. tradend.* 8
Diotrephēs, first of *Alogoi* 173, 209
Doceticism of Marcion 30, 57, 180
Domitian, Emperor 92, 97, 135, 140
Donatist heresy 118
Dositheus, gnostic 118, 174
dust from John's grave 117

earth breathing over St. John's tomb 116 f.
earthquake, Rev. xi. 13 99
Ebionites 14, 29, 150
ἐκκλησία μεγάλη in Ephesus 126
ecclesiasticae historiae 50
Ecclesius, Bishop of Ravenna 158, 162 f.
ἠγαπημένος 148
   see καλός 115
Egypt, Jewish revolutionaries in 167
Egyptianism, an, in Apoc. xii. 5 109
Egyptian Messiah 166
ἐκδιδόναι, διδόναι = *edere, dare* 146
ἐκεῖνος in John xix. 35 = the author John 194 f.
Elder John 28, 106, 138, 139, 141, 144, 204
   and Papias 138 f., 141, 144, 150, 189
   writer of epistles 171
   idioms of 194
'Eleʻazar—
   s.o. Annas II 41
   s.o. Deinaeus 40, 202
   the beloved disciple, *see* Lazarus of Bethany
   Rabbi, son of Ṣadōq 202
elementa turbare, a crime 91
Elijah, prophet 87
   drought of 94, 101
   and Moses 89, 101
   redivivus 97, 98
Elisabeth, St., flight to desert 133

ANALYTIC INDEX

Encratites, sect 29, 111 f.
Enoch and Elijah 87
Ephesus—
  aqueducts of 122
    see Basilica of St. John in catacombs of 120 ff.
  council of 124
  ἐκκλησία μεγάλη of 126
  high-priest living at 42, 50
  hydraulic air-blast 122
  Metropolis of Asia 36
  rock-tomb of St. John in 126, Pl. IX
  sack of, A.D. 1090 163
  Seven Sleepers' tomb in 124
Epimenides, sleeper 135
ἐπιστήθιος, see bosom-friend
Epistle—
  Hebrews, to 37
  of John, 1st 31, 48, 125, 166, 169, 204
  addressed ad Parthos 169, 170 ff., 174
  covering letter to Gospel of John 170
  2nd and 3rd 144, 170 f., 194
  quoted by Polycarp 170
  2nd rectifies Gospel John xiii. 34 171
  1st, of Peter v. 1 188
epitomae of ancient books 130
ἐραστής and ἐρώμενος see καλός and ἠγαπημένος 115
Eratosthenes 47
ἔρως παιδαγωγικός 147
Essenes, misogyny of 112 f.
Ethiopic calendar 61
Eudoxos, beloved disciple of Theomedōn 148
'eunuch of the Christ' 115
Euripides' secretary 150
  the Younger 24
excavations, see Austrian exc.
Exegetica of Papias corr. *exoterica, exotorica* 146
expurgation of John's martyrdom 77
ἐξωτερικοὶ διάλογοι of Plutarch 146
—λόγοι of Aristotle 146
eye-witness of crucifixion 3
  see John, Evangelist 204
  see Lazarus and Beloved Disciple
  of arrest of Jesus, St. John 196 ff., 204, 206

famine 89, 97
  under Claudius 103, 202

fairy-tale of marvellous vine told by Jesus to John 206
fertility, marvellous—Messian age 138
'Foreign God' of Marcion 177
forger of 'Acts of Paul' convicted before John of Ephesus 107
Fortunatianus Afer, *Breves* of 8, 9, 11, 13, 22, 23, 35, 144, 145, 146, 153, 156, 158 f., 160 f., 196
  rustic style of 9, 154, 155
Fourth Gospel, authenticity denied 32
French MSS. of Vulgate Bible 159
fruges excantare, see magia, maleficium 91
full-stop in wrong place 160, 162

Gaius, Presbyt. of Rome 47, 54, 57, 92, 94, 107, 112, 153, 173
Galatians ii. 9 79 ff., 81 ff.
  Chronology of 84 f.
g'bar = τις idiom 195
gebhirah = Lady 171
ghost-writing 129
Gophnitis and Acrabatēnē, John commander of 41, 43, 46, 114, 207
Gospel, Ebionite—
  of John 51
  -harmony 48, 50
  of Hebrews 51
gospels 'falsified by evangelists' 153
  see Marcion
γράμματα = *scripta vel epistula* 162
  see letters of introduction 162

Hadrian, Emperor 168, 169, 209
hadha, hahu gabra = ἐκεῖνος, John xix. 35, idiom 195
Hedibia, on style of Peter 143
Herod—
  see Agrippa I 66, 69, 75, 77, 88, 95, 99, 106, 135, 202
  the Great 99
Heron of Alexandria 122
ἱερεύς, ἱερεῖς, see *kohanîm* 37
High-priests—
  see John, Annas, etc. 38
  see list of 39, 43 f.
  present at crucifixion 202
Hilarius Pseudo-Africanus 46, 48 f., 51, 198 f.
Hilary of Poitiers 49
Hrabanus Maurus 69

'illiterate', John Zeb. 32, 132, 133
infancy-gospels 133
instrumentum Johanneum 144

Isaac (= Hilarius) *see* Ambrosiaster 41
Ishmaʻel b. Phiabi, High-priest 43
  see Scaeva, Σκευᾶς
Isis and Horus 109
Isocrates 21

Jago, San, di Compostella 63
James, St., *see* Zebedee 30, 73
  beheaded 21, 62, 74, 76, 91, 135
  the Just subst. for St. James Zebedee 62, 67
Jameses two, confused? 81 ff.
Jerusalem, Pauline journeys to 78ff.
Jesus b. Gamaliel, High-priest 101
Jesus, son of Daianaiah, High-priest 41, 43
Jesus Naṣorean—
  king of Jews xx, 203, 205, 209
  body, human, of 183
  Protean body of 29 ff.
  saying on marvellous vine to boy John 139
  Sayings and Doings 211
  sojourn 'with animals' in desert omitted by John 176
Jesus b. Saphia 41
Jews—
  Egyptian—and Claudius 96
  names of 44
  slay SS. John and James 66
Jōḥanan, *see* John 39
Jōḥenis, Jōḥanan changed to 70
John Baptist—
  = Jōḥanan *ha-maṭbil* 207
  substituted for John the Zebedaid 60 f., 66
John the Essene 114
John the Evangelist—
  see Elder John, Presbyter John, Younger John, *Ἀνανίου Ἰωάννης*
  Acts iv. 6, in 39
  archbishop of Asia? 173
  = 'beloved disciple'? 197
  a boy 47 ff., 167, 196-200
  criticises Marc 142
  disciple of the Lord 2, 34 ff.
  in Ephesus 36 ff.
  eyewitness of arrest and crucifixion of Jesus 3, 196 ff., 204
  familiar to high-priest 48, 52, 137
  identified with John son of Zebedee 30, 57, 158
  in Josephus Flav. 40, 202
  not John Marc 196
  minimus apostolorum 50
  martyr 63, 205

John the Evangelist (*contd.*)—
  old age of 173
  poison cup, drinks 175
  saw and touched Jesus 185
  sitting as judge 194, cp. 107
  self-burial of 118, 174
  a 'virgin' 115
  see Virginity of
John the second, Bishop of Ephesus 23 f.
John Marc of Jerusalem 45, 136 f.
  not the Evangelist 196
John son of Zebedee—
  adopted by St. Mary 137
  beheaded 75
  see Zebedaids, Beheading of
John the 'Pillar' 27
John, a 'robber chief' 70 f.
Jōnathan (= *Theodotos*) High-priest 40, 43
Joseph Kabi, High-priest 43
Joshuʻa = Jesus 165 f.
Josippon 69
Judas Iscariot 27
Judas Thomas 27
Justin Martyr 184
Justinian, Emperor xvii, 120, 125, 126
  see Basilica of

Kalendae Jan. 95
καλός 115
  see ἐραστής and ἐρώμενος
Karos on island of Patmos 163
Katapausis, Mountain xix, 163
Keiroussis, Evangeliary of xviii, 185, Pl. xiii
Kephisophōn, Euripides' secretary 150
Kombabos, emasculated 115
kohanîm, see ἱερεύς 37
κύρια, *see* Lady and *gebhirah* 170, 171

lad (νεανίσκος) in night-wrap = John Evangelist 196 ff.
Lady, elect = Palestine 170 f.
Lamb of God 193, 206
latrones = λῃσταί, *pārišîm* 71
Law—
  Jewish 28, 29, 83
  Roman 91, 93
Lazarus xx, xxi
  the Beloved Disciple 190 ff., 193, 197
  book of 202
lemma historicum 105
Leningrad miniature of St. John, Pl. XIV, 185

ANALYTIC INDEX

Lèse-majesty 71, 93
Lessons for St. John's Day omitted 63, 75, 103
λῃστής, see bandit 71
letters of introduction 162
Leucian Acts of John 25, 29-35, 56, 57, 117 f., 125 f., 133, 168, 174
Library-notes, bio-bibliogr. 4, 24
Logia Kyriaka 64
'Love each other' saying of John 172, 207
God is 178
Lucinius of Baetica 9 f., 13, 21, 61
Luke—
  anti-Marcion. prologue to 77, 131, 144, 149
  dedicates book to John-Theophilus 208, 211
Luke's—
  authorship of Acts 143
  text curtailed by Marcion 211
Lukuas (= Lycian), Andreas, Pseudo-Messiah 166 f.
Maccabaean Zealots 176 f.
Lycia, Jewish revolution in 209

magia, crime 91
Manichaeans 29, 118
Marcion of Sinope xviii, xix, xx, 11 f., 29, 81, 132 f., 135, 145, 153, 175
  excommunicated 135, 210
  excommunicated by his father 162, 185
  on forged gospels 152
  rejects warrior-Messiah of Jews 177
  in Rome 185
  secretary of John Evangelist 150, 159, 161 f., 164, 170, 183 ff.
Marcion's *contraria* 161
— *inquieta curiositas* 186
Marcionism in Fourth Gospel 178-186
Marcionite—
  Acts of John 34, 51, 54, 55, 56, 58, 71, 111, 133, 208 ff.
  Bible 11
  heresy 13, 14, 31 f., 130, 153, 162, 184
  quotation of John xv. 10; xiii. 34 171
Marcius Turbo 166
Marcus, Marcionite heretic 171, 180
Mark, St. (*Colobodactylus*)—
  Marcionite preface to Gospel of 7, 11, 13, 144
  Gospel of, criticized by St. John 142

Mark, St. (*contd.*)
  Gospel of, written after Peter's death 161
  interpreter of Peter 142, 145
  xiv. 51 f., ref. to John Ev. not Mark 196 ff.
  'Stumpfingers' 196, 202
Marriage—
  a pollution 110 ff.
  a duty 113 f.
Martyrologies 59 ff.
  Armenian 60
  of Carthago 60, 63, 64, 118
  of Gellone 62
  Syrian 60
Mary, St., Virgin 137
μαθητής καὶ ἐρώμενος = *discipulus et carus* 148
Matthew, son of Annas, High-priest 44
Maurine Congregation 3
Measuring the temple, oracle on 100
Mediumistic impersonation 129, 132
  see Cerinthus
Megethius, Marcionite 180
Melchisedec 37
Memorial chapel of St. John 120, 125
Menahem, Pseudo-Messiah 166
Menander of Kapparathea, gnostic 118
Mesopotamia 171
  Christians of 169
  Jews of 169, 209
Messengers, seven 103, 105, 134
Messiah—
  of Jews, warrior reject. by Marcion 177
  Menahem, Pseudo— 165, 166
Messianic child born (in Rev.) 139
Messiahs, several, in 1 John ii. 18 166
Messianist agitators 96
Methodius 66
  of Constantinople 22
milleniarism—
  of Apocalypse 138
  of Papias 151
Miltiades, Marcionite psalms by 30
Monarchianist prologues 6, 90, 118, 199
Montanists 29
Moses—
  120 years old 166
  and Elijah 89, 101, 117, 132, 134
  and prophets included among 'thieves and robbers' 182
Mosis, Ascensio 147

Musaeus, Orpheus' scribe xviii, 150

Names double—
of Jews 44
changed 70, 191
Natalis Caesaris 95
νεανίσκος in Mk. xiv. 51 = St. John 200
see lad; night-wrap
Nepos of Arsinoe 23
Nero redivivus 106
Nicolaitans 14
night-wrap (see σινδών) of lad in Mark xiv. 51 f., 196 ff., 201
Nonnos of Panopolis 52
North Africa, Jewish Revolution in 180, 209
Number, mystic of 'Beast' 139

Orpheus, dictating to Musaeus xviii, 150
ὄρυγμα, see rock-tomb of St. John 126

παιδία idiom of old John 172
Papias of Hierapolis 13, 56, 65 ff., 104, 140, 142–145, 153, 188, 193, 197, 204, 207
  bishop? 146
  discipulus Johannis carus 147
  Exegetica 145 f., 148
    see Exegetica and corruptions
  hearer of John 139, 160, 164, 187
  on Apocalypse 138 ff., 144
  on first Epistle of John 171
  on Marcion's ἀλλότριαι ἐντολαί 180
  on Marcion secretary of John 178
  milleniarist 151
  pilgrimage to John 207 f.
  secretary of John? 149 ff., 152, 156, 159
  'unintelligent'? 141
  witness to Fourth Gospel restored 161
  writing under Trajan 189
Papyrus of Fourth Gospel xix, 163, 168, Pl. XVI
Parthian Empire 169
Parthians addressed by John 170 f., 209
partibus in (idiom) 11
Paschal controversy 59
Patmian visions 111, 133
  quoted by Papias 138, 140, 142

Patmos 22, 90, 92 f., 113, 129, 133, 134
  Codex N of 52, 163
  see Karos, Katapausis, and Christodulos, Abbot of
Patricius presb. of Ravenna 158 f., 159 f., 162
Paul, St.—
  and Barnabas 84, 104
  and John Marc 196
  'John halfway between — and Marcion' 178
  meeting the 'Pillars' 78 ff.
Paul's, St., Epistle to Titus 81 f., 135
Paulinist quietism 175, 207, 209
Pax Romana 207
Persecution of Christian books 8
pest, world-wide (Naṣorean) 97
πέταλον of high-priest 36, 38, 42
  see diadem
Peter, St.—
  see Simon 30, 79, 141, 202
  epistles of 143
  interpreters of 142 f., 145
  outlived by John 141
Phiabi = Scaeva, High-priest, see Ishmaʻel 42
Philastrius of Brescia 188, Folder 1, col. 1 (**)
Philip, apostle 36, 67
Philo Alexandrinus 67
  Sophia in— 133
  vita contemplativa 112
Pillar-apostles 78 ff., 81 ff.
Pinhas b. Šamuʻel, High-priest 101
pirhej kehunah 201
Plato 26, 135
pneumatic gospel 2, 53
poison-cup drunk by John 210
Polycarp 36, 56, 59, 118, 135, 139, 142, 145, 151
  quotes Epistles of John 170
Polycrates—
  of Athens 21
  of Ephesus 36 f., 43, 46, 52, 53, 54, 55, 56, 57, 59, 67, 104, 124, 173
Pontic scriptures brought to John by Marcion xviii, 156, 185, 203, 205, 211
Presbyter John 28, 144
  see Elder
prices, high, of books 131
Primasius 99
Priscillianists 29
Prochoros, St., secretary of St. John xix, 31, 163, Pl. XV

ANALYTIC INDEX

Prochoros Pseudo-, 'Wanderings of John' 168
ψευδὴς ἱστορία 30, 51, 58
  see vie romancée
Pseudo-Messiah, see Antichrist 165
publisher's 'blurb' 148
  note to Gospel of Luke in Cod. Bodl. 200
punctuation, see διαστελλειν, διαστολή 141
  no — in Merovingian, Visigothic and Lombard MSS.
  of preface to John 155 ff., 157 ff., 159
  see Patricius of Ravenna

Quartodeciman rite 59
Quietist politic tendency of Fourth Gospel 175 f.
Quietus Lusus 166, 169, 174

Ravenna 158 ff., 159 f., 162 f.
rebellis, John sentenced velut 71
Resurrection of Christ, self-caused (Marcion) 179
Revelation of John, see Apocalypse 11, 94, 133
  excluded from Canon 108
  two beginnings, two ends 104
  on Mt. Sinai denied by Gospel of John 182
reversio illicita, crime 94
Rhetoric literature, Gospels classified as 21
Rich young man, see Beloved Disciple xxi, 191
Righteous Father, John xxvii. 25, 183
rock-tomb of St. John xvii, 126, Pl. IX
Romulus and Rufus, Messiahs, sons of Bar Cochba 166 f.

Sagaris, Martyr 118
Samaritan women in Fourth Gospel 182
σαφῶς = 'certainly' 141
Sarah, symbolism of 171
Scaeva, see Σκευᾶς High-priest 42
Salome, mother of Zebedaids 136
'Salvation comes from the Jews' 182
Schlettstadt, lectionary of 75 f.
scribes, Spanish, sent to Palestine 9
scripta vel epistulas = γράμματα 12, 161
Secretaries—
  see συνεργοί 132
  of Democritus 150

Secretaries (contd.)—
  of Euripides 150
  of John 144, 149 f., 151, 159, 163
  of Josephus 143 f.
  of Lykon 150
  of Peter and Paul 143, 184
secretary abusing confidence 185
self-burial of John 174
senility of John Evangelist 173
Seven Sleepers of Ephesus 124
Seventy-two apostles 23
Sexual abstinence 114
Shammai, school of, on marriage 114
shortened edition of Scriptures 129
Silos, missal of 76
  see Comicus, liber
Simon the Boethusian, High-priest 97
  son of Clophas, 120 years old 166, 173
  Magus 118, 174
  Peter 27
  Zelotes 27
σινδών, see night-wrap 197, 200
Siōn, Hagia, church in Jerusalem 136 f.
Skeuas, see Scaeva = Phiabi 42
Solomon of Basra 23
Sons of—
  Thunder (see Zebedaids) 103
  Fire from the mouth 87, 89
  Twins 68
Sophia 133
Sophronios, patriarch 137
spado Christi, St. John 56, 115
Spanish bibles 154, 159
  see Luciniys of Baetica
Spanish liturgy 62 f.
sphragis, author's seal 187
Spica, star 109
spies, Herodian 79
Spirit, God a 178
Stephen—
  protomartyr 60, 61, 76
  stoning of — omitted 76
στοιχεῖα 36
style and language 142, 144
subscriptions and superscriptions 5, 24
Suidas' Lexicon 4, 47, 166
Summaries—
  of Gospels 5, 8, 75, 76
  Benedictine edition of 76
Supper, Last 27, 52, 59, 152, 197
συνεργοί 132
Synoptic Gospels and Fourth Evang. 33
syphōn 122

Syrian bishops in Ephesus   124
Syrian superscription of Fourth Gospel in MS.   24

Talmud, Babylon marriage   113
τέκνια idiom of old St. John   173
Temple, heavenly   102
Tertullian   14, 57, 69, 81, 104, 107, 115, 135, 186
  a Montanist   56
Tetraevangel   33
Teukros of Babylon (in Egypt)   109
θεηγόρος John a   55, 65
Theoderic the Great   158
Theodor Mopsuestieus   26, 108
Theodoret of Cyrrhus   108
θεογλώσσος   65
θεολόγος—
  St. John   65 f.
  Moses   66
  Orpheus   66
Theophilus s. o. Annas, High-priest   53 ff., 46, 80, 206
  see John, High-priest
  deposed by Herod Agrippa I   97, 207
Theophylactus   58
Theudas, Pseudo-Messiah   165
Thraseas, Martyr   118
Thrasyllus   26
Tiberius—
  Emperor   85, 93, 209
  —Alexander   66, 92
Timothy, St., secretary of St. John?   163
Tiro, Cicero's secretary   149
tituli = summaries   9, 75
Titus, Emperor   101
Toldoth Jeshu   69 ff.
Tombs, two of St. John   125 ff.
torture in Roman law   71
Trajan, Emperor, 166, 168, 169, 174, 189, 209
trance-script of Cerinthus   132
Transfiguration   30
translation of relics   126
transposition of leaves in 'Acts'   80
Twelve, one of the   23 f., 34 f., 36, 77, 131, 144, 150
Typhon, dragon in Rev.   109

Unknown God of Marcion   178
unnamed disciples   26

Valentinians   14, 67, 184
Valentinus   30
Vaticanus Cod. Gr. 1209 = B, antiMarcionite correction in   181
ventilator system of Ephesian catacombs   122 f.
Victor, Pope   36, 54, 57, 59
vie romancée of John, see ψευδής ίστορία   30, 58, 174
Virgin, Constellation of   109, 132
virginity of St. John   57, 113 f., 133
Virgins 144000   110 ff.
'Visigothic' Bibles   13, 21, 159

'we', subject of οἴδαμεν in John xxi. 24   187 ff., 193 f.
'Whore, drunken', Rome called—in Rev.   209
witness and superwitness, idioms of St. John   194, 203
Witnesses, Two, in Rev. xi. 3–11   86 ff., 100, 139

Younger John, see Elder and Presbyter   24, 28

Zebedaid brothers   xvii, 2, 21, 26, 30 f., 33, 135
  see Beheading of
  execution of   101, 135
  illiterate   32
  martyrdom of   59, 60 ff., 64 ff., 125, 141
  martyrdom of—delete   69 ff., 76 ff., 132
  mother of   136
  'pillars'   78 ff.
  'slain by Jews'   66, 88
  twins   27
  see 'Sons of Thunder'
Zeno of Elea, beloved disciple of Parmenides   148
Zephyrinus, Pope   92
Zosimus   21

For Product Safety Concerns and Information please contact our EU representative GPSR@taylorandfrancis.com
Taylor & Francis Verlag GmbH, Kaufingerstraße 24, 80331 München, Germany